Communications in Computer and Information Science

2735

Series Editors

Gang Li , *School of Information Technology, Deakin University, Burwood, VIC, Australia*

Joaquim Filipe, *Polytechnic Institute of Setúbal, Setúbal, Portugal*

Zhiwei Xu, *Chinese Academy of Sciences, Beijing, China*

Rationale

The CCIS series is devoted to the publication of proceedings of computer science conferences. Its aim is to efficiently disseminate original research results in informatics in printed and electronic form. While the focus is on publication of peer-reviewed full papers presenting mature work, inclusion of reviewed short papers reporting on work in progress is welcome, too. Besides globally relevant meetings with internationally representative program committees guaranteeing a strict peer-reviewing and paper selection process, conferences run by societies or of high regional or national relevance are also considered for publication.

Topics

The topical scope of CCIS spans the entire spectrum of informatics ranging from foundational topics in the theory of computing to information and communications science and technology and a broad variety of interdisciplinary application fields.

Information for Volume Editors and Authors

Publication in CCIS is free of charge. No royalties are paid, however, we offer registered conference participants temporary free access to the online version of the conference proceedings on SpringerLink (http://link.springer.com) by means of an http referrer from the conference website and/or a number of complimentary printed copies, as specified in the official acceptance email of the event.

CCIS proceedings can be published in time for distribution at conferences or as post-proceedings, and delivered in the form of printed books and/or electronically as USBs and/or e-content licenses for accessing proceedings at SpringerLink. Furthermore, CCIS proceedings are included in the CCIS electronic book series hosted in the SpringerLink digital library at http://link.springer.com/bookseries/7899. Conferences publishing in CCIS are allowed to use our online conference service (Meteor) for managing the whole proceedings lifecycle (from submission and reviewing to preparing for publication) free of charge.

Publication process

The language of publication is exclusively English. Authors publishing in CCIS have to sign the Springer CCIS copyright transfer form, however, they are free to use their material published in CCIS for substantially changed, more elaborate subsequent publications elsewhere. For the preparation of the camera-ready papers/files, authors have to strictly adhere to the Springer CCIS Authors' Instructions and are strongly encouraged to use the CCIS LaTeX style files or templates.

Abstracting/Indexing

CCIS is abstracted/indexed in DBLP, Google Scholar, EI-Compendex, Mathematical Reviews, SCImago, Scopus. CCIS volumes are also submitted for the inclusion in ISI Proceedings.

How to start

To start the evaluation of your proposal for inclusion in the CCIS series, please send an e-mail to ccis@springer.com

Yen-Chia Hsu · Kari Systä · In-Young Ko ·
Filippo Gramegna

Editors

The Inclusive Web

Realizing Safe, Accessible, Inclusive, and Sustainable Web Engineering

25th ICWE 2025 International Workshops, BECS, SWEET
Delft, The Netherlands, June 30–July 3, 2025
Revised Selected Papers

 Springer

Editors
Yen-Chia Hsu
University of Amsterdam
Amsterdam, The Netherlands

Kari Systä
Tampere University
Tampere, Finland

In-Young Ko
Korea Advanced Institute of Science
and Technology
Daejeon, Korea (Republic of)

Filippo Gramegna
Polytechnic University of Bari
Bari, Italy

ISSN 1865-0929   ISSN 1865-0937 (electronic)
Communications in Computer and Information Science
ISBN 978-3-032-11232-3   ISBN 978-3-032-11233-0 (eBook)
https://doi.org/10.1007/978-3-032-11233-0

Preface

The ICWE conference series aims to promote research and scientific exchange related to Web Engineering, and to bring together researchers and practitioners from various disciplines in academia and industry in order to tackle emerging challenges in the engineering of Web applications and associated technologies, as well as to assess the impact of those technologies on society, media, and culture.

The ICWE conference has traditionally included co-located workshops that facilitate more detailed discussion on emerging topics. In 2025, we accepted two workshops, whose revised papers are included in this volume:

- The Fifth International Workshop on Big Data Driven Edge Cloud Services (BECS 2025) brought researchers and practitioners together to exchange ideas, share experiences, and explore recent advances in developing intelligent, data-driven services in edge-cloud environments.
- The Third International Workshop on the Semantic WEb of EveryThing (SWEET 2025) focused on integrating, optimizing, and exploiting artificial intelligence in WoT and pervasive computing scenarios. This will help push the Web Engineering boundary toward a Web of Smart Things, and particularly toward the Semantic Web of Things.

All articles included in this volume underwent a rigorous single-blind peer review process, with at least 3 reviews per submitted article. For BECS 2025, a total of 10 submissions were received using the EasyChair submission system, of which 6 were accepted as full papers. For SWEET 2025, a total of 6 submissions were received using the EasyChair submission system, of which 6 were accepted as full papers. Accepted papers were presented during the workshops on June 30, 2025. After the workshop, the authors got the opportunity to update their paper and produce the final version included in these proceedings, taking into account the comments received during the workshop.

We would like to thank the large number of people who made all this possible: workshop organizers, organizers of the main conference, reviewers, paper contributors, and workshop participants. We extend our gratitude to all the technical program committee members for their dedicated efforts in delivering high-quality reviews and valuable feedback. We thank the authors who submitted and presented their research work at the workshop, as well as all the participants whose contributions played a pivotal role in the workshop's success.

Specifically for BECS 2025, the workshop was supported by the IITP (Institute of Information & Communications Technology Planning & Evaluation)-ITRC (Information Technology Research Center) grant funded by the Korean government (Ministry of Science and ICT) (IITP-2025-RS-2020-II201795).

Specifically for SWEET 2025, we would like to express our sincere thanks to Savio Sciancalepore, Assistant Professor at the Eindhoven University of Technology (TU/e), for his insightful invited talk on the challenges and solutions for securing critical infrastructures in the Web of Things. His contribution provided valuable perspectives and stimulated fruitful discussions.

September 2025

Kari Systä
Yen-Chia Hsu
Filippo Gramegna
In-Young Ko

Organization

ICWE 2025 Workshop Co-chairs

Kari Systä	Tampere University, Finland
Yen-Chia Hsu	University of Amsterdam, Netherlands

BECS 2025 Workshop Co-chairs

In-Young Ko	Korea Advanced Institute of Science and Technology, South Korea
Michael Mrissa	InnoRenew CoE, University of Primorska, Slovenia
Juan Manuel Murillo	University of Extremadura & COMPUTAEX Foundation, Spain
Abhishek Srivastava	Indian Institute of Technology Indore, India

SWEET 2025 Workshop Co-chairs

Filippo Gramegna	Polytechnic University of Bari, Italy
Saverio Ieva	Polytechnic University of Bari, Italy
Giuseppe Loseto	LUM "Giuseppe Degennaro" University, Italy
Agnese Pinto	Polytechnic University of Bari, Italy
Ivano Bilenchi	Polytechnic University of Bari, Italy
Davide Loconte	Polytechnic University of Bari, Italy

BECS 2025 Workshop Technical Program Committee

Cheyma Ben Njima	Université Jean Moulin Lyon 3, France
Eunkyoung Jee	Korea Advanced Institute of Science and Technology, South Korea
Min-Soo Kim	Korea Advanced Institute of Science and Technology, South Korea
Jemin Lee	Yonsei University, South Korea
Faïza Loukil	Université Polytechnique Hauts-de-France, France

Ayan Mondal	Indian Institute of Technology Indore, India
Martin Musicante	Federal University of Rio Grande do Norte, Brazil
Jihun Park	Chungnam National University, South Korea
Placido Souza Neto	IFRN, Brazil
Jongse Park	Korea Advanced Institute of Science and Technology, South Korea
Kiran K. Patnaik	Indian Institute of Information Technology, Design, and Management, India
Duksan Ryu	Jeonbuk National University, South Korea

SWEET 2025 Workshop Technical Program Committee

Eugenio Di Sciascio	Polytechnic University of Bari, Italy
Francesco M. Donini	University of Tuscia, Italy
Nicola Epicoco	LUM "Giuseppe Degennaro" University, Italy
Corrado Fasciano	Polytechnic University of Bari, Italy
Hasan Ali Khatthak	National University of Sciences and Technology, Pakistan
Alessandro Massaro	LUM "Giuseppe Degennaro" University, Italy
Michele Ruta	Polytechnic University of Bari, Italy
Floriano Scioscia	Polytechnic University of Bari, Italy
Arnaldo Tomasino	Polytechnic University of Bari, Italy

Contents

5th International Workshop on Big data driven Edge Cloud Services (BECS 2025)

Adaptive ML-Enabled Edge-Cloud System Framework for Safe and Efficient Autonomous Systems

Eunho Cho$^{(\boxtimes)}$ and In-Young Ko

Korea Advanced Institute of Science and Technology (KAIST),
Deajeon, Republic of Korea
`{ehcho,iko}@kaist.ac.kr`

Abstract. Machine Learning (ML)-enabled systems like Autonomous Driving Systems (ADSs) face challenges meeting safety and performance requirements in diverse environments, especially in resource-constrained, latency-sensitive edge-cloud settings. These challenges often arise from ML models' limitations, including poor generalization to unseen conditions. Adaptive algorithms using ML system switching have been proposed, but existing approaches frequently lack generalizability, support for common black-box systems, and effective use of distributed edge-cloud resources. This paper presents a novel adaptive ML-enabled Edge-Cloud system framework to address these shortcomings. Our framework combines cloud-based pre-runtime analysis, which leverages simulation for behavioral understanding and scenario-to-system mapping, with collaborative edge-cloud runtime adaptation featuring dynamic ML model switching. It supports black-box systems and aims to balance safety and efficiency by utilizing appropriate edge and cloud resources situationally. Preliminary CARLA-based evaluation of the edge runtime component suggests our framework can potentially improve the safety-efficiency trade-off compared to single-model ADSs in some scenarios. This work offers insights for designing adaptive edge-cloud systems and identifies future directions, including robust cloud analysis and effective edge-cloud collaboration. Findings suggest this edge-cloud approach can advance the feasibility and reliability of adaptive ML systems for real-world autonomous applications.

Keywords: ML-Enabled Systems · Autonomous Driving Systems · Edge-Cloud Computing · Adaptive Systems · Simulation-Based Testing

1 Introduction

Autonomous systems, particularly Autonomous Driving Systems (ADSs), are increasingly integrated within the broader edge-cloud computing ecosystem. Modern ADSs generate substantial sensor data at the edge, selectively offload data to the cloud for large-scale analysis and model refinement, and receive

Y.-C. Hsu et al. (Eds.): ICWE 2025, CCIS 2735, pp. 3–15, 2026.
https://doi.org/10.1007/978-3-032-11233-0_1

updated models back at the edge. This collaborative edge-cloud architecture aims for safer roads, reduced congestion, and more efficient mobility services [14].

ADSs rely on machine learning (ML) components for perception, decision-making, and control tasks. However, these ML components face challenges due to the unpredictable nature of real-world scenarios—including diverse traffic patterns, unexpected behaviors, and varying environmental conditions [16,17]. Ensuring reliable performance, especially under edge constraints (resource limits, latency requirements), remains an open challenge.

Frameworks like Autoware [11] and Apollo [1] use modular designs with independently optimized components. Despite such architectures, achieving consistent safety and efficiency across diverse driving scenarios with a fixed set of ML models is difficult. ML models risk being too large for practical computational budgets or too small and overfitting specific scenarios [9]. Static ML systems, therefore, often struggle with adaptability, particularly when facing scenarios unseen during training, highlighting the need for dynamic solutions in edge-cloud environments.

Adaptive approaches using runtime ML system switching have been proposed to mitigate these challenges [6,13]. However, most existing approaches assume white-box accessibility, requiring predictable model behaviors and limiting practical applicability. This limits practical applicability because many state-of-the-art ML models used in ADSs, particularly deep neural networks, function as complex black boxes, making their internal states difficult to predict or analyze directly for adaptation purposes. Moreover, these methods often don't fully leverage both cloud computational strengths and edge real-time capabilities simultaneously. Thus, frameworks that seamlessly integrate edge-cloud collaboration for effectively handling black-box ML systems under varying conditions are critically needed.

To address the limitations of static models in diverse/unseen scenarios and the applicability constraints of existing white-box adaptive approaches, particularly concerning black-box systems and effective edge-cloud collaboration, we present an adaptive ML-enabled edge-cloud system framework designed to overcome these limitations. Our approach combines a cloud-driven pre-runtime phase (leveraging extensive simulations for behavioral analysis and scenario mapping) with a collaborative runtime phase where edge and cloud systems jointly identify scenarios and dynamically select optimal ML systems. This two-phase strategy maximizes cloud resources for exhaustive pre-runtime analyses and edge speed for real-time adaptability. Our prototype implementation using the CARLA simulation platform [7] integrates both a high-performance deep-learning agent and a computationally efficient rule-based agent, showing promising preliminary results regarding safety-efficiency trade-offs.

The main contributions of this study are:

- **Edge-cloud adaptive framework**: Formalized an edge-cloud adaptive framework supporting black-box ML systems, defining cloud roles (pre-runtime analysis) and edge-cloud collaboration roles (runtime adaptation).

- **Empirical validation**: Quantified safety-efficiency trade-offs of adaptive ML switching via preliminary CARLA-based validation.
- **Insights and future research directions**: Provided insights and future directions for scenario generation, knowledge base maintenance, and deployment in practical edge-cloud environments.

The remainder of this paper is structured as follows: Sect. 2 reviews relevant literature. Section 3 introduces our proposed adaptive framework. Section 4 describes the experimental setup and presents preliminary results. Section 5 discusses implications, limitations, and future research. Finally, Sect. 6 summarizes our findings.

2   Related Work

The adaptive system framework, employing system or model switching, is critical for ensuring ML system adaptability in dynamic environments. This technique dynamically transitions between models/systems to maintain optimal performance, safety, and quality under varying circumstances.

Several studies explore adaptive frameworks. For instance, researchers have proposed strategies like predictive control with reconfigurable models [4], model selection using transfer reinforcement learning (RL) in Open IoT [15], anomaly-aware adaptation via RL for cyber-physical systems [6], and QoS-based switching to manage performance uncertainties [13].

However, these valuable studies often have limitations. Many frameworks are constrained to specific environments or predefined scenarios, limiting generalizability. Some depend on accessible system behaviors, making them unsuitable for black-box systems. It is very difficult or impossible to determine in which situation the system behavior will react as desired for many high-performance ML models used in practice. Furthermore, existing works frequently focus on specific aspects like efficiency or anomaly detection, often neglecting the complex interplay with other critical factors such as overall system safety.

Recent research explores Edge AI optimization considering resource constraints [20] and novel cloud-edge collaborative architectures [10]. Yet, these often do not directly tackle the specific challenge of dynamically adapting black-box ML models for safety-critical autonomous driving systems. Our work aims to bridge this gap by proposing a framework integrating adaptive black-box ML switching within a structured Edge-Cloud approach tailored for ADS safety and efficiency.

3   Adaptive ML-Enabled Edge-Cloud System Framework

Our framework utilizes an Edge-Cloud architecture comprising two main phases: a pre-runtime phase executed on cloud resources and a runtime phase operating across edge and cloud infrastructure. This section first discusses the overall approach, followed by detailed examinations of the pre-runtime and runtime phases.

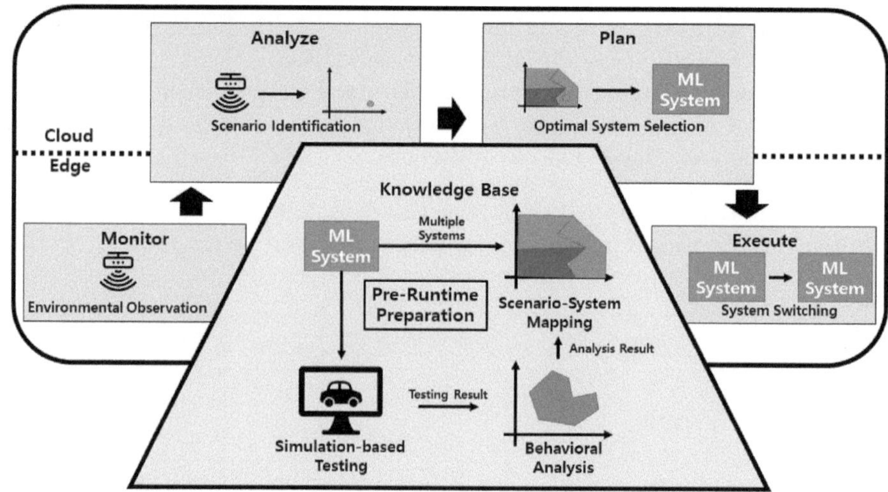

Fig. 1. Overall Adaptive ML-Enabled Edge-Cloud System Framework

Figure 1 illustrates the framework's flow, divided into two phases. The lower section depicts the cloud-based pre-runtime phase, which involves simulation-based testing, behavioral analysis, and scenario-system mapping to prepare the system knowledge base. This phase evaluates candidate ML systems through extensive simulation, analyzes their behavior to identify optimal operating subspaces, and maps the most suitable system to each subspace within the knowledge base, leveraging cloud computational power.

The upper section shows the runtime phase, based on the distributed MAPE-K loop [12], a standard model for self-adaptive systems. The edge monitors the environment (Monitor); edge and cloud collaboratively identify the current scenario subspace (Analyze); they collaboratively select the optimal ML system using the knowledge base (Plan); and the edge executes the system switch (Execute). This combination of cloud pre-runtime preparation and distributed runtime adaptation enables stable and effective adaptation in complex environments.

In this framework, a 'Scenario' represents the specific operational context, often captured as a vector encompassing environmental factors such as weather and road type, system goals like waypoints, and current system state variables including speed and position. We assume multiple ML systems exist, each optimized for different scenarios or data distributions. The primary goal of the pre-runtime phase is to analyze system behavior across diverse scenarios via large-scale simulations, identify the scenarios best suited for each system's operation, and systematically compile this information into a knowledge base that informs runtime decision-making.

3.1   Pre-runtime Phase

Executed on the cloud due to computational demands, the pre-runtime phase includes three key steps: simulation-based testing, behavioral analysis, and scenario-system mapping.

Simulation-Based Testing. First, we evaluate ML system performance using extensive simulations (e.g., using CARLA) across diverse environments. These scenarios, encompassing complexities like varying weather, road networks, and traffic in ADS contexts, enable the collection of performance data for each ML system. Scenario generation prioritizes diversity to cover a broad spectrum of operating conditions, grounding the identification of suitable operating scenarios for each system.

Simulation-based testing is crucial for evaluating ML systems, especially when real-world testing is risky or infeasible. It allows systematic performance evaluation under diverse, controlled conditions. Platforms like CARLA [21] offer realistic physics-based simulations suitable for analyzing safety and efficiency metrics in autonomous systems like Autonomous Driving Systems (ADSs). The scale and computational demands of such simulations are well-suited for cloud execution. Simulation testing characterizes ML system performance. Prior work includes surrogate model-based frameworks [8] and search-based approaches to identify hazard boundaries [19], demonstrating simulation's ability to define operational limits. In our framework, simulation testing is a key component of the cloud-based pre-runtime phase.

Behavioral Analysis. Next, each ML system's behavior is analyzed using the simulation data, focusing on safety and efficiency. For ADSs, safety metrics might include detailed collision types, involving pedestrians or vehicles for example, off-road excursions, route completion ratio, and compliance with traffic regulations such as traffic signal adherence and stop sign compliance. Efficiency metrics cover computational cost, like average inference time per frame or peak memory usage, and network resource consumption required by each ML system. This analysis assesses whether systems meet safety requirements and satisfy QoS criteria within different scenario subspaces.

Scenario-System Mapping. This mapping step is crucial because different ML systems exhibit varying performance trade-offs, notably between safety and efficiency, under different scenarios. Based on the behavioral analysis, this step systematically assigns the best-performing system to each identified scenario subspace according to pre-defined objectives, for instance prioritizing safety over efficiency, creating a reliable decision guide known as the knowledge base for the runtime phase. This involves cloud-based multi-objective optimization, potentially using evolutionary algorithms or rule-based heuristics. The resulting mapping is stored in the knowledge base, possibly as a compact decision tree or a hash map for efficient runtime lookup, and potentially cached at the edge for runtime access, directly enabling the system's adaptive capabilities.

3.2   Runtime Phase

The runtime phase operates using the distributed MAPE-K (Monitor, Analyze, Plan, Execute, Knowledge) loop across edge and cloud resources. We assume the edge device is equipped with necessary sensors. Each step leverages edge and cloud strengths to maintain safety and efficiency in complex environments.

Environmental Observation. The runtime process begins with observing the environment in real-time using onboard edge sensors (e.g., cameras, LiDAR, radar). This collected data forms the input for the subsequent analysis step.

Scenario Identification. Following observation, the current scenario subspace is determined using the observed edge data. A scenario involves initial environment/system states and operational goals. Observations identify the current state and goals, but unobservable variables may lead to multiple possible scenarios, thus forming a scenario subspace. This analysis is performed collaboratively on edge and cloud. Rapid analysis of immediate sensor data is performed by the edge device for local context identification, potentially using lightweight convolutional neural networks to identify environment, or other cars. The cloud leverages larger datasets or more powerful models for deeper analysis, perhaps employing Long Short-Term Memory networks for predicting traffic or accessing aggregated complex mobility data, providing broader context or predictions. The result is an identified scenario subspace incorporating both edge and cloud perspectives.

Optimal System Selection. Based on the identified scenario subspace, the most suitable ML system is selected by referencing the knowledge base. This planning step also occurs collaboratively on edge and cloud. A quick selection is made by the edge using the identified local context and the potentially cached knowledge base to address immediate needs. A more sophisticated selection or refinement is performed by the cloud, considering broader goals or complex trade-offs. This decision can potentially update the edge's initial plan, for instance, based on predicted traffic congestion patterns or system-wide energy optimization goals. The final decision on the optimal ML system combines edge and cloud inputs, aiming for optimal safety and efficiency based on both immediate needs and longer-term objectives.

System Switching. Finally, the execution step involves switching to the selected ML system on the edge device. This transition must occur in real-time with minimal disruption. The execution requires edge technologies capable of minimizing transition delays and ensuring system stability post-transition. Furthermore, the performance of the newly activated ML system should ideally be monitored, with results potentially reported to the cloud to refine the knowledge base for future decision-making improvement.

4   Investigation

This section presents a preliminary evaluation of the runtime adaptation component within our proposed adaptive ML-enabled edge-cloud framework. A simple prototype adaptive ADS assesses practical applicability, focusing on safety and efficiency. As discussed in the Introduction, achieving both safety and efficiency consistently across diverse driving scenarios is a primary challenge for ADSs, especially considering edge resource constraints and the limitations of static or existing adaptive approaches. Our proposed framework aims to improve this balance through adaptive ML switching in an edge-cloud context. Therefore, this preliminary evaluation focuses on quantifying the potential benefits regarding these two critical aspects, guided by the following research questions (RQs):

RQ1 (Safety): What advantages does the adaptive ADS offer in terms of safety compared to conventional ADS, either holistically or in specific scenarios?

RQ2 (Efficiency): What advantages does the adaptive ADS provide in terms of efficiency compared to conventional ADS?

Experiments ran on Ubuntu 22.04 (Intel Xeon 4215R, 3x RTX A5000 GPUs 24GB, 128GB RAM). The replication kit containing the source code used in this study is publicly available at [3].

4.1   Experiment Design

We implemented a simple adaptive ADS prototype focusing on runtime adaptation at the simulated edge. The prototype uses CARLA [7], our simulated edge environment, and Leaderboard benchmarks [2] to evaluate safety and efficiency across various scenarios. We compared the adaptive mechanism against single ML systems regarding safety and efficiency at the edge.

CARLA [7] is a widely used open-source ADS simulator providing diverse maps and dynamic components. We used CARLA datasets, originally from Transfuser [5] and InterFuser [18] training, for testing. Key test scenarios included 'longest6', '42routes', 'town05_short/long', 'town06_long', and 'town10_short'. The CARLA Leaderboard [2] executes these scenarios under predefined conditions using modules like scenario runner.

Evaluation focused on safety and efficiency. Safety metrics from the CARLA Leaderboard included: *Route Score*, representing the percentage of the route completed; *Penalty Score*, reflecting points deducted for incidents where 1 is perfect; and *Composed Score*, providing an overall safety measure. We also introduced *Scenario Dominance Count*, measuring the number of scenarios where an agent achieved the highest composed score. Efficiency was measured by the decision time ratio, calculated as CARLA simulation time divided by real-world time.

The prototype combines Transfuser [5] and the NPC Agent sourced from the CARLA Leaderboard, simulating edge runtime adaptation. Transfuser is a complex DNN agent utilizing camera and LiDAR fusion via self-attention; it is capable of handling challenging scenarios but computationally heavy for continuous edge execution. The NPC Agent is a simple, computationally efficient rule-based baseline suitable for edge resources but limited in complex situations. The prototype activates Transfuser near intersections, defined as within 50 m, and uses the NPC Agent otherwise, simulating edge-based scenario identification and system selection. This logic prioritizes safety with Transfuser in higher-risk intersections and efficiency with NPC on simpler road segments, balancing the trade-offs within the edge environment.

The prototype employs a simple rule-based knowledge base, simulating the output of the envisioned cloud pre-runtime analysis. The underlying principle is that Transfuser offers higher safety at greater computational cost, while NPC is efficient but less safe. The mapping reflects this: Transfuser is selected for high-risk intersections prioritizing safety, and NPC for other roads prioritizing efficiency. This allows the prototype to dynamically adapt at the edge, balancing safety and efficiency based on simple scenario detection.

4.2   Experiment Result

We evaluated the adaptive ADS prototype against the NPC and Transfuser ADS to address RQ1 (Safety) and RQ2 (Efficiency).

Table 1. Safety and Efficiency Metrics for ADS Systems

Scenarios	NPC					Transfuser					Adaptive				
	Route	Penalty	Composed	Dominance	Time	Route	Penalty	Composed	Dominance	Time	Route	Penalty	Composed	Dominance	Time
longest6	39.8	0.237	5.4	1	0.157	42.7	0.799	24.4	14	0.094	61.7	0.419	24.4	21	0.110
42routes	75.1	0.315	21.7	0	0.078	85.5	0.901	79.3	23	0.074	69.4	0.490	37.6	1	0.074
town05_short	79.6	0.375	27.9	2	0.129	97.0	0.877	85.5	29	0.101	93.4	0.856	80.8	1	0.104
town05_long	63.2	0.136	5.1	0	0.133	100.0	0.459	45.9	9	0.098	92.5	0.330	30.2	1	0.119
town06_long	66.0	0.088	1.6	0	0.174	94.5	0.613	56.8	9	0.103	92.5	0.177	16.6	1	0.106
town10_short	31.2	0.406	18.0	0	0.098	100.0	0.810	81.0	8	0.069	83.7	0.653	58.9	1	0.074

Regarding RQ1 (Safety), Table 1 and Fig. 2 present the safety and efficiency results. Transfuser consistently achieved the highest composed scores, while NPC performed poorly, highlighting the inherent trade-off between performance and computational simplicity relevant to edge suitability. Although the adaptive ADS often scored below the pure Transfuser, it demonstrated robustness. Notably, it matched Transfuser's composed score in the 'longest6' scenario and achieved the highest score, indicating dominance, in 21 scenarios overall according to Table 1. This result suggests that, concerning RQ1, the potential effectiveness of edge-based adaptation. However, lower scores in specific scenarios, such as 'town06_long,' indicate limitations of the prototype's simple adaptation rule, pointing to the need for refinement through the full edge-cloud framework involving, for example, more sophisticated scenario identification or a richer knowledge base.

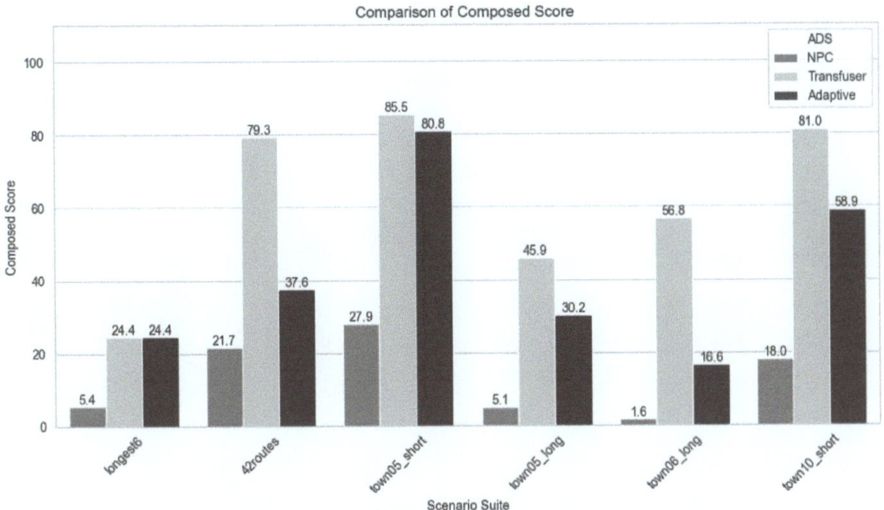

Fig. 2. Comparison of Composed Score for ADS Systems

In relation to RQ2 (Efficiency), Fig. 3 illustrates computational efficiency via time ratios. Transfuser's consistently low time ratio signifies high computational cost, potentially problematic for resource-constrained edge devices. Conversely, NPC was the most efficient but demonstrated poor safety performance. The adaptive ADS achieved intermediate efficiency. This result indicates that, concerning RQ2, the adaptive approach successfully balanced safety needs with edge resource usage by selectively engaging the computationally heavier Transfuser only when necessary, thus demonstrating a clear efficiency advantage over running Transfuser continuously.

In summary, addressing RQ1 and RQ2, these preliminary results suggest that edge-based adaptation, as demonstrated by the prototype, can offer safety performance comparable to the best-performing single model (Transfuser) in specific scenarios while achieving significantly greater computational efficiency suitable for edge deployment. This indicates the potential of the edge adaptation component within our broader edge-cloud framework to address the core challenge of balancing safety and efficiency. However, the observed limitations underscore the need for future work focusing on the complete framework implementation, including cloud-based pre-runtime analysis and more sophisticated edge-cloud coordination mechanisms to improve the adaptation strategy and achieve robust performance across a wider range of scenarios.

5   Discussion

5.1   Investigation Analysis

Our preliminary evaluation indicates the framework's edge runtime adaptation component can potentially balance safety and efficiency across diverse scenarios.

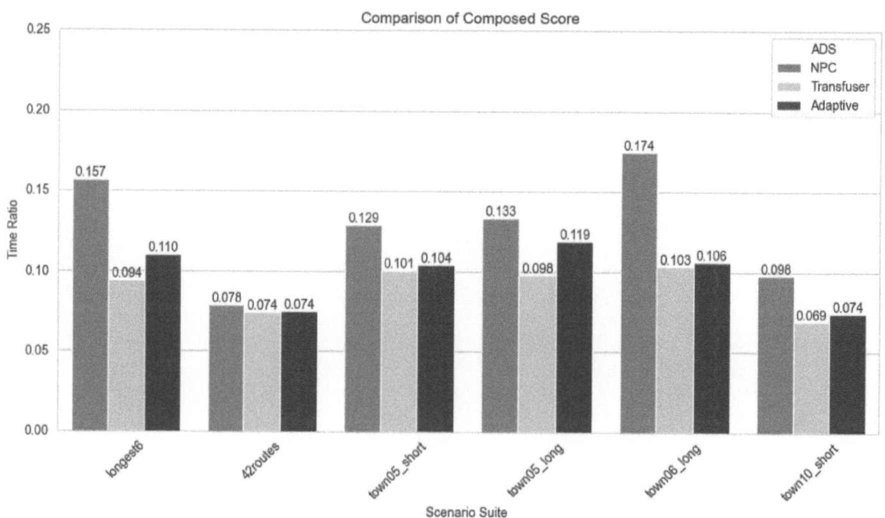

Fig. 3. Comparison of Time Ratio for ADS Systems

The adaptive prototype outperformed monolithic systems by dominance count in some scenarios (Table 1) and matched Transfuser's safety score in 'longest6' while being more computationally efficient (Fig. 3). This suggests dynamic edge switching, guided by scenario perception, is a promising approach for adapting ADS performance under varying edge conditions.

However, the experiments also revealed limitations, emphasizing the importance of cloud-based pre-runtime analysis and careful component selection for edge execution. The NPC Agent's struggles with unexpected events (e.g., pedestrians, obstacles) negatively impacted safety when it was selected by the simple edge adaptation logic in non-intersection scenarios. This issue stems from the NPC's design as a simple rule-based algorithm, highlighting the challenge of relying solely on simple edge models for complex, unforeseen events and underscoring the need for robust cloud-based pre-analysis to identify such weaknesses or provide mechanisms for escalating to more capable models or cloud intervention.

Similarly, Transfuser's occasional safety failures in certain intersection scenarios, despite high overall scores, demonstrate that the adaptive system's performance is ultimately bounded by the capabilities and potential flaws of the underlying models deployed at the edge. While edge switching can optimize system selection based on known characteristics derived from pre-analysis, it inherits the drawbacks of its constituent systems if the cloud pre-runtime analysis fails to adequately characterize these limitations or if the edge cannot reliably detect the critical conditions requiring a specific model.

Consequently, these observed limitations underscore the critical role of the cloud-based pre-runtime phase, involving extensive simulation-based testing and behavioral analysis, in building a comprehensive and accurate knowledge base.

This knowledge base is essential for informing effective edge runtime adaptation logic, enabling accurate mapping of scenarios to the most suitable edge-executable systems, and understanding the operational boundaries and limitations of each component. Therefore, while this study validates the potential of the edge-based adaptive approach, it simultaneously highlights the critical need for thorough cloud-based pre-analysis as an indispensable element for optimizing both safety and efficiency in the design of adaptive edge-cloud ADS systems.

5.2 Future Directions

To overcome the limitations identified and fully realize the framework's potential, future work should first address robust scenario generation techniques for the cloud pre-runtime analysis. Simulation scenarios are critical for evaluating the performance and identifying the limitations of candidate ADS models intended for edge deployment. Cloud-based scenario generation methods should systematically explore the operational boundaries of these models by designing diverse scenarios including edge cases, such as unexpected obstacles or highly complex intersections. These methods need to balance criticality (exploring key boundary conditions) and variety (covering diverse environments), while enabling automation to reduce the time and cost associated with building the pre-runtime knowledge base.

Second, mapping scenarios to optimal system behaviors and identifying the scenario subspaces where specific edge models excel or fail remain significant challenges, primarily addressed within the cloud component during pre-runtime analysis. Addressing these requires advanced techniques. Exploration-based techniques can automatically identify critical scenarios within cloud simulations, efficiently pinpointing model weaknesses. Reinforcement learning is well-suited for training adaptive switching policies governing edge behavior, allowing the edge component to learn and respond effectively based on cloud-derived models or policies.

Furthermore, effective collaboration mechanisms between the edge and the cloud require in-depth research. Defining clear criteria for when scenario analysis should be handled solely by the edge versus requiring cloud interaction is a key challenge in designing the collaboration logic. This includes designing efficient communication protocols, maintaining data consistency, managing potential conflicts between edge and cloud decisions, and developing strategies for dynamic task allocation and resource management considering real-time requirements, communication constraints, and computational loads at both edge and cloud.

Future research will prioritize integrating comprehensive cloud-based behavioral analysis with sophisticated self-adaptive techniques executed at the edge, ensuring effective edge-cloud collaboration. Such efforts aim to maximize the safety and efficiency of autonomous driving systems by leveraging the strengths of both edge and cloud resources, while ensuring reliable performance in complex environments. Ultimately, advancing edge-cloud adaptive frameworks is expected to improve the feasibility of autonomous driving technologies for commercialization and play a critical role in developing safe and efficient autonomous systems.

6   Conclusion

We proposed an adaptive ML-enabled Edge-Cloud framework to enhance autonomous system safety and efficiency. It combines cloud pre-runtime analysis with collaborative edge-cloud runtime adaptation (including ML switching) to handle diverse requirements. Preliminary CARLA evaluation validated the edge adaptation component's effectiveness. The experimental results demonstrated that the proposed framework, through edge adaptation potentially improved trade-off between safety and efficiency compared to conventional single ML system approaches in certain scenarios.

A simplified prototype confirmed the edge adaptation's applicability and highlighted future work: improving test scenario generation for cloud analysis, developing robust scenario-system mapping (e.g., using search or RL), and refining edge-cloud collaboration. Implementing and evaluating the complete framework is the crucial next step.

Acknowledgments. This work was partly supported by the Institute of Information & communications Technology Planning & Evaluation(IITP) grant funded by the Korea government(MSIT)(RS-2025-02218761, 50%), IITP grant funded by the Korea government(MSIT)(RS-2024-00406245, 25%), Samsung Electronics(25%).

References

1. Baidu apollo team. apollo: Open source autonomous driving (2017). https://github.com/ApolloAuto/apollo. Accessed 09 Dec 2024
2. Carla autonomous driving leaderboard. https://leaderboard.carla.org/. Accessed 09 Dec 2024
3. Replication kit. https://github.com/EunhoCho/AdaptiveADS/. Accessed 17 Apr 2025
4. Amir, M., Vahid, F., Givargis, T.: Switching predictive control using reconfigurable state-based model. ACM Trans. Des. Autom. Electron. Syst. (tODAEs) **24**(1), 1–21 (2018). https://doi.org/10.1145/3267126
5. Chitta, K., Prakash, A., Jaeger, B., Yu, Z., Renz, K., Geiger, A.: Transfuser: imitation with transformer-based sensor fusion for autonomous driving. IEEE Trans. Pattern Anal. Mach. Intell. **45**(11), 12878–12895 (2023). https://doi.org/10.1109/TPAMI.2022.3200245
6. Cho, E., Yeo, G., Jee, E., Bae, D.H.: Anomaly-aware adaptation approach for self-adaptive cyber-physical system of systems using reinforcement learning. In: 2022 17th Annual System of Systems Engineering Conference (SOSE), pp. 7–12. IEEE (2022). https://doi.org/10.1109/SOSE55472.2022.9812671
7. Dosovitskiy, A., Ros, G., Codevilla, F., Lopez, A., Koltun, V.: Carla: an open urban driving simulator. In: Conference on Robot Learning, pp. 1–16. PMLR (2017)
8. Haq, F.U., Shin, D., Briand, L.: Efficient online testing for dnn-enabled systems using surrogate-assisted and many-objective optimization. In: Proceedings of the 44th International Conference on Software Engineering, pp. 811–822. IEEE (2022). https://doi.org/10.1145/3510003.3510188

9. Hestness, J., et al.: Deep learning scaling is predictable, empirically. arXiv preprint arXiv:1712.00409 (2017). https://doi.org/10.48550/arXiv.1712.00409

10. Ji, X., Gong, F., Wang, N., Xu, J., Yan, X.: Cloud-edge collaborative service architecture with large-tiny models based on deep reinforcement learning. IEEE Trans. Cloud Comput. (2025)

11. Kato, S., et al.: Autoware on board: enabling autonomous vehicles with embedded systems. In: 2018 ACM/IEEE 9th International Conference on Cyber-Physical Systems (ICCPS), pp. 287–296. IEEE (2018). https://doi.org/10.1109/ICCPS.2018.00035

12. Kephart, J.O., Chess, D.M.: The vision of autonomic computing. Computer **36**(1), 41–50 (2003). https://doi.org/10.1109/MC.2003.1160055

13. Kulkarni, S., Marda, A., Vaidhyanathan, K.: Towards self-adaptive machine learning-enabled systems through qos-aware model switching. In: 2023 38th IEEE/ACM International Conference on Automated Software Engineering (ASE), pp. 1721–1725. IEEE (2023). https://doi.org/10.1109/ASE56229.2023.00172

14. Muhammad, K., Ullah, A., Lloret, J., Del Ser, J., de Albuquerque, V.H.C.: Deep learning for safe autonomous driving: current challenges and future directions. IEEE Trans. Intell. Transp. Syst. **22**(7), 4316–4336 (2020). https://doi.org/10.1109/TITS.2020.3032227

15. Noguchi, H., Isoda, T., Arai, S.: Shared trained models selection and management for transfer reinforcement learning in open iot. In: 2021 IEEE International Conference on Systems, Man, and Cybernetics (SMC), pp. 2170–2176. IEEE (2021). https://doi.org/10.1109/SMC52423.2021.9658890

16. Serban, A.C.: Designing safety critical software systems to manage inherent uncertainty. In: 2019 IEEE International Conference on Software Architecture Companion (ICSA-C), pp. 246–249. IEEE (2019). https://doi.org/10.1109/ICSA-C.2019.00051

17. Shafaei, S., Kugele, S., Osman, M.H., Knoll, A.: Uncertainty in machine learning: a safety perspective on autonomous driving. In: Gallina, B., Skavhaug, A., Schoitsch, E., Bitsch, F. (eds.) SAFECOMP 2018. LNCS, vol. 11094, pp. 458–464. Springer, Cham (2018). https://doi.org/10.1007/978-3-319-99229-7_39

18. Shao, H., Wang, L., Chen, R., Li, H., Liu, Y.: Safety-enhanced autonomous driving using interpretable sensor fusion transformer. In: Proceedings of the 6th Conference on Robot Learning, vol. 205, pp. 726–737. PMLR (2023)

19. Sharifi, S., Shin, D., Briand, L.C., Aschbacher, N.: Identifying the hazard boundary of ml-enabled autonomous systems using cooperative coevolutionary search. IEEE Trans. Softw. Eng. **49**(12), 5120–5138 (2023). https://doi.org/10.1109/TSE.2023.3327575

20. Surianarayanan, C., Lawrence, J.J., Chelliah, P.R., Prakash, E., Hewage, C.: A survey on optimization techniques for edge artificial intelligence (AI). Sensors **23**(3), 1279 (2023)

21. Zhang, J.M., Harman, M., Ma, L., Liu, Y.: Machine learning testing: survey, landscapes and horizons. IEEE Trans. Softw. Eng. **48**(1), 1–36 (2020). https://doi.org/10.1109/TSE.2019.2962027

E-VaaS: Edge-Enabled Vehicle-as-a-Service for Smart Transportation Systems

Priyanshu Jogdand[1] , Anjani Kumar[1] , Ayan Mondal[1(✉)] ,
and Erkki Harjula[2]

[1] Indian Institute of Technology Indore, Indore, India
{cse210001055,cse210001004,ayanm}@iiti.ac.in
[2] Centre for Wireless Communications, University of Oulu, Oulu, Finland
erkki.harjula@oulu.fi

Abstract. Traffic congestion and low vehicle occupancy rates pose significant challenges in urban areas, highlighting the need for efficient, shared transportation systems. Hence, in this work, we introduce an Edge-Enabled Vehicle-as-a-Service scheme, named E-VaaS, designed to improve traffic flow, reduce travel times, and enhance user satisfaction in intelligent transportation networks. By combining the *Gale-Shapley stable matching* algorithm with edge computing, the proposed E-VaaS system effectively schedules and matches riders to vehicles based on metrics that include travel time, distance, and cost. With the help of edge computing, E-VaaS enables low-latency processing, ensuring that ride-matching decisions are made swiftly and improving system responsiveness and user experience. Experimental results validate the effectiveness of the model, showing improved vehicle occupancy, reduced travel times and costs, and a balanced distribution of shared vehicles across the transportation network. This research advances the development of stable, scalable, and efficient ride-sharing solutions for urban environments.

Keywords: Edge networks · Ride-Sharing · Stable matching · Smart transportation · Game Theory

1 Introduction

In modern urban environments, the challenges of traffic congestion and inefficient vehicle usage are becoming increasingly critical. With growing urban populations, the traditional model of private vehicle ownership has led to substantial under-utilization of transportation resources, where individual vehicles frequently operate with low occupancy rates. This contributes to environmental issues and economic inefficiencies, as congested roads result in wasted time and higher fuel consumption. For example, according to the 2021 TomTom Traffic Index [2], cities such as Istanbul, Moscow, and Kyiv, suffer from severe traffic congestion, leading to hours of delay for commuters annually. Addressing these

Y.-C. Hsu et al. (Eds.): ICWE 2025, CCIS 2735, pp. 16–27, 2026.
https://doi.org/10.1007/978-3-032-11233-0_2

challenges requires a shift from individual vehicle ownership toward shared transportation solutions that optimize vehicle occupancy and improve traffic flow.

We argue that ride-sharing can be one of the promising solutions to these issues by encouraging individuals with similar destinations or routes to share a single vehicle. Various digital platforms have facilitated this practice, but traditional ride-sharing models often rely on centralized cloud-based systems, which can struggle to process requests efficiently during peak times. This also contributes heavily to a high carbon footprint. These systems typically use basic matching algorithms that focus on geographic proximity rather than a more holistic measure of user satisfaction, which includes factors like travel time, cost, and route efficiency. Consequently, they may fall short of providing the quick response and optimal matches that urban travelers expect.

To address these limitations, we introduce an Edge-Enabled Vehicle-as-a-Service (E-VaaS) system that combines the Gale-Shapley stable matching algorithm with edge computing to deliver a more efficient and user-centered ride-sharing experience. This novel E-VaaS framework is designed to improve traffic efficiency by maximizing vehicle occupancy, minimizing travel costs, and optimizing travel time, thereby enhancing traveler satisfaction. By integrating edge computing, the E-VaaS system reduces latency by processing data closer to end-users at edge nodes rather than solely relying on centralized cloud resources. This distributed architecture enables faster response times, allowing the system to match riders and vehicles in real time, essential in dynamic and high-demand urban contexts. In summary, our primary contributions are as follows:

1. We introduce a novel E-VaaS system that combines the Gale-Shapley stable matching algorithm with edge computing to achieve stable, real-time ride-sharing.
2. We present a satisfaction-driven matching framework that considers travel time and cost, enabling personalized matches that improve vehicle occupancy and user satisfaction.
3. We propose an edge-based ride request transmission mechanism, which reduces latency and ensures timely, responsive service for riders and drivers alike.
4. We evaluated and validated experimentally the effectiveness of the model, improvement of vehicle occupancy, reduced travel times and costs, and a balanced distribution of shared vehicles across the transportation network.

2   Related Works

There are a few existing works that focus on the concept of ride-sharing. Additionally, the integration of edge computing into public vehicle (PV) systems has garnered significant attention in recent years, aiming to enhance traffic efficiency, optimize vehicle occupancy ratios, and reduce overall congestion. Zhang et al. [6] presented a comprehensive Edge Computing Based Public Vehicle (ECPV) system designed to address these challenges by leveraging edge devices for real-time ride-sharing and vehicle scheduling. Their approach emphasizes the reduction of decision-making latency through distributed computing, thereby improving the quality of experience (QoE) for travelers. Previous research on the matching problem in ride-sharing systems has primarily addressed optimization challenges in route planning, dynamic pricing, and cost-sharing mechanisms. For instance, Guan *et al.* [4] examined ride-sharing trade-offs from a multi-objective perspective, aiming to maximize trip-sharing willingness and minimize total vehicle usage costs. Other studies have focused on dynamic pricing schemes, highlighting how fluctuating demand can result in pricing imbalances, leading to inefficiencies in matching and incentivizing drivers. Notably, Xie *et al.* [5] proposed a cost-sharing approach utilizing a double auction mechanism to maximize cost savings for drivers and passengers within specific timing constraints. Troyan *et al.* [1] proposed another approach that contrasts with standard commercial models by focusing on stable matching. Using the Gale–Shapley algorithm, adapted to accommodate different driver and passenger capacities, the authors demonstrate that the algorithm always reaches a stable matching. The experimental simulations of their model reinforce its effectiveness by validating stable matches across multiple randomly generated test cases, emphasizing the model's stability and scalability.

The proposed E-VaaS builds on the iterated version of the Gale-Shapley algorithm by introducing refined utility functions tailored to the cost-time trade-offs in ride-sharing systems, enhancing matching efficiency. By leveraging edge computing, we also reduce latency in real-time matching processes, addressing a critical gap in existing systems where rapid response times are essential for optimal user experience and system performance. This unique approach aims to deliver a robust, low-latency matching solution that improves stability and operational speed.

3   System Model

We consider a road network abstracted as a directed multi-graph $G = (N, E)$, where N and E represent the set of nodes corresponding to intersection points and the set of directed edges representing road segments between these nodes, respectively. Each user u, traveling along a path in G, follows a sequence

$$P_{0k} = n_0 \xrightarrow{e_{01}} n_1 \xrightarrow{e_{12}} \cdots \xrightarrow{e_{jk}} n_k$$

where $n_i \in N$, $e_{jk} \in E$, and $0 \leq i, j, k \leq k$. e_{jk} represents the directed edge connecting two nodes n_j and n_k. A sub-path $P_{ij} = n_i \cdots \xrightarrow{e_{ij}} \cdots n_j$ is considered a proper segment of a path P_{0k} if $\{e_{ij}\} \subseteq \{e_{0k}\}$. A weighting function $\omega : E \to \mathbb{R}^+$ is defined to represent the cost, e.g., travel time and distance, associated with each edge of the graph. The total cost of traversing the path P_{ij} is given by

$$\omega(P_{ij}) = \sum \omega(e_{ij})$$

In E-VaaS, we consider the roadside units (RSUs) as edge devices that ensure operational efficiency. Vehicles exchange real-time route and scheduling information with the closest RSUs over wireless networks. The cloud data center communicates with these edge devices via wired connections for global data aggregation and analysis. This distributed architecture allows edge devices to process and respond to ride requests while reducing latency significantly.

Each node $n \in N$ in the road network hosts an edge device or RSU, ensuring comprehensive coverage. These edge devices facilitate real-time communication with vehicles and handle localized data processing, thereby alleviating the load on central cloud servers and improving the scalability and responsiveness of the system.

4 E-VaaS: The Proposed Edge-Enabled Vehicle-as-a-Service System

4.1 Justification of Using Gale-Shapley Stable Matching Algorithm

A central component of the proposed E-VaaS system is adapting the Gale-Shapley stable matching algorithm [3]. It is traditionally used to solve matching problems with participants having individual preferences. Hence, it is particularly effective in situations requiring stable matches, ensuring that no rider-vehicle pair would prefer a different matching over the one assigned. In ride-sharing, the Gale-Shapley algorithm is adapted to consider the preferences of both riders and vehicles based on a utility function that incorporates travel time, distance, and cost. Each rider and vehicle has preferences calculated using a weighted sum of these factors, where time and cost often have the highest weights. The goal is to create stable matches that align with the preferences of both parties, reducing the likelihood of mid-trip cancellations or disruptions.

4.2 Mathematical Model Formulation

The utility function in E-VaaS aims to balance travel time and cost. For instance, travelers with more flexibility in timing may prefer routes with lower costs, while those on tight schedules might prioritize shorter travel times. This preference-based approach allows the system to generate personalized matches that increase user satisfaction. Additionally, using the Gale-Shapley algorithm enables the system to dynamically adjust matches as new requests are received, which is particularly beneficial during peak times when demand is high. By optimizing for both time and cost, the E-VaaS model increases the likelihood of achieving stable matches and incentivizes more users to participate in the ride-sharing service, as their preferences are accounted for.

To further enhance efficiency, our E-VaaS system leverages edge computing to handle the processing and decision-making closer to the users, thus reducing the dependency on a central server. In traditional cloud-based ride-sharing systems, requests are sent to a centralized server, which may result in significant latency due to network delays and heavy computational loads. Edge computing mitigates these issues by distributing the computational tasks across multiple edge nodes near end-users. This proximity allows edge nodes to quickly process ride requests and make matching decisions locally, thus enabling real-time response and reducing the load on cloud resources. With edge nodes handling the bulk of the processing, latency is minimized, which is critical for a responsive ride-sharing system that operates efficiently under fluctuating demand.

Dynamic Zone Management with Edge Devices. A specific edge device manages each geographic area or zone within the city. The edge device serves as a local computational hub, responsible for handling the matching requests, processing waiting lists, and monitoring vehicles within its designated zone.

Vehicles entering or leaving a zone inform the respective edge device of their status. When a vehicle (driver) enters a zone, it sends an entry message to the edge device, signaling that it is now available for matching within that zone. Similarly, when a vehicle exits, it sends a departure message informing the edge device, which removes it from the list of available drivers in that zone.

Matching Process and Edge Computation. The matching algorithm is run locally on each edge device, which handles requests from passengers and drivers within its specific zone. Each edge device represents the system as a bipartite graph, where nodes represent passengers and drivers in the zone, and edges signify potential matches with weights based on preference and utility levels.

4.3   Handling the Waiting List with Edge Devices

In cases where passengers are not matched within a few iterations, they are placed on a waiting list within the edge device's queue. Suppose a passenger remains on the waiting list without a match after a set number of iterations. The waiting list data is forwarded to nearby edge devices to explore broader matching options. This forwarding mechanism leverages the proximity of other edge devices, which may have nearby drivers that could pick up the unmatched passenger. In a hierarchical or peer-to-peer configuration, the closest edge devices can include the waiting passenger in their following matching process.

Inter-zone Coordination via Edge Devices. Edge devices maintain lightweight communication with neighboring edge devices, allowing passengers on the waiting list to have a greater chance of finding a driver even if their zone lacks available vehicles. When a new driver enters a zone and registers with the local edge device, the system checks if any passengers are still on the waiting list, locally or from nearby zones. Inter-zone coordination can help resolve cases where passengers in low-density areas might have experienced delays.

5   Theoretical Framework for E-VaaS

In our study, we introduce an **enhanced utility function** to assess and optimize ride-sharing matches between drivers and passengers. The utility function is a core concept in economic and mathematical optimization, representing a measure of preference or satisfaction. Here, our utility function quantifies the collective benefit or satisfaction that a potential ride-sharing arrangement brings to both drivers and passengers. The main aim of this utility function is to ensure that each match not only reduces costs and travel times for both parties but also respects individual rationality, where both driver and passenger benefit positively from the shared ride. This optimization is further supported by theoretical constraints and efficiency principles, ensuring the proposed matching process is practical and effective.

5.1   Utility Function Definition

The utility function $U(d,p)$ captures the net benefit of a shared ride between a driver d and a passenger p by considering cost savings and time efficiencies. Formally, this function is represented as follows:

$$U(d,p) = w_c \cdot [C_d(p) + C_p(d)] + w_t \cdot [T_d(p) + T_p(d)]$$

where w_c and w_t are weight coefficients for cost and time, constrained by $w_c + w_t = 1$ and $w_c, w_t \in [0,1]$; $C_d(p)$ and $C_p(d)$ represent the cost-related functions for the driver and passenger, respectively; and $T_d(p)$ and $T_p(d)$ represent the time-related functions for the driver and passenger, respectively.

By balancing cost and time through these weighted terms, the function allows us to quantify the **overall utility** of a ride-sharing match. This model aims to maximize $U(d,p)$ for pairs of drivers and passengers to determine optimal, mutually beneficial matches.

5.2   Cost Savings Analysis

Cost savings are crucial for drivers and passengers considering ride-sharing, as both are motivated by potential reductions in travel expenses.

Driver's Cost Function $C_{d(p)}$. For a driver, the cost function $C_d(p)$ represents the difference between the revenue received from the passenger $R_d(p)$ and any additional operational costs incurred due to the shared ride, denoted $O_d(p)$. Mathematically:

$$C_d(p) = R_d(p) - O_d(p)$$

where $R_d(p) = \beta \cdot d_p \cdot r$, with β as a fare share coefficient that defines the proportion of revenue received by the driver, d_p as the trip distance of the passenger, and r as the base fare rate; and $O_d(p) = (d_{det} \cdot c_r) + (t_{det} \cdot c_t)$, where d_{det} is the detour distance incurred to accommodate the passenger, c_r is the cost per distance unit, and $t_{det} = \frac{d_{det}}{v}$ is the detour time at average velocity v, multiplied by a time-based cost c_t.

Passenger's Cost Function $C_{p(d)}$. For a passenger, the cost function $C_p(d)$ quantifies the savings achieved by sharing the ride instead of bearing the full cost of a solo trip. It is represented as:

$$C_p(d) = C_s - C_r$$

where $C_s = d_p \cdot r$ is the cost of a solo trip; and $C_r = d_p \cdot r \cdot (1 - \delta)$ represents the reduced cost in the shared trip, with δ as a discount factor.

Thus, the passenger's utility from cost savings stems from the difference between the solo trip cost and the discounted shared trip cost.

5.3   Latency Analysis

In addition to cost, both drivers and passengers seek time efficiencies in ride-sharing. Time functions capture the impact of shared travel on each party's total journey duration.

Driver's Time Function $T_{d(p)}$. The driver's time-related benefit is calculated based on any additional time incurred from the detour and waiting time for the passenger:

$$T_d(p) = -(t_{det} + t_{wait})$$

where t_{wait} represents the waiting time for the passenger. A negative value indicates that these elements reduce the driver's utility.

Passenger's Time Function $T_{p(d)}$. The passenger's time savings function compares the time for a solo trip with that of a shared ride:

$$T_p(d) = T_s - T_r$$

where $T_s = \frac{d_p}{v}$ represents the solo travel time. $T_r = \frac{d_p + d_{det}}{v} + t_{wait}$ is the shared trip time, factoring in the detour and waiting time. This function captures how much travel time the passenger saves (or loses) by sharing a ride with the driver.

5.4   Theoretical Analysis

To ensure the effectiveness of the utility-based ride-sharing model, we establish two primary theorems [3]: **Individual Rationality** and **Route Efficiency**.

Theorem 1: Individual Rationality A ride-sharing match between driver d and passenger p is deemed rational if both benefit positively from the shared ride. Formally, this condition is satisfied if:

$$U(d, p) > 0 \iff U_d(p) > 0 \wedge U_p(d) > 0$$

Proof:

1. **Forward Direction** ($\Rightarrow$): If $U(d, p) > 0$, then both the driver's and passenger's components of utility must also be positive.

2. **Reverse Direction** ($\Leftarrow$): If both driver and passenger utilities are positive, then the overall utility $U(d, p)$ is also positive.

Theorem 2: Route Efficiency Route efficiency ensures minimal detours, keeping the shared route convenient and cost-effective. This is characterized by the **detour ratio** $\frac{d_{det}}{d_p}$, which should be bounded by a constant ϵ:

$$\exists\, \epsilon > 0 : \frac{d_{det}}{d_p} \leq \epsilon \iff \text{match is route-efficient}$$

Proof:

1. **Forward Direction** ($\Rightarrow$): Given $\frac{d_{det}}{d_p} \leq \epsilon$, the total time remains within acceptable bounds, ensuring route efficiency.
2. **Reverse Direction** ($\Leftarrow$): If the match is route-efficient, then $\frac{d_{det}}{d_p} \leq \epsilon$ must hold to maintain bounded travel times.

Corollary 1: Cost-Time Trade-off Balancing cost and time effectively within the utility function is crucial for maximizing matches. The optimal weights w_c^* and w_t^* for cost and time, respectively, can be derived as:

$$w_c^* = \frac{T}{C + T}, \quad w_t^* = \frac{C}{C + T}$$

where $C = C_d(p) + C_p(d)$ and $T = T_d(p) + T_p(d)$ are the combined cost and time components, respectively. This yields the highest possible utility for the given weight constraints.

This utility-based model provides a structured, theoretically sound framework for maximizing mutual benefit in ride-sharing arrangements. By balancing cost savings and time efficiencies, and applying constraints for rationality and route efficiency, this model guides an optimal ride-sharing matching process, effectively implemented through the Gale-Shapley algorithm. This approach improves user satisfaction and enhances system efficiency, encouraging broader adoption of shared mobility solutions.

5.5   Algorithm

This work proposes a new algorithm to address the stable matching problem in ride-sharing systems, adapting the well-known Gale-Shapley algorithm to a unique context. The proposed algorithm iterates over the Gale-Shapley method, modifying the traditional constraints on matching. Here, unlike in the original algorithm, the number of drivers and passengers need not be equal, and the algorithm can accommodate incomplete or non-strict preference lists, which more realistically reflect real-world ride-sharing environments.

To set up the matching framework, we define the users in the system as either passengers (type p) or drivers (type d). Each driver d has a limited number of seats available in their vehicle, denoted by s, and each passenger p seeks to occupy a seat. A total seat count, N_{seats}, represents all available seats in the ride-sharing system, and the number of passengers n_p should not exceed this capacity.

The algorithm introduces a "waiting list" for unmatched passengers, ensuring that any unmatched passenger is given a final option to join this list. If a passenger p is on the waiting list, it implies they could not find a driver, and in the model, this waiting list serves as a fallback with minimal priority for matching purposes.

To implement this matching process, the proposed algorithm represents the system as a bipartite graph, where nodes represent users (passengers and drivers), and edges represent possible pairings. Each edge between a passenger p_i and a driver d_j has a weight, which reflects the utility or preference level that p_i has for d_j, and vice versa. This setup allows us to represent the relationships between passengers and drivers as directed edges with weights for each direction, capturing each user's utility.

In every iteration of the modified Gale-Shapley process, a matching is conducted between passengers and drivers based on these preferences and available seats. If a stable matching is not yet achieved, the algorithm iterates further, updating the bipartite graph and reducing the set of edges by eliminating unstable or lower-priority pairings.

The algorithm continues to iterate until no further pairings improve stability, ensuring a convergent, stable matching for the ride-sharing system. By allowing for a flexible number of drivers and passengers and the option for passengers to wait if they are unmatched, this approach adapts Gale-Shapley to the complexities of real-world ride-sharing, prioritizing efficient seat allocation and maximizing utility for users.

6   Performance Evaluation

In this study, we designed a 3×3 grid comprising nine equal squares, with edges representing roads, as shown in Fig. 1. Each square has an edge device as a local computational hub for efficient communication and processing. Once a vehicle enters a zone, it notifies the edge device of its presence and the number of available seats, enabling real-time coordination for ride-sharing requests. All passengers and drivers are positioned on the edges, facilitating quick interactions with the corresponding edge device. This setup allows a comprehensive comparison of solo trips versus ride-sharing, with ride-sharing shown to be more cost-effective due to optimized shared expenses.

For the analysis, we examined two scenarios—one with a fixed number of passengers and varying drivers, and the other with a fixed number of drivers and varying passengers, as presented in Fig. 2. Results highlight that ride-sharing significantly reduces costs compared to solo trips by distributing expenses across multiple passengers. Additionally, if a zone lacks an available driver for a ride request, the edge device forwards the request to adjacent zones anticlockwise until a match is found. This dynamic, grid-based edge-device coordination ensures that passengers experience minimal delays even when no drivers are initially in their starting zone.

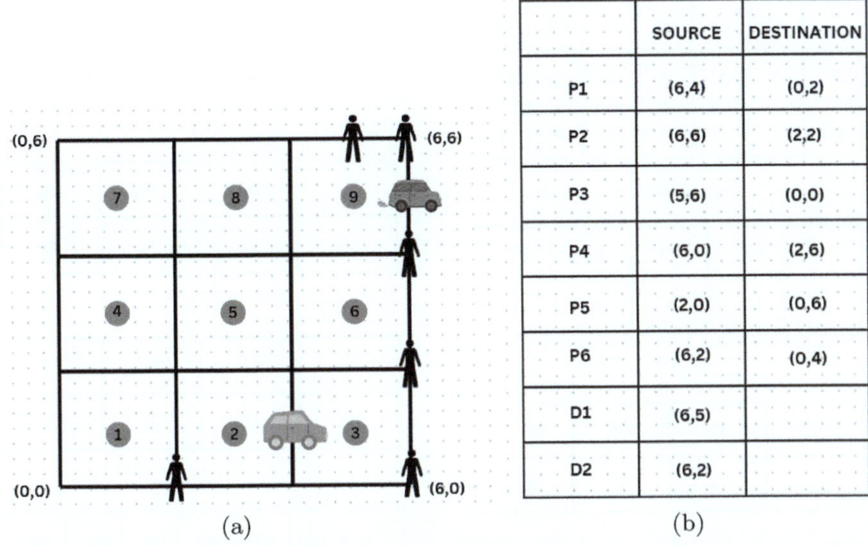

	SOURCE	DESTINATION
P1	(6,4)	(0,2)
P2	(6,6)	(2,2)
P3	(5,6)	(0,0)
P4	(6,0)	(2,6)
P5	(2,0)	(0,6)
P6	(6,2)	(0,4)
D1	(6,5)	
D2	(6,2)	

(b)

Fig. 1. Simulation Setup

We visualize the comparative performance of solo and shared trips for both scenarios. The findings underscore the efficiency and cost benefits of the ride-sharing model, primarily as the grid-based system supports rapid matching and minimizes redundant detours by systematically forwarding unmet requests across the grid. With zone-specific edge devices, this grid design demonstrates a scalable and responsive approach to optimizing urban ride-sharing networks.

We take a case of *six* passengers and *two* drivers. The current coordinates of passengers and drivers are given in Fig. 1(b). We evaluate the performance of ride-sharing in terms of cost and time efficiency. The distances of all passengers from the driver are calculated as shown in the figure. For solo riding drivers, D1 and D2 will pick up the nearest passenger and drop them at their location. The initial distances of drivers from passengers are given in Fig. 2(a). The one who drops first will then look on for the nearest passengers near them, and so on. The total time and cost for passengers are 43 s and Rs. 159(Considering unit distance on grid costs Rs. 3). In ride sharing, drivers broadcast their location and seat availability to their nearest edge device. Similarly, the ride request of passengers is also taken on the nearest edge device governing that area. If any driver or passenger is located equidistant from two edge devices, the requests are taken to the edge devices anticlockwise.

For example, in the given case, P1 is on (6,4), hence its request is forwarded to edge device 6. If any edge device has a request from a passenger, but there is no driver in the area, then the request is forwarded to the next edge device until the area covered by some edge device has a driver in it. For example, the ride request of P5 is taken on E1, but as there is no driver there, it is forwarded to E2, which

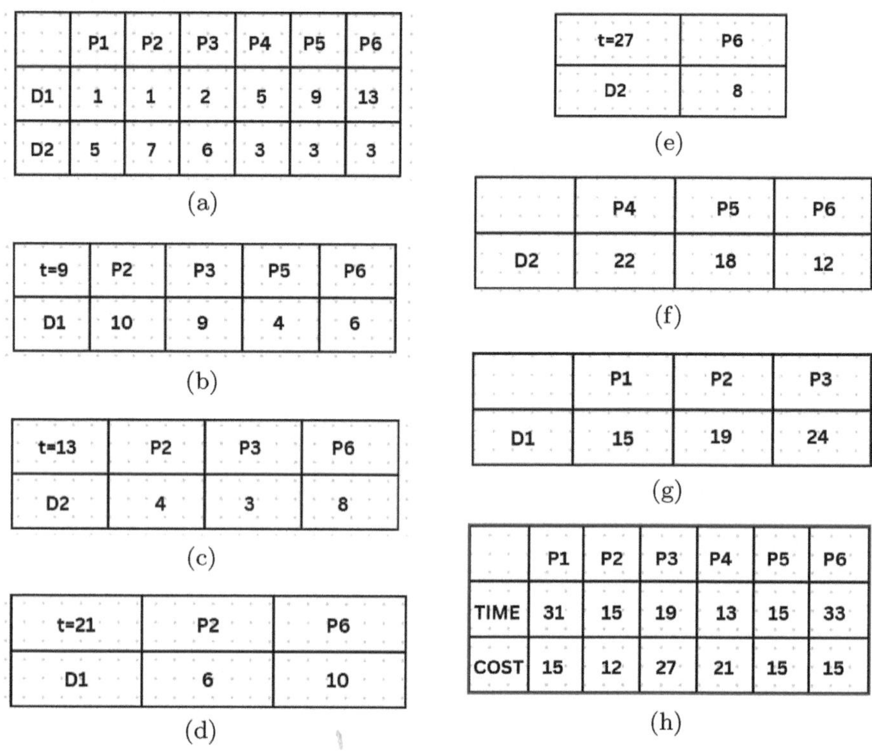

Fig. 2. Evaluation Scenarios

has a driver in that area. After this consideration, D1 received the requests from P1, P2, and P3 as shown in Fig. 2(g). Based on utility functions and applying the Gale-Shapley algorithm (considering cost coefficients as 0.7 and time as 0.3, discount factor as 0.5) on this, D1 will take P3 and P2 with it; similarly, D2 will take P4 and P5. There will be cost reduction for passengers as there are some common subroutes. Figure 2(h) shows the time at which each passenger is dropped and their effective cost. Finally, after calculations, the cumulative time and cost for passengers are 33 secs and Rs. 107.

7   Conclusion

This study introduces a novel, utility-optimized ride-sharing framework that leverages edge computing for dynamic, responsive matching between drivers and passengers. By integrating enhanced utility functions into a modified Gale-Shapley algorithm, the proposed system adapts traditional stable matching principles to better address the unique challenges of real-world ride-sharing, such as variable passenger-driver ratios and non-strict preferences. Adding edge devices in a distributed grid configuration improves matching efficiency and latency, enabling faster, localized decision-making and inter-zone coordination. In some cases, we demonstrate that ride-sharing using this edge-computing approach significantly reduces both costs and travel time when compared to solo trips. This system improves users' cost-effectiveness and offers a scalable solution that minimizes resource strain on central cloud servers. As urban mobility demands continue to evolve, the proposed model provides a practical, efficient solution that can enhance the adoption of shared mobility services, benefiting both individual users and the broader transport infrastructure.

Acknowledgment. This research was partially supported by the 6G Flagship (grant number 369116) funded by the Research Council of Finland.

References

1. Troyan, P., Delacrétaz, D., Kloosterman, A.: Essentially stable matchings. Games Econ. Behav. **120**, 370–390 (2020)
2. Beedham, M.: Here are the world's most congested cities according to the 2021 tomtom traffic index (2022). https://www.tomtom.com/newsroom/explainers-and-insights/the-most-congested-cities-in-2021/
3. Gale, D., Shapley, L.S.: College admissions and the stability of marriage. Am. Math. Monthly **69**(1), 9–15 (1962). http://www.jstor.org/stable/2312726
4. Guan, L., Pei, J., Liu, X., Zhou, Z., Pardalos, P.M.: Ridesharing in urban areas: multi-objective optimisation approach for ride-matching and routeing with commuters' dynamic mode choice. Int. J. Prod. Res. **60**(5), 1439–1457 (2022). https://doi.org/10.1080/00207543.2020.1859635
5. Xie, H., Yan, P., Bai, M., Chen, Z.: An efficient parking-sharing program through owner cooperation with robust slot assignment and incentive revenue distribution. Transp. Res. Part E: Logist. Transp. Rev. **191**, 103697 (2024)
6. Zhu, M., et al.: Public vehicles for future urban transportation. IEEE Trans. Intell. Transp. Syst. **17**(12), 3344–3353 (2016). https://doi.org/10.1109/TITS.2016.2543263

Underwater Object Identification with Edge Computing Paradigms

Shekhar Tyagi$^{(\boxtimes)}$ [iD], Akshat Shah [iD], and Abhishek Srivastava [iD]

Indian Institute of Technology Indore, Indore, India
`shekhartyagicse@gmail.com, asrivastava@iiti.ac.in`

Abstract. In this work, we propose a solution that simplifies the complex process of underwater object detection, surveillance and environmental monitoring. The approach proposed harnesses an Underwater Acoustic Sensor (UAS) system to detect and analyze objects within a three-dimensional underwater environment incorporating constraints through acoustic path loss models. The approach integrates three core components - Delaunay's Convex Hull-Based Reconstruction, Laws of Magnetic Equilibrium and Doppler's Effect in doing so. The UASs are optimally deployed in a grid format with each grid consisting of 8 sensors. The grid is equipped with an Insulated Magnetometer at the center to measure the net magnetic field intensity. The detected information is transmitted to a surface anchor/sink node for further analysis and detection.

Keywords: Wireless Sensor Network · Sensor deployment · Object Identification

1 Introduction

Several methods are in use for monitoring underwater environments. These are mainly utilised for biodiversity research, defense, resource prospecting, and infrastructure monitoring [12]. Climate change and marine ecosystem deterioration make the exercise of underwater monitoring imperative. Underwater Acoustic Sensor (UAS) networks are a widely used method for such monitoring [2].

Investigating and observing underwater environments is not easy amid poor visibility and signal attenuation. Traditional technologies such as sonar, imaging and ROVs/AUVs (Remotely Operated Vehicles/Autonomous Underwater Vehicles) have certain limitations. Sonar is efficient over larger distances but is affected by interference, whereas, imaging, requires good lighting and is often too expensive. ROVs and AUVs are efficient, but they use a lot of energy and equipment-setups. Current underwater object detection methods provide a strong foundation in UAS networks but most of them are dependent on machine learning (CNN [13], YOLO [15]) and computer vision (OpenCV) [4], which require better visibility conditions, lack bathymetric analysis and fail to address

Y.-C. Hsu et al. (Eds.): ICWE 2025, CCIS 2735, pp. 28–40, 2026.
https://doi.org/10.1007/978-3-032-11233-0_3

path losses. Their accuracy is limited and are only feasible in regions with good visibility.

For example Fossum et al. [9] and Fayaz et al. [8] used CNN and YOLO (You Only Look Once) based techniques for underwater tracking respectivey. However, these techniques are dependent on visual data sets and are not effective ($<=75\%$ accuracy) in underwater conditions with high depth and low visibility. Also, they do not consider path loss models, which is crucial for acoustic detection. Hayat et al. [11] and Zhang et al. [20] explored underwater object detection using OpenCV and YOLO-based techniques. These were also limited with an accuracy $<= 76.8\%$.

The proposed approach overcomes these challenges in the following manner:

1. It starts with bathymetric analysis and subsequently utilises path loss models to accurately deploy the sensors at optimal, known locations.
2. The object detection phase includes, Delaunay's Convex Hull-Based Point Cloud Reconstruction [14], the Law of Magnetic Equilibrium [16] and Doppler's Effect [17] to gain enhanced and accurate perception of object type (living or non - living), shape, location and state (rest or motion).
3. The data collected by the sensors is transmitted to a surface anchor/sink, enabling real-time processing.

The remainder of this paper is organized as follows: Sect. 2 discusses the proposed methodology in detail; Sect. 3 comprises comprehensive experiment description and results that validate the efficiency of the proposed approach through comparisons with existing methods and real-world deployment. Finally, Sect. 4 concludes the paper.

2 Proposed Methodology

This section describes the step-by-step approach to detect and analyze objects present underwater using the proposed sensor system.

2.1 Extraction of RoI and Topography Analysis

As shown in Fig. 1a the approach is initiation by selection of the Region of Interest (RoI) using Google Earth tools [10] by carefully placing coordinate points which can be exported as a KML (Keyhole Markup Language) file. The KML file includes information about the latitudes and longitudes of the points of interest. To obtain depth information on the points we utilise an Advanced Converter API [1]. The values thus obtained are stored in a CSV (Comma Separated Values) file. Finally, the data in the CSV file is plotted as a bathymetric distribution using a specialized tool named QuickGrid [7], showing depths, which helps in further calculations required for topography analysis, as illustrated in Fig. 1b.

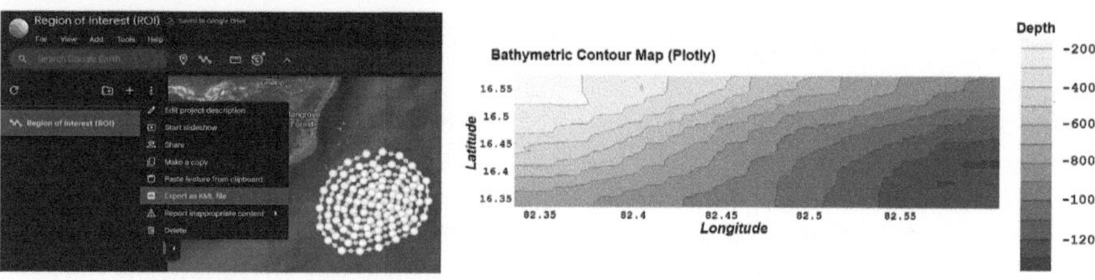

(a) Extracting RoI for Topography   (b) Bathymetric Distribution of Extracted RoI

Fig. 1. Extracted RoI and its Bathymetric Distribution

The bathymetric map enables the evaluation of the locations of the detected objects with good accuracy. The UAS system is able to determine whether an object is resting on the seabed or suspended in the water based on its location. They can also be used for varied tasks such as identification of stationary debris/wreckage, tracking underwater vehicles or aquatic organisms, tracking suspicious underwater activities and so on.

2.2 Path Loss Calculations for Underwater Environnments

Acoustic propagation is one of the most accepted methods for underwater monitoring. However, it has several prominent drawbacks that include and are not limited to absorption and transmission losses [18]. These are due largely to factors like frequency, pH, temperature, salinity, turbidity, depth and flow of waves and tides. In UAS networks, attenuation is significantly affected by these losses and leads to reduction of intensity of sound as it travels through water.

Absorption loss refers to the loss of acoustic energy as sound waves move through water. This energy is turned into heat due to the properties of the water and the frequency of the sound wave. Larger the frequency of sound, greater the absorption loss.

Transmission loss on the other hand is the total loss of acoustic energy in the medium. This loss occurs due to the spread of wave and absorption losses. Greater the distance between the source and the receiver, higher is the transmission loss.

The Anslei-McColm acoustic path loss model [3] provides mechanisms to compute how sound waves behave underwater. It computes that sound absorption increase with acidity(pH decreasing) and decreases with higher salinity at lower frequencies. Temperature generally reduces absorption, except near specific relaxation frequencies f_b and f_m for boric acid and for magnesium sulfate, where absorption increases. Whereas, at greater depths, high-frequency absorption decreases, but waves increase both absorption and transmission losses. This model calculates relaxation frequencies f_b and f_m using the following equations:

$$f_b = 0.78 \left(\frac{S_w}{35}\right)^{1/2} e^{T_w/26} \text{(for boron)} \tag{1}$$

$$f_m = 42e^{T_w/17} \text{(for magnesium)} \tag{2}$$

noindent where S_w is the salinity of water in parts per thousand (ppt), and T_w is the temperature of water in degrees Celsius (°C).

Based on the calculated relaxation frequencies, the absorption coefficient A can be calculated using [3]:

$$\alpha = 0.106\frac{f_b f^2}{f_b^2 + f^2}e^{\frac{\text{pH}-8}{0.56}} + 0.52\left(1 + \frac{T_w}{43}\right)\left(\frac{S_w}{35}\right)\frac{f_m f^2}{f_m^2 + f^2}e^{-\frac{Z}{6}} + 0.00049f^2 e^{-\left(\frac{T_w}{27} + \frac{Z}{17}\right)} \tag{3}$$

noindent where A is the absorption coefficient (in dB/km), Z is the depth (in km), and f is the frequency of acoustic signals (in kHz).

Further Transmission Loss T_L can be calculated using:

$$T_L = 10\log_{10}(R_1) + A.R_1 \tag{4}$$

noindent where T_L is the transmission loss (in dB), R_1 is the propagation range (in km), and A is the absorption coefficient (in dB per km).

These loss calculations are necessary to determine the new propagation ranges due to the changed behaviour of the sensors and acoustic signals in the real-time underwater environment which may also require to modify the grid arrangement.

2.3   System Arrangement for Object Identification

In this section, we will discuss underlying sensor modifications and the deployment strategy.

Components of UAS Modification: Figure 2 shows the construction of the UAS. The sensor has been modified and equipped with four components and are described as follows:

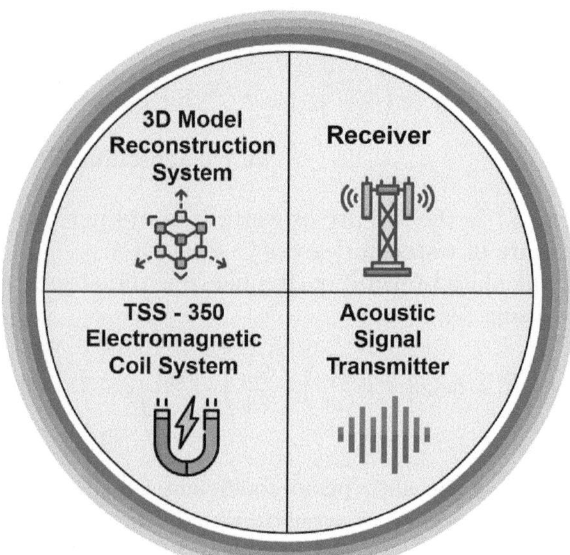

Fig. 2. Components of Sensor

1. *Reconstruction System* - The sensors produce sound waves, which pass through water and hit the surface of the object and then return to the sensor. Based on the velocity of acoustic signals in underwater and the time taken by the sound waves to collide the object and return (as calculated by the receiver itself), the system determines the distance D_{ij} from the sensor to the point of reflection on the object's surface. Finally, using the known coordinates of sensor's location $S_i(X_i, Y_i, Z_i)$, distance between the sensor and the point of reflection and the unit vector $\boldsymbol{r_{ij}}$ along that direction, the coordinates of that point $P_{ij}(x_j, y_j, z_j)$ are calculated. This is applicable to compute coordinates of several points on the object's surface from where the acoustic signals are reflected. Mathematically define as follows:

$$D_{ij} = c_w * TOF_j \tag{5}$$

$$x_j = X_i - D_{ij}.\hat{r_x} \tag{6}$$

$$y_j = Y_i - D_{ij}.\hat{r_y} \tag{7}$$

$$z_j = Z_i - D_{ij}.\hat{r_z} \tag{8}$$

where,

- $i, j > 0; i <= 8; i, j \in Z$,
- D_{ij}: Distance between i^{th} sensor and j^{th} point of reflection (in m),
- c_w: Velocity of sound in water i.e. $344\,\text{m/s}$,
- TOF: Time taken by acoustic signal to travel D_{ij} (in seconds).
- (X_i, Y_i, Z_i): Coordinates of ith sensor,
- (x_j, y_j, z_j): Coordinates of jth point of reflection,

- $r_{ij}(\hat{r_x}, \hat{r_y}, \hat{r_z})$: Unit vector in direction of reflected signal.

After computing the reflection points, a point cloud is formed on the object's surface within the sensor's range. Delaunay's triangulation then connects these points, creating an optimal and stable structure. Figure 3a depicts the 3D region with reflection points, while Fig. 3b illustrates the Delaunay triangulation process [14]. Note that the dimensions are in meters.

1. A set of reflection points $P(P_{1\ 1}, P_{1\ 2}, ..., P_{1\ n_r})$, where n_r is the number of reflection points, and each P_{ij} has coordinates (x_j, y_j, z_j) in 3D space is obtained from the above process. The convex hull is the smallest convex polygon (or polyhedron in 3D) that contains all the points.
2. Initially, a tetrahedron that contains all the points is constructed. The convex hull helps to determine the boundary of the triangulation. The triangulation starts with an initial set of tetrahedrons. New points are inserted one by one into the triangulation and the tetrahedrons which are already present in the space are updated to include the new point.
3. Multiple tetrahedrons are formed in the space by considering any three points such that no other point lies inside the circumcircle of these three points.
4. The algorithm iteratively keeps on connecting the points and edges and keeps on constructing tetrahedrons that satisfy the above property until it is ensured that no such set of three points is left in which condition of Delaunay's triangulation is satisfied.

Finally, a mesh is obtained where the minimum angles are maximized with iterations. By applying this method, a 3D mesh is obtained which shows the geometry of a part of the object. By collectively analyzing results of all the sensors, it gives a strong perception of the shape and size of the object.

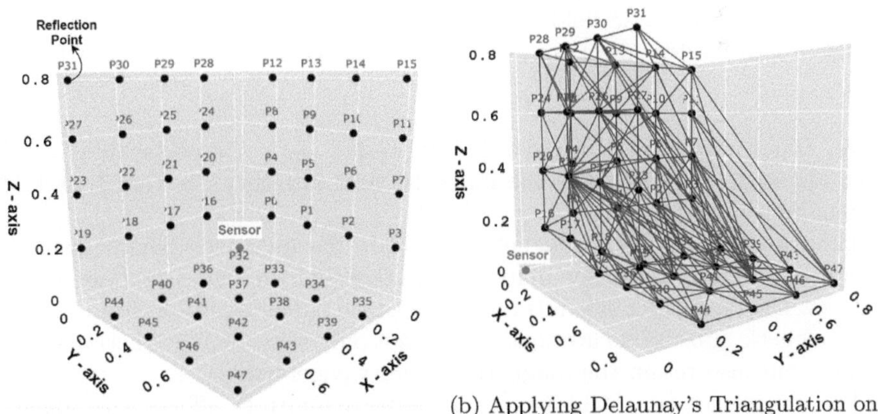

(a) Demonstration of Reflection points

(b) Applying Delaunay's Triangulation on Reflection points

Fig. 3. Visualization of Reflection Points and Delaunay Triangulation

2. *Receiver* - The first task of the receiver component is to measure the frequency of the signal echoed or reflected from the object. This frequency may be less than or equal to the original frequency of the signal emitted from the sensor. This can be confirmed using Doppler's Effect [6], which is a fundamental principle in physics. It describes the change in frequency of wave (sound or light) due to the relative motion between source and the object. In contrast to this, if the receiver detects change in frequency and assuming the source at rest, the velocity of the object can be determined using the Doppler's Effect. The formulation is shown below:

$$v_0 = c_w \cdot \left(\frac{f - f'}{f + f'} \right) \tag{9}$$

where, v_0 is the velocity of the object with respect to the source (in m/s), and f' is the frequency received by the receiver (in kHz).

The second task of the receiver is to figure out the time of flight and the direction of the emitted signal using the direction of the reflected signal. The receiver senses the reflected signal and then calculates unit vector r_{ij} along that direction. This information is shared with the reconstruction system that is required to calculate the locations of points of reflection.

3. *Electromagnetic Coil System (ECS)* - It uses a magnet(electromagnet) that creates a magnetic field with the help of electric current. The TSS-350 ECS [19] is used here over permanent magnets as its magnetic strength can be dynamically controlled by changing the electric current. An ECS is present within each of the sensors and produces a strong and steady magnetic field surrounding the corresponding sensor. The magnetometer will measure the magnetic field at equilibrium. As soon as an underwater object enters the region common to sensor's range and the magnetic field, equilibrium is disturbed and fluctuations are observed in the magnetometer reading. These fluctuations will provide a perception of the object that it is not a living organism but a ferromagnetic object. This is because magnetic field does not change drastically by intervention from weakly or non-ferromagnetic materials. Mathematically represented as follows:

$$B = \mu_0(H + M) \tag{10}$$

where, B is the magnetic flux density (in Tesla), μ_0 is the permeability of free space ($4\pi \times 10^{-7}$ H/m), H is the magnetic field intensity (in Tesla), and M is the magnetization (in A/m).

There are three types of magnetic materials: Paramagnetic, Diamagnetic and Ferromagnetic. Paramagnetic materials are those which have attraction towards magnets. Diamagnetic materials are those which suffer repulsion from magnets. Ferromagnetic substances are those which not only show high attraction towards magnets but also retain the magnetic property.pagebreak

The magnetic susceptibility (χ) and its magnitude affects the magnetic strength of a substance. Weakly Diamagnetic materials have negative χ with a lower magnitude, whereas strongly diamagnetic materials have negative χ with a higher magnitude. Similarly, weakly paramagnetic materials have small positive χ and strongly paramagnetic materials have high positive χ. Ferromagnetic materials are similar to strongly paramagnetic materials but can also retain magnetic properties. Most elements in the periodic table are diamagnetic. The tables can be reffered to for further details on the magnetic behavior of elements [5].

Most biological tissues are weakly diamagnetic in nature. This property can be useful for determining whether the object in water is the body of a living organism. Diamagnetic materials have a negative magnetization which is proportional to the magnetic field.

$$M_{dia} = -\chi_{dia}H \tag{11}$$

There is also a high chance where paramagnetic materials get encountered. These may be wreckage or part of some machinery. Paramagnetic materials have a positive magnetization which is proportional to the magnetic field.

$$M_{para} = \chi_{para}H \tag{12}$$

Using (10), (11) and (12), we get,

$$B = \mu_0 H(1 + \chi) \tag{13}$$

$$\Delta B = \mu_0 H \chi \tag{14}$$

For very small value of χ, ΔB becomes very small which implies that there is negligible effect on magnetic field intensity caused by the object and thus, $B_{total} \approx B$.

4. *Acoustic Signal Transmitter* - The acoustic signal transmission is by default set to spherical mode of propagation. These signals are transmitted in the form of concentric spheres outwards the sensor.

Deployment Strategy for UASs: Figure 3a represents the deployment strategy of the sensors using the proposed approach. The sensors are deployed within a uniform grid, each grid consisting of 8 sensors. Each sensor is equipped with the modifications as discussed above. In the center, lies a magnetometer to measure the overall magnetic field equilibrium within the grid (Fig. 4).

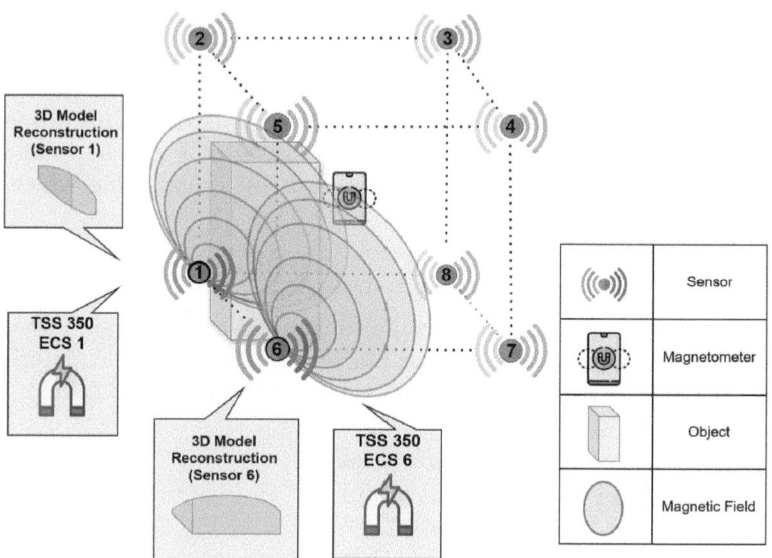

Fig. 4. Deployment Architecture

Time Complexity Analysis: The complexity of entire process is contributed by the four main components.

1. The reading of the magnetic field fluctuations through the magnetometer can be understood as a constant time complexity of $O(1)$.
2. The process of determining object motion through the Doppler's Effect also has a constant time complexity of $O(1)$ as it involves direct mathematical computation of object's velocity.
3. The process of calculating all the reflection points involves first calculating the time of flight of the number of signals emitted with complexity of $O(N)$(for N being number of signals emitted). The signals reaching back after collision from the object have complexity of $O(n)$ (for n being number of signals returned) making the total $O(N+n)$. Moreover, the time complexity to compute X,Y and Z coordinates for each reflection point is $O(3n)$ (for n being the number of reflection points). Adding all of them simplifies to linear time complexity of $O(n)$.
4. Finally the process of Delaunay's Triangulation has the most optimal time complexity of $O(n \log n)$ (for n being the number of reflection points in the point cloud).

The analysis of the accuracy of the reconstruction system is significant in the entire process. It is important to note that accuracy can be calculated by dividing the number of points in the point cloud that participate in Delaunay's Triangulation by the total number of points in the point cloud as in Eq. 15.

$$A_{\text{overall}} = \frac{No.\ of\ connected\ points\ in\ point\ cloud}{Total\ no.\ of\ points\ in\ point\ cloud} \tag{15}$$

However, there may be some points present on the boundary of the part of object in the sensor's range . This can have a negative but negligible effect on overall accuracy and the perception accuracy still stays 100 % as it depends on the clarity of the shape of the object which is still understandable.

3 Results and Evaluation

3.1 Simulation Environment

We have developed a simulation environment for this using Python 3.10.11 on a Notebook Computer equipped with an Intel i7 12th-gen processor, 16 GB RAM, and a dedicated NVIDIA graphics card. The simulation process is shown in Fig. 5a where a 3-D underwater region of $100\,\text{m} \times 100\,\text{m} \times 100\,\text{m}$ is assumed at a random location. Inside the region an imaginary object is considered using Convex Hull at coordinates $(20, 40, 40)$.

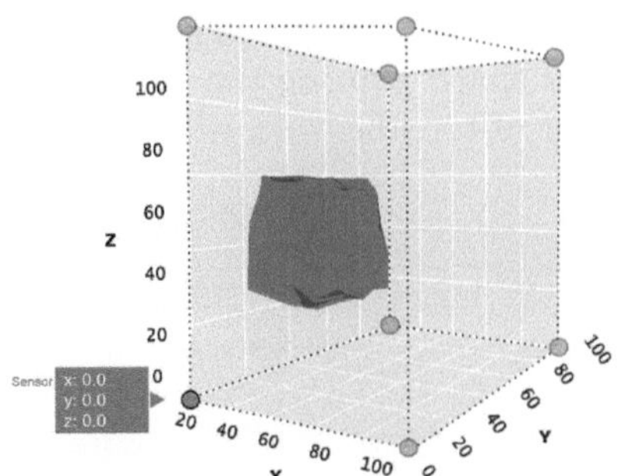

(a) A 3-D underwater region with an object

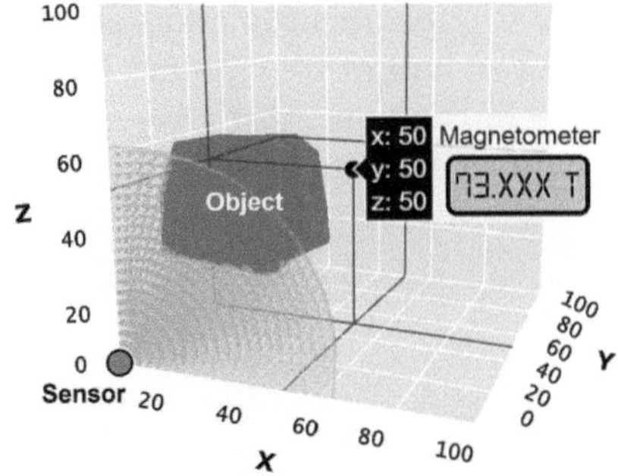

(b) Point cloud of the object obtained from a single sensor view

Fig. 5. Simulation Process

The sensors are placed at all extreme corners of the grid. However, the sensors' position may vary a little with consideration of the path loss model. Also, to reduce complexities, further simulations are carried out for a single sensor placed at coordinates $(0, 0, 0)$. A magnetometer is placed at the center of the grid which measures the equilibrium magnetic field intensity. The readings are shared to the sink node managing the grid.

38   S. Tyagi et al.

The process begins by determining sensor locations using bathymetric analysis. When an underwater object enters the grid, magnetometer readings may fluctuate due to disturbances in the magnetic field, indicating whether the object is ferromagnetic. Doppler's Effect then determines the object's velocity and helps calculate reflection points of acoustic signals. Based on magnetometer fluctuations and velocity, the object is classified as living, non-living, or machinery. Delaunay's Point Cloud Triangulation reconstructs the object's surface within the sensor's propagation range, with green tetrahedrons filling the point cloud Fig. 5b. Data from all eight sensors is analyzed collectively for higher perception accuracy and sent to the sink node for transmission to the base station.

Figure 8 represents nearly linear variation of total number of triangulations as we increase number of reflection points. Figure 9 represents time taken to construct final object with different number of triangulations. Figure 6 represents percentage of area covered for different numbers of reflection points. Figure 7 represents percentage of area covered at reaching different number of simplices. A **simplex** is a fundamental building block of the triangulation. A 0-simplex is a point, 1-simplex is a line segment connecting two points, 2-simplex a triangle and 3-simplex a tetrahedron and so on. We can also say that n-simplex is nothing but the convex hull of n+1 points in n-dimensional space. During the triangulation process in the point cloud we achieve a number of tetrahedrons which increases the number of simplices.

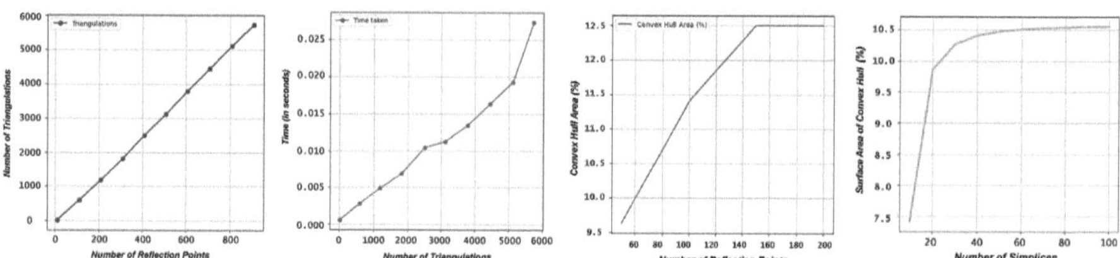

Fig. 6. Covered area of Convex Hull vs Number of reflection points.

Fig. 7. Covered area of Convex Hull vs Number of simplices.

Fig. 8. Number of triangulations vs Number of reflection points.

Fig. 9. Time taken vs Number of triangulations.

3.2 Comparative Analysis with Existing Underwater Object Detection Techniques

In this section, we compare the outcomes of our approach with several existing methods based on key performance parameters. Although a direct comparison is challenging due to variations in experimental setups and results, we have considered several important criteria, including accuracy, depth limit, time complexity, real-time monitoring capability, dependency on datasets, and the use of imaging and videography equipment. The comparative analysis is presented in Table 1.

Table 1. Comparative analysis of the proposed method with existing methods based on different parameters.

Parameter	Proposed Approach	Fossum et al. [9]	Fayaz et al. [8]	Hayat et al. [11]	Zhang et al. [20]
Imaging/Video Architecture	None	CNN	CNN, YOLO	OpenCV	OpenCV, YOLO
Bathymetric Analysis	Yes	No	No	No	No
Path Loss Consideration	Yes	No	No	No	No
Real-time Monitoring	Yes	Yes	Yes	No	Yes
Dataset	None	J-EDI	Heriot-Watt Dataset	None	Robot Target Catching Dataset
Depth Limit	Only pressure constraint	300 m	Until Visibility	Until Visibility	Until Visibility
Time Complexity	$O(n \log n)$	$> O(n^2)$	$O(n^3)$	$O(n^3)$	$O(n^3)$
Accuracy	100%	75%	$< 75\%$	Low	76.8%

4 Conclusion

Underwater exploration faces challenges with traditional methods like imaging and videography based ones, as these are ineffective in unclear regions and lacks bathymetric analysis and path loss models. To overcome this, we use acoustic detection with strategically placing sensors in a grid set-up. Techniques like Delaunay's Convex Hull, Magnetic Equilibrium, and Doppler's Effect enhanced our object detection scheme.

Acknowledgment. The authors would like to acknowledge support from the Research Council of Norway through their INTPART DTRF project.

References

1. Advanced Converter: Find depth by coordinates. Webpage (2024). https://www.advancedconverter.com/map-tools/find-altitude-by-coordinates. Accessed 28 Jan 2025
2. Aguzzi, J., et al.: New technologies for monitoring and upscaling marine ecosystem restoration in deep-sea environments. Engineering (2024)
3. Ainslie, M.A., McColm, J.G.: A simplified formula for viscous and chemical absorption in sea water. J. Acoust. Soc. Am. **103**(3), 1671–1672 (1998)

4. Bradski, G.: Learning opencv: computer vision with the opencv library. O'REILLY Google Schola **2**, 334–352 (2008)
5. Contributors, W.: Diamagnetism, paramagnetism, and ferromagnetism (2025). https://en.wikipedia.org/wiki/Diamagnetism. https://en.wikipedia.org/wiki/Paramagnetism. https://en.wikipedia.org/wiki/Ferromagnetism. Accessed 05 Feb 2025
6. Contributors, W.: Doppler effect (2025). https://en.wikipedia.org/wiki/Doppler_effect. Accessed 05 Feb 2025
7. Coulthard, J.: Quikgrid (version 5.4.4). Computer software (2007). Accessed 22 Jan 2025
8. Fayaz, S., Parah, S.A., Qureshi, G.: Underwater object detection: architectures and algorithms-a comprehensive review. Multimedia Tools Appl. **81**(15), 20871–20916 (2022)
9. Fossum, T.O., Sture, Ø., Norgren-Aamot, P., Hansen, I.M., Kvisvik, B.C., Knag, A.C.: Underwater autonomous mapping and characterization of marine debris in urban water bodies. arXiv preprint arXiv:2208.00802 (2022)
10. Google: Google Earth (2024). https://earth.google.com/. Accessed 28 Jan 2024
11. Hayat, M.A., Yang, G., Iqbal, A., Saleem, A., Mateen, M.: Comprehensive and comparative study of drowning person detection and rescue systems. In: 2019 8th International Conference on Information and Communication Technologies (ICICT), pp. 66–71. IEEE (2019)
12. Huy, D.Q., Sadjoli, N., Azam, A.B., Elhadidi, B., Cai, Y., Seet, G.: Object perception in underwater environments: a survey on sensors and sensing methodologies. Ocean Eng. **267**, 113202 (2023)
13. LeCun, Y., Bottou, L., Bengio, Y., Haffner, P.: Gradient-based learning applied to document recognition. Proc. IEEE **86**(11), 2278–2324 (1998)
14. Rakotosaona, M.J., Guerrero, P., Aigerman, N., Mitra, N.J., Ovsjanikov, M.: Learning delaunay surface elements for mesh reconstruction. In: Proceedings of the IEEE/CVF Conference on Computer Vision and Pattern Recognition, pp. 22–31 (2021)
15. Redmon, J.: You only look once: unified, real-time object detection. In: Proceedings of the IEEE Conference on Computer Vision and Pattern Recognition (2016)
16. Sorensen, C.: Magnetism. In: Nanoscale Materials in Chemistry, pp. 169–221 (2001)
17. Toman, K.: Christian doppler and the doppler effect. EOS Trans. Am. Geophys. Union **65**(48), 1193–1194 (1984)
18. Tsuchiya: Acoustic absorption coefficient in seawater. Webpage (2010), https://tsuchiya2.org/absorption/absorp_e.html. Accessed 25 Jan 2025
19. Zhang, J., Xiang, X., Li, W.: Advances in marine intelligent electromagnetic detection system, technology, and applications: a review. IEEE Sens. J. **23**(5), 4312–4326 (2021)
20. Zhang, L., Li, C., Sun, H.: Object detection/tracking toward underwater photographs by remotely operated vehicles (rovs). Futur. Gener. Comput. Syst. **126**, 163–168 (2022)

LLM-Driven Multi-agent Recommendation for QoS-Aware Edge Server Selection in Mobile Environments

Eunjeong Ju[1], Jeonghwa Lee[1], Duksan Ryu[1(✉)], and Jongmoon Baik[2]

[1] Department of Software Engineering, Jeonbuk National University,
Jeonju, South Korea
`{jeju3146,dlwjdghk133,duksan.ryu}@jbnu.ac.kr`
[2] School of Computing, Korea Advanced Institute of Science and Technology,
Daejeon, South Korea
`jbaik@kaist.ac.kr`

Abstract. Mobile Edge Computing (MEC) environments present significant challenges for edge server selection due to user mobility, varying network conditions, and diverse service intents. Traditional static Quality of Service (QoS)-based methods often fail to adapt to these dynamic, context-sensitive scenarios. The objective of this paper is to improve server selection quality by incorporating user intent and predicted future conditions into the decision-making process. To this end, we propose an LLM-driven multi-agent recommendation framework. The system is composed of agents responsible for user context interpretation, mobility prediction, QoS estimation, and final server selection, coordinated through a central controller. A Large Language Model (LLM) is used to infer the relative importance of QoS metrics—such as response time, throughput, server load, and failure rate—from natural language preferences, and to reason about optimal server choices. Experimental results demonstrate that our method significantly outperforms baseline approaches in server selection accuracy. The LLM successfully identifies user-prioritized QoS dimensions even from minimal input and enhances decision quality through contextual reasoning. These findings suggest that LLMs offer a promising approach to enabling adaptive, personalized, and explainable edge server recommendations in future MEC systems.

Keywords: Mobile Edge Computing · LLM-based Multi-Agent System · Context-Aware Recommendation

1 Introduction

MEC has emerged as a foundational infrastructure for supporting latency-sensitive and computation-intensive services, including real-time streaming, autonomous driving, smart cities, and augmented reality. A central challenge in MEC environments is the dynamic selection of the most suitable edge server for each user, particularly under user mobility and fluctuating network conditions.

Y.-C. Hsu et al. (Eds.): ICWE 2025, CCIS 2735, pp. 41–53, 2026.
https://doi.org/10.1007/978-3-032-11233-0_4

Traditional server selection approaches predominantly rely on static heuristics such as physical proximity or average QoS metrics (e.g., response time, throughput). While computationally efficient, these methods often overlook application specific requirements and user intent. For instance, video conferencing demands low latency, whereas music streaming emphasizes stable throughput. Consequently, applying uniform selection policies across diverse contexts can degrade Quality of Experience (QoE).

Moreover, selecting servers based solely on the user's current location neglects temporal dynamics and evolving server-side conditions. Anticipating the user's future location and proactively assessing server states—such as system load and failure probability—can improve decision quality, albeit at the cost of increased computational complexity.

The objective of this study is to enhance the quality of server selection by incorporating both user intent and predicted server conditions into the decision-making process. To this end, we propose a context-aware, multi-agent server recommendation framework that leverages the reasoning capabilities of a LLM. The proposed system is composed of specialized agents responsible for: (i) inferring QoS priorities from high-level user context, (ii) predicting future mobility and corresponding server conditions, and (iii) selecting the optimal server via LLM-based reasoning in a flexible and explainable manner.

We validate the proposed method using a hybrid dataset and address three research questions (RQ1–RQ3). Experimental results show that our method consistently outperforms conventional baselines, effectively infers user-specific QoS preferences from minimal context, and improves selection accuracy by replacing fixed scoring logic with contextual LLM-driven reasoning.

The remainder of this paper is organized as follows. Section 2 reviews related work. Section 3 presents the proposed procedure. Section 4 describes the experimental setup. Section 5 reports and analyzes the results. Section 6 discusses threats to validity, and Sect. 7 concludes the paper.

2   Related Work

2.1   Edge Server Selection Strategies

In MEC environments, selecting the optimal edge server is critical for ensuring QoS and delivering a seamless user experience. Early approaches primarily relied on distance-based heuristics [1,2], which are computationally lightweight but insufficient for handling dynamic network conditions such as server load and fluctuating latency.

To improve upon this, QoS-aware selection techniques were introduced that combine metrics like response time and throughput into a weighted score [3,4]. While more accurate, these approaches typically assume static or uniform weight assignments for all users, which limits their adaptability to individualized user contexts [5,6].

Recent efforts have introduced dynamic server state monitoring and mobility-aware predictions [7,8], often incorporating machine learning models to better anticipate user movement or network performance. However, most still lack the capability to flexibly interpret user intent or dynamically adjust QoS priorities in real time.

2.2   QoS Prediction and Imputation Techniques

A common approach to server recommendation is computing a weighted combination of QoS metrics using predefined weights [9,10]. However, such methods often overlook user-specific preferences [11]. To address this, optimization-based strategies such as Analytic Hierarchy Process, Genetic Algorithms, and Particle Swarm Optimization have been explored for weight learning [12,13]. Despite their personalization benefits, these methods often suffer from scalability issues and are less suitable for real-time inference.

Table 1. Performance comparison of QoS prediction models under 10% missing rate

Model	Throughput		Response Time	
	MAE	RMSE	MAE	RMSE
UIPCC	22.84	55.34	0.582	1.380
LMF-PP	16.91	48.14	0.486	1.322
DCALF (SOTA)	**15.83**	**47.42**	**0.492**	**1.275**

Additionally, QoS datasets frequently include missing entries, motivating the development of robust imputation techniques. Traditional collaborative filtering (CF), matrix factorization, and deep learning-based models such as DCALF (Dual Collaborative Autoencoder for Latent Factorization) have demonstrated effectiveness in imputing incomplete QoS values [14,15].

Based on our preliminary evaluations, DCALF outperformed alternative models in both throughput and response time prediction under 10% missing data conditions. Consequently, DCALF was selected as the primary QoS imputation method in our system, as summarized in Table 1.

2.3   Context-Aware Inference and LLM-Based Reasoning

While metrics such as latency, throughput, and availability are fundamental to QoS, their relative importance varies depending on the user's application context. For example, streaming services typically emphasize throughput and reliability, whereas real-time communication demands low response time [16,17].

To reflect this diversity, recent work has explored context-aware server recommendation using factors such as application type, user location, and temporal patterns [18,19]. However, many of these systems rely on rule-based logic or fixed heuristics, limiting their generalization to new or complex user needs.

Our work addresses this limitation by introducing a LLM-driven reasoning framework [20,21]. Given a minimal natural language input (e.g., "music streaming"), the LLM infers user intent and dynamically assigns weights to QoS elements. Furthermore, the LLM exhibits strong generalization and robustness in handling cold-start scenarios or sparse data, providing reliable decisions even in underrepresented conditions.

In summary, although prior studies have investigated mobility-aware edge selection, QoS prediction, and context-aware decision-making, they largely rely on fixed heuristics, rule-based mechanisms, or static weight configurations. Such methods fall short in adapting to diverse user intents or real-time network conditions. Our work addresses these limitations by employing a LLM to infer QoS preferences directly from natural language input and integrating this capability into a modular multi-agent architecture. This enables flexible, personalized, and explainable edge server recommendations that extend beyond traditional heuristic- or optimization-based approaches.

3   Methodology

This study proposes an LLM-based multi-agent system for adaptive edge server recommendation. The system is designed to select the most suitable server by integrating user context, mobility prediction, and real-time server status.

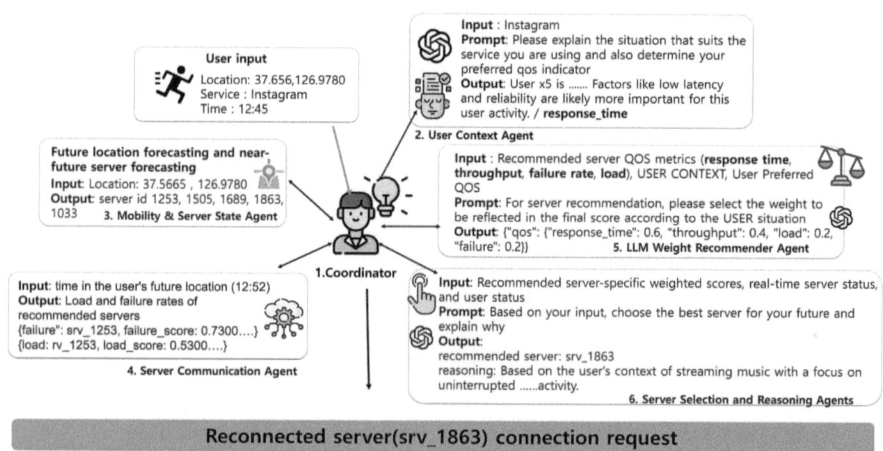

Fig. 1. System Overview

It consists of five modular agents coordinated by a central **Coordinator**, which governs the information flow between agents. Each agent performs a specialized task, and their collective output leads to an explainable and personalized recommendation. The overall system architecture is shown in Fig. 1.

3.1   Coordinator Agent

The **Coordinator Agent** manages the execution pipeline and communication between all other agents (**line 1**). It receives the initial input (l, t, s) and sequentially activates the user context agent (lines 2–5), mobility prediction (lines 6–9), server state querying (lines 10–14), and the subsequent reasoning modules. After receiving the final output from the *Server Selection and Reasoning Agent* (lines 27–29), the Coordinator finalizes the server recommendation.

Algorithm 1. LLM-Driven Multi-Agent Edge Server Recommendation Procedure

---

Require: User location l, time t, service name s
Ensure: Recommended server $\hat{s}$
1: **Coordinator Agent:** Manage execution and communication across all agents.
2: **Step 1: User Context Agent**   *// Infer user context*
3:     Input: (s, t)
4:     Use LLM to generate contextual description C of user service intent.
5:     Example output: "User is listening to music and expects stable playback."
6: **Step 2: Mobility & Server State Agent**   *// Predict user mobility*
7:     Input: (l, t)
8:     Predict future location l_{fut} using LSTM.
9:     Identify top-k nearby servers $S = \{s_1, ..., s_k\}$ around l_{fut}.
10: **Step 3: Server Communication Agent**   *// Collect server metrics*
11: **for** each $s_i \in S$ **do**
12:     Query predicted load $LD(s_i, t_{fut})$
13:     Query predicted failure rate $FR(s_i, t_{fut})$
14: **end for**
15: **Step 4: QoS Completion Module**   *// Fill missing QoS data*
16: **if** $RT(s_i)$ or $TP(s_i)$ is missing **then**
17:     Apply DCALF or collaborative filtering to estimate missing values
18: **end if**
19: **Step 5: LLM Weight Recommender Agent**   *// Infer QoS importance*
20:     Input: Context C
21:     Use LLM to infer weights for QoS factors:
        $w_{\text{resp}}, w_{\text{thr}}, w_{\text{load}}, w_{\text{fail}}$
22: **Step 6: QoS Scoring Module**   *// Compute score per server*
23: **for** each $s_i \in S$ **do**
24:     Compute:
        $\text{Score}(s_i) = w_{\text{resp}} \cdot RT(s_i) + w_{\text{thr}} \cdot TP(s_i) + w_{\text{load}} \cdot LD(s_i) + w_{\text{fail}} \cdot FR(s_i)$
25: **end for**
26: **Step 7: Server Selection and Reasoning Agent** *// Final decision*
27:     Input: C, QoS scores, server metrics
28:     Use LLM to select server $\hat{s}$ and generate explanation
29: **return** $\hat{s}$

3.2   User Context Agent

This agent interprets high-level user intent using a Large Language Model (**lines 2–5**). It receives the service name and time as input and produces a semantically enriched context C (e.g., "User is listening to music and expects stable playback"). This context is forwarded to the weight inference step and serves as the basis for determining QoS importance in downstream agents.

3.3   Mobility and Server State Agent

The **Mobility & Server State Agent** forecasts the user's future location l_{fut} using a mobility prediction model (e.g., LSTM), and identifies the top-k edge servers near that location (**lines 6–9**). This enables the system to anticipate where the user will be and focus server selection on relevant candidates.

3.4   Server Communication Agent

This agent retrieves predicted server-side metrics—load and failure rate—for each candidate server $s_i \in S$ using forecasting or monitoring tools (**lines 10–14**). These metrics are essential inputs for the scoring and selection process.

3.5   Missing QoS Data Imputation

To handle missing data, this module imputes unavailable values for response time $RT(s_i)$ or throughput $TP(s_i)$ using either DCALF or collaborative filtering techniques (**lines 15–18**). This ensures robustness in environments with sparse measurements.

3.6   LLM Weight Recommender Agent

Based on the contextual information C, the LLM infers the relative importance of QoS metrics: response time, throughput, server load, and failure rate (**lines 19–22**). These weights—w_{resp}, w_{thr}, w_{load}, w_{fail}—are used in the scoring formula to reflect user-specific QoS priorities.

3.7   QoS Scoring Module

For each candidate server, a weighted score is calculated by combining the predicted QoS values and the LLM-inferred weights (**lines 23–25**). The score quantifies how well a given server matches the user's preferences and expected conditions.

3.8   Server Selection and Reasoning Agent

This final agent receives the candidate servers, their QoS scores, and the context C (**lines 26–29**). It constructs a prompt for the LLM to semantically reason over the inputs and return the most appropriate server $\hat{s}$ along with an explanation. This step enables flexible and interpretable server selection based on context-aware logic.

4 Experimental Setup

4.1 Research Questions

To assess the effectiveness of the proposed system in terms of accurate, personalized, and context-aware server recommendation, we define the following research questions:

- **RQ1:** Does LLM-based context-aware recommendation outperform traditional static QoS-based selection methods?
- **RQ2:** Can the LLM accurately infer the primary QoS priority from user preferences alone?
- **RQ3:** Does LLM-based reasoning yield more accurate server selection than traditional score-based logic?

4.2 Dataset

We construct a hybrid evaluation dataset by integrating two publicly available sources, each serving a complementary role in simulating a MEC scenario:

- **Shanghai Telecom:** Provides user mobility traces and base station connection logs, which are essential for modeling user movement over time. These logs enable prediction of future locations and identification of top-k nearby edge server candidates [22].
- **WSDream:** Offers real-world QoS measurements collected from 300 users and 5,200 web services [9]. These measurements are critical for simulating server-side network conditions in a data-driven manner.

By combining mobility data and service quality metrics, we emulate both user-side dynamics and server-side variability, which are central to evaluating context-aware server recommendation. For each simulated user movement instance, a corresponding QoS record is assigned. The **ground truth server** is defined as the top-k closest server with the highest weighted QoS score (with equal weights of 0.5 for response time and throughput), independent of any LLM inference. This serves as the baseline reference for evaluation.

4.3 Evaluation Metric

We adopt **Top-1 Accuracy** as a unified evaluation metric for all research questions. It reflects the proportion of cases where the top-ranked prediction $\hat{y}_i$ matches the ground truth label y_i:

$$\text{Top-1 Accuracy} = \frac{1}{N} \sum_{i=1}^{N} \mathbb{K}\left(\hat{y}_i = y_i\right) \tag{1}$$

Here, $\mathbb{K}(\cdot)$ is the indicator function, returning 1 if the condition is true and 0 otherwise.

- For **RQ1** and **RQ3**, $\hat{y}_i$ is the server selected by the system, and y_i is the ideal server.
- For **RQ2**, $\hat{y}_i$ is the QoS priority inferred by the LLM, and y_i is the expected ground-truth QoS element.

This consistent metric enables direct comparison across different types of reasoning tasks.

4.4 Implementation Details

We implemented the proposed system using the OpenAI GPT API as the backbone for LLM-based reasoning. The LLM is integrated into a multi-agent decision-making pipeline and performs three key roles: (1) inferring context-aware QoS weights from natural language user input, (2) predicting or imputing missing QoS metrics for candidate servers, and (3) selecting the optimal server through contextual reasoning.

To ensure fair comparison, all baseline and LLM-based methods were tested under identical user inputs and simulated environmental conditions. We consistently used Top-1 Accuracy across all evaluations to quantify how accurately each method selected the correct server.

Baseline models corresponding to each research question—including static QoS-based selection, response-time-only, throughput-only, and score-based logic were independently implemented. Detailed descriptions of each baseline are provided in Sect. 5 alongside their respective experimental results.

5 Experimental Results

5.1 RQ1: Effectiveness of LLM-Based Context-Aware Recommendation

To evaluate the effectiveness of our proposed recommendation system, we compared it with four representative baselines, each reflecting a traditional strategy in QoS-aware edge server selection:

- **Distance-Based Selection**: Selects the server that is physically closest to the user's predicted future location, without considering any QoS attributes. This approach represents classical heuristics based on user mobility only.
- **Response Time Only**: Selects the server with minimal predicted latency, ignoring context and other QoS dimensions. This captures latency-optimized but context-independent decision-making.
- **Throughput Only**: Chooses the server with the highest predicted throughput, disregarding latency or failure risk. This corresponds to bandwidth-optimized strategies.
- **Static QoS Weights**: Computes a server score using fixed weights (0.5 for response time and 0.5 for throughput) and selects the server with the highest score. This simulates conventional QoS aggregation approaches commonly used in prior studies.

Unlike these fixed, non-adaptive baselines, our LLM-based approach infers user intent from natural language and dynamically prioritizes QoS metrics through contextual reasoning. This enables personalized and adaptive server selection tailored to diverse service needs and real-time conditions.

Results and Analysis. Table 2 summarizes the Top-1 Accuracy across all methods. The proposed LLM-based system outperformed all baselines, achieving an accuracy of **84.67%**, while the best-performing baseline (Response Time) recorded **73.33%**. Notably, the distance-based strategy failed to identify any correct selections.

Table 2. Top-1 Accuracy Comparison

Method	Correct	Total	Top-1 Accuracy (%)
LLM (Proposed)	254	300	**84.67**
Response Time	220	300	73.33
Throughput	210	300	70.00
Static QoS Weights	196	300	65.33
Distance	0	300	0.00

To confirm significance, chi-squared tests were conducted between the proposed method and each baseline. As shown in Table 3, all p-values fall below the 0.05 threshold, indicating that the observed improvements are significant.

Table 3. Chi-Squared Test Results: LLM vs. Baselines

Comparison	χ^2	p-value	Significant (p<0.05)
Response Time	12.31	0.0005	Yes
Throughput	19.27	<0.0001	Yes
Static QoS Weights	30.98	<0.0001	Yes
Distance	442.03	<0.0001	Yes

These findings confirm the advantage of the LLM-based system, which dynamically adjusts QoS priorities in alignment with user intent. Unlike fixed strategies, our approach adapts to context, delivering personalized and accurate recommendations in dynamic edge computing environments.

5.2   RQ2: QoS Priority Inference from User Preferences

To evaluate the LLM's ability to infer the most relevant QoS dimension from minimal user input, we designed an experiment involving 56 simulated user scenarios. Each scenario corresponds to a specific service type—such as video conferencing or music streaming—and was manually annotated with an expected primary QoS requirement: either `response_time` or `throughput`. The goal is to assess whether the LLM can accurately identify the dominant QoS preference implied by the service context without any explicit guidance or rules.

The ground-truth labels were assigned based on commonly accepted application characteristics: latency-sensitive services (e.g., video conferencing, online gaming) were associated with `response_time`, while bandwidth-intensive services (e.g., music or video streaming) were labeled with `throughput`. We did not include any additional rule-based or model-based baseline in this experiment, as our focus is to evaluate the LLM's reasoning capabilities in isolation, independent of prior heuristics or engineered logic.

Results and Analysis. As shown in Table 4, the LLM correctly inferred the primary QoS factor in **76.79%** of cases. It achieved perfect accuracy for `response_time` inference (34/34), but performance dropped to **40.91%** (9/22) for `throughput`-focused scenarios.

Table 4. LLM Inference Accuracy by QoS Priority (RQ2)

Category	Correct	Total	Accuracy (%)
Overall	43	56	76.79
response_time	34	34	100.00
throughput	9	22	40.91

These results illustrate the LLM's capability to interpret latency-sensitive service intents with high precision. However, inference accuracy declined in more ambiguous cases, suggesting the need for additional prompt refinement or data augmentation to better handle non-obvious QoS contexts (Fig. 2).

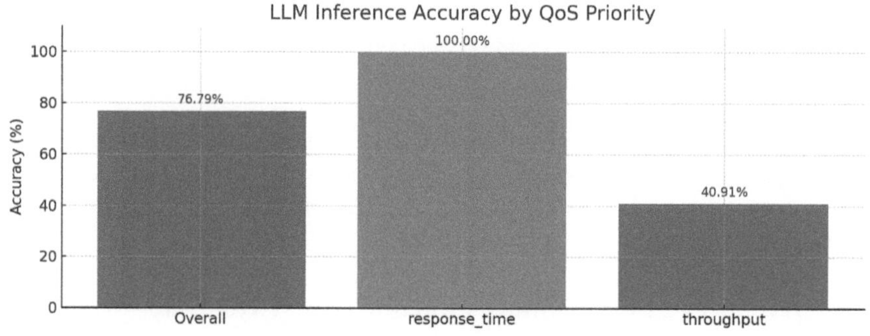

Fig. 2. LLM inference performance: overall and per-QoS accuracy (RQ2)

5.3 RQ3: Impact of LLM Reasoning on Final Server Decision

To evaluate whether LLM-based reasoning improves final server selection, we compared two decision strategies under identical input conditions:

- **LLM-Based Decision**: This method leverages the full user context, QoS scores, and server metrics as input to a language model, which selects the most appropriate server through contextual reasoning and justification.
- **Score-Based Decision**: This approach selects the server with the highest weighted QoS score, computed using fixed weights derived from the LLM's prior output (e.g., `w_resp`, `w_thr`, etc.). The decision is purely based on numerical aggregation without additional semantic reasoning.

Both strategies were evaluated using user scenarios, candidate server sets, and QoS inputs. The distinction lies in the final decision logic: while the score-based method applies a deterministic scoring rule, the LLM-based approach interprets context and prioritization cues to generate an explainable recommendation.

Table 5. Top-1 Accuracy: LLM-Based vs. Score-Based Decision Logic (RQ3)

Method	Correct	Total	Accuracy (%)
LLM-based Decision	254	300	**84.67**
Score-based Only	224	300	74.67

Results and Analysis. As shown in Table 5, LLM-based decision-making outperformed the score-based approach by **10% points**. These results suggest that the LLM's ability to reason over user context and dynamic server conditions provides a tangible advantage in selecting the most appropriate server.

Overall, these experiments demonstrate that integrating LLMs into the decision making pipeline enhances both personalization and recommendation accuracy under realistic MEC conditions.

6 Threats to Validity

This study has several limitations that may affect its generalizability.

First, the ground-truth labels were generated using fixed QoS weights (0.5 for response time and throughput). While this offers a neutral evaluation baseline, it may not fully reflect diverse user preferences or real-world application needs.

Second, our framework relies on GPT-4, a LLM. Although it performs well, its black-box nature and sensitivity to prompt phrasing limit interpretability. The use of external APIs also raises privacy and deployment concerns.

Finally, the current system operates in a single-user simulation without modeling concurrent users or inter-agent coordination in large-scale settings. Future work will explore multi-user scenarios and scalable deployment strategies.

7 Conclusion

In this study, we proposed a context-aware edge server recommendation framework that leverages a LLM to interpret user intent and reason over QoS priorities in a dynamic, personalized manner. Unlike traditional rule-based or static score-based approaches, our system integrates both user preferences and predicted server-side conditions into a unified, LLM-enabled decision pipeline.

To evaluate its effectiveness, we conducted a series of experiments guided by three research questions. First, we demonstrated that LLM-based recommendations significantly outperform traditional QoS-weighted strategies in server selection accuracy. Second, we showed that LLMs can successfully infer context-appropriate QoS priorities from user preferences, particularly in latency-sensitive scenarios. Third, we confirmed that replacing static scoring with contextual reasoning substantially improves recommendation quality when nuanced understanding is required.

These results collectively highlight the potential of LLMs as intelligent intermediaries that bridge user intent with system-level optimization in mobile edge computing. By enabling flexible, explainable, and user-adaptive decision-making, our approach offers a new perspective on personalized service delivery in dynamic environments.

Future work will focus on addressing current limitations and expanding system capabilities. Specifically, we plan to (1) integrate open-source LLMs to support local and privacy-preserving inference, (2) incorporate real behavioral traces from actual usage scenarios to improve realism and robustness, and (3) extend the system into a scalable multi-agent architecture that supports edge-to-edge collaboration and concurrent multi-user scenarios in practical MEC deployments.

Acknowledgment. This research was supported by the MSIT (Ministry of Science and ICT), Korea, under the ITRC (Information Technology Research Center) support program (IITP-2025-RS-2020-II201795) supervised by the IITP (Institute for Information & Communications Technology Planning & Evaluation).

References

1. Mach, P., Becvar, Z.: Mobile edge computing: a survey on architecture and computation offloading. IEEE Commun. Surv. Tutor. **19**(3), 1628–1656 (2017)
2. Wang, S., Zhang, J., Liu, B.: Dynamic service placement for mobile micro-clouds with predicted future costs. IEEE Trans. Parallel Distrib. Syst. **28**(4), 1002–1016 (2017)
3. Skarlat, O., Nardelli, M., Schulte, S., Borkowski, M., Leitner, P.: Towards qos-aware fog service placement. In: Fog and Edge Computing: Principles and Paradigms, pp. 215–230. Wiley (2017)
4. Dinh, H.T., Lee, C., Niyato, D., Wang, P.: A survey of mobile cloud computing: architecture, applications, and approaches. Wirel. Commun. Mob. Comput. **13**(18), 1587–1611 (2013)

5. Sun, Y., Zhang, D., Wang, Y.: Qos-aware service recommendation in edge computing environments. IEEE Access **8**, 122889–122901 (2020)
6. Zhang, Y., Liu, M., Zhao, H.: A context-aware edge server selection approach for mec based on user preferences. Futur. Gener. Comput. Syst. **128**, 368–380 (2022)
7. Mei, J., Zhou, Z., Wang, X.: Learning-based adaptive edge service placement for mobile users. IEEE Trans. Netw. Serv. Manag. **18**(1), 325–338 (2021)
8. Xu, X., Liu, W., Zhao, J.: Reinforcement learning for dynamic edge server selection in mec. Comput. Netw. **225**, 109570 (2023)
9. Zheng, Z., Ma, H., Lyu, M.R., King, I.: QoS-aware web service recommendation by collaborative filtering. IEEE Trans. Serv. Comput. **4**(2), 140–152 (2011)
10. Zhao, Y., Wang, S., Huang, L., Xu, J., Hsu, C.-H.: Context-aware QoS prediction for mobile users in edge computing. Futur. Gener. Comput. Syst. **108**, 180–190 (2020)
11. Xie, S., Ma, H., Wang, Q., Lyu, M.R.: A cloud-based QoS ranking prediction framework for web services. IEEE Trans. Parallel Distrib. Syst. **25**(4), 775–784 (2012)
12. Mei, J., Zhang, W., Liu, X.: AHP-based cloud service selection method considering user preferences and QoS requirements. Soft. Comput. **22**(11), 3535–3547 (2018)
13. Liu, H., Wu, J., Li, M.: Multi-objective optimization for QoS-aware service recommendation using PSO. IEEE Access **9**, 117880–117891 (2021)
14. Fan, J., Chen, W., Zhang, K.: Dcalf: dual collaborative autoencoder for QoS prediction. IEEE Trans. Serv. Comput. **14**(6), 1774–1787 (2019)
15. Ye, Y., Chen, L., Yang, J.: Matrix factorization-based QoS prediction: a comparative study. Knowl.-Based Syst. **220**, 106929 (2021)
16. Wang, S., Zhao, Y., Huang, L., Xu, J., Hsu, C.-H.: A context-aware service selection and recommendation framework for mobile users in edge computing. IEEE Access **8**, 63513–63524 (2020)
17. Wu, H., Chen, J., Zomaya, A.Y.: Towards smart service allocation in edge computing. Futur. Gener. Comput. Syst. **92**, 1022–1034 (2019)
18. Chen, M., Zhang, Y., Li, Y.: Mobility-aware edge computing in 5g networks. IEEE Commun. Mag. **56**(5), 26–33 (2018)
19. Samanta, T., Li, M., Yang, Y.: Proactive edge service migration with mobility prediction in smart city environments. IEEE Trans. Netw. Serv. Manag. **19**(1), 571–584 (2022)
20. OpenAI. Gpt-4 technical report. OpenAI, Technical Report (2023). https://openai.com/research/gpt-4
21. Zhuang, S., Liu, W., Li, C., Tong, Y.: Llm4qos: context-aware QoS preference modeling using large language models. In: Proceedings of the 32nd International World Wide Web Conference (WWW) (2023)
22. Wang, S., Zhao, Y., Huang, L., Xu, J., Hsu, C.-H.: QoS prediction for service recommendations in mobile edge computing. J. Parallel Distrib. Comput. **127**, 134–144 (2019)

ECGTwinMentor: Enhancing Cardiology Education in ECG with Digital Twins

Daniel Flores-Martin[1]([✉])[iD], Francisco Díaz-Barrancas[2][iD], Pedro J. Pardo[2][iD], Javier Berrocal[2][iD], and Juan M. Murillo[2][iD]

[1] COMPUTAEX, Extremadura Supercomputing Center, Cáceres, Spain
`daniel.flores@computaex.es`
[2] University of Extremadura, Badajoz, Spain
`{frdiaz,pjpardo,jberolm,juanmamu}@unex.es`

Abstract. Electrocardiograms (ECGs) are essential diagnostic tools in cardiology, yet access to practical ECG interpretation training remains limited, especially in resource-constrained educational environments. Addressing this gap, we present ECGTwinMentor, an intelligent digital twin system designed to enhance cardiology education through interactive and personalized learning. The system integrates a Deep Learning model capable of predicting potential cardiac abnormalities based on simulated ECG parameters and user interactions. ECGTwinMentor supports deployment across multiple platforms—including edge devices-offering students a versatile tool to explore various ECG configurations, visualize waveforms, and receive automated diagnostic feedback. The model was trained using synthetically generated ECG data to ensure controlled variability and pedagogical suitability. Preliminary results demonstrate accurate prediction performance and low-latency inference on low-power hardware. ECGTwinMentor contributes to closing the gap between theoretical knowledge and practical ECG interpretation skills, offering a scalable and accessible solution for modern cardiology training.

Keywords: Electrocardiogram · Digital Twins · Edge Computing · Simulation · Deep Learning · Formation

1 Introduction

Cardiology remains a critical area of medicine due to the global impact of cardiovascular diseases, which continue to be the leading cause of mortality worldwide. Although advances in research and technology offer new opportunities to improve care, medical trainees often lack the necessary skills to interpret ECGs effectively, highlighting the need for better educational approaches [7].

Innovations in medical technologies, such as diagnostic tools and treatment techniques, have significantly enhanced the understanding and management of heart-related conditions. The application of cutting-edge technologies has led to more precise diagnostics, better patient outcomes, and increasingly personalized

Y.-C. Hsu et al. (Eds.): ICWE 2025, CCIS 2735, pp. 54–67, 2026.
https://doi.org/10.1007/978-3-032-11233-0_5

treatments, which ultimately improve public health and the quality of life for millions of people [15]. Also, the artificial intelligence (AI) enhances ECG interpretation by identifying subtle patterns in large datasets, enabling early detection of cardiac and non-cardiac conditions—even in asymptomatic patients [13]. There are many fundamentals of supervised AI models and key applications, such as identifying left ventricular dysfunction, silent atrial fibrillation, and structural heart diseases [14]. Despite the rapid advancements, there is a lack of relevant resources for personalized learning and a disconnect between AI technologies and their application in medical education [4].

Education and training in cardiology are crucial for healthcare students, as a solid understanding of cardiovascular diseases is vital for accurate diagnosis and treatment. Traditional methods—lectures, textbooks, and clinical rotations— provide foundational knowledge [10], but face limitations such as limited access to diverse ECG data, insufficient hands-on practice, and restricted exposure to varied pathologies. Clinical settings can also be stressful and time-constrained. During the COVID-19 pandemic, many students were unable to complete rotations due to restricted hospital access, reducing opportunities for practical learning [6].

In recent years, digital twins have emerged as an innovative tool with the potential to revolutionize education across various disciplines, including healthcare [1]. A digital twin is a virtual representation of a physical system or environment, which can simulate real-world conditions and allow for interactive learning and experimentation. The use of digital twins in healthcare has gained significant attention, as they can model complex medical systems, simulate patient conditions, and provide immersive, hands-on learning experiences. Research has demonstrated the potential of digital twins in cardiology, with applications ranging from virtual heart models to simulations of cardiac interventions [5]. These innovations have significantly contributed to the advancement of cardiology education by providing students with a dynamic, interactive environment in which they can practice diagnostic reasoning, analyze diverse ECG patterns, and explore complex cardiovascular conditions without clinical risk. By simulating real-world scenarios and offering immediate feedback, the system promotes experiential learning, reinforces theoretical concepts, and helps bridge the gap between classroom instruction and clinical application.

This paper introduces **ECGTwinMentor** as a solution to the challenges identified in traditional cardiology education. The system combines DL with a digital twin approach to create an interactive learning platform for ECG interpretation and diagnosis. The main contributions of this work are the development of a DL model for predicting cardiopathies based on variable simulated ECG data, the creation of a web-based application for ECG interpretation, and the implementation of a simulator that allows students to interact with and diagnose simulated ECGs that can be deployed on the cloud or in edge devices. The novelty of ECGTwinMentor lies in its integration of ECG simulation, diagnostic prediction, and real-time visualization into a unified, lightweight digital twin for cardiology education. Designed for deployment on edge devices, it offers a modular and scalable platform that supports interactive, hands-on learning across diverse settings.

The remainder of this paper is organized as follows: Sect. 2 presents the background and motivations behind the development of ECGTwinMentor, highlighting existing challenges in cardiology education and the advantages of digital twin technology. Section 3 provides a detailed description of the ECGTwinMentor system, including the DL model, the web-based application, and the simulator. Then, Sect. 4 presents the results of the system's validation and user testing, demonstrating its effectiveness as an educational tool. Finally, Sect. 5 concludes with a conclusion of the project's implications and future work.

2   Background and Related Work

Cardiology faces several challenges in medical education. One of them is the limited access to real clinical data and the complexity of ECG interpretation [3]. Although ECGs are widely used in clinical practice, the variability in patient conditions and the diverse real-life examples make learning challenging.

Existing solutions focus on ECG classification through DL but often lack integration into educational platforms or fail to simulate realistic patient scenarios. Furthermore, these models do not offer an interactive. In [12], the authors introduce ECG-Image-Kit, an open-source toolkit designed to generate synthetic multi-lead ECG images with realistic artifacts from time-series data. Its primary goal is to automate the conversion of scanned ECG images into structured ECG datapoints. While this tool has broad applications, such as supporting the development of models for ECG image digitization and classification, it currently lacks a user-friendly interface, limiting its accessibility—especially for educational purposes aimed at training new medical professionals.

Paper-based ECG interpretation is addressed in [17], where an automated digitization tool is developed to convert scanned paper ECGs into digital signals. Although paper-based ECG interpretation remains clinically relevant, the digitization of this process still requires more comprehensive and integrated solutions. In this context, ECG interpretation is a critical skill for nursing staff in cardiology. One of the widely adopted instructional models is BOPPPS (Bridge-in, Objective, Pre-assessment, Participatory Learning, Post-assessment, and Summary), evaluated in [16]. This highlights the growing demand for digital tools that support ECG interpretation using modern technologies.

From a real-time monitoring perspective, ECG data acquisition and interpretation are explored in [9]. The authors propose a Cybertwin-based multimodal network for continuous ECG pattern monitoring during daily activities. This architecture integrates a cloud-centric network with several Cybertwin communication endpoints and incorporates a deep convolutional neural network-based human activity recognition classifier to enhance pattern recognition accuracy. The study is particularly valuable due to its comparative analysis of various neural network algorithms, emphasizing the potential of DL models for effective ECG pattern identification in dynamic environments.

The limitations of traditional methods hinder the development of expertise in ECG interpretation. This is where ECGTwinMentor comes into play, offering a flexible, interactive platform for learning ECG interpretation and diagnosis through simulated ECG data. Beyond its use in centralized environments, ECGTwinMentor is also designed to operate on edge devices such as Raspberry Pi or embedded systems integrated into clinical training stations. This edge-based deployment paradigm minimizes network latency, enhances system responsiveness, and reinforces data privacy by performing computations locally rather than transmitting sensitive health data to remote servers. By leveraging edge computing, the application becomes more resilient, scalable, and suitable for real-world educational scenarios in hospitals, classrooms, or field settings where connectivity may be limited or regulated.

3   ECGTwinMentor: System Overview

This section describes ECGTwinMentor, an intelligent educational system composed of three main components: (1) a Deep Learning model trained on ECG data to predict potential cardiopathies, (2) an interactive application that provides diagnostic feedback and supports student training—available via a web API, graphical frontend, or deployable on edge devices such as Raspberry Pi or Android, and (3) a parameter-based ECG simulator that allows students to explore different waveform configurations and interpret diagnostic patterns. These components are seamlessly integrated to form a comprehensive digital twin platform that enhances the learning experience by combining theoretical knowledge with practical, hands-on interaction. The architecture is shown in Fig. 1 and detailed in the following sections.

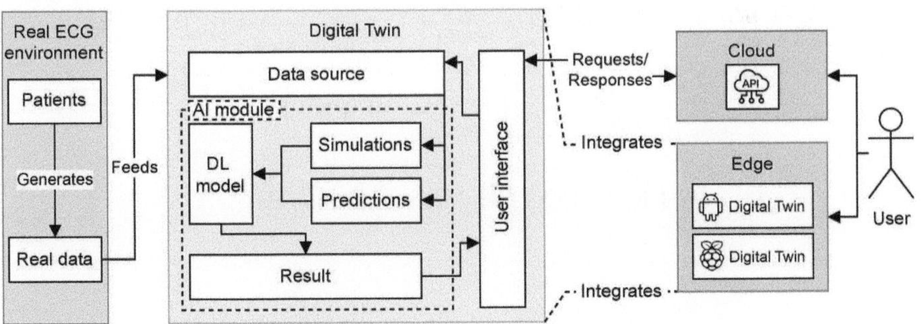

Fig. 1. ECGTwinMentor system architecture

- **Real ECG environment**: represents the physical environment where the digital twin aims to replicate real patients and their ECG information.
- **Digital Twin**: the digital representation of the real-world ECG environment. It is composed of the following components:

- **User interface**: allows users to interact with the digital twin.
- **Data source**: provides the input data for the AI-based algorithm.
- **AI module**: responsible for processing the input data. It includes:
  - **Simulations**: enables users to generate ECG simulations.
  - **Predictions**: provides diagnostic predictions based on the user-inputs.
  - **DL model**: processes the input and producing an output.
  - **Result**: the output or diagnostic result returned to the user.
- **Cloud**: the digital twin can be accessed via cloud infrastructure through a custom web application and REST API.
- **Edge**: the digital twin can also be deployed on edge devices, allowing local execution and offline operation without the need for internet connectivity.

3.1 Deep Learning Model for Cardiopathy Prediction

The heart of ECGTwinMentor is the AI module (Fig. 2). In cloud environments (red), this module resides in the Cloud and is responsible for generating predictions and ECG images, as well as exporting the model to the Lite version for edge environments. In edge environments (purple), this module is integrated within the device and can infer predictions and update its local model (*ecg_model.tflite*). This environment does not require an internet connection (except to update the model) and offers an additional layer of security by not exposing the user's data.

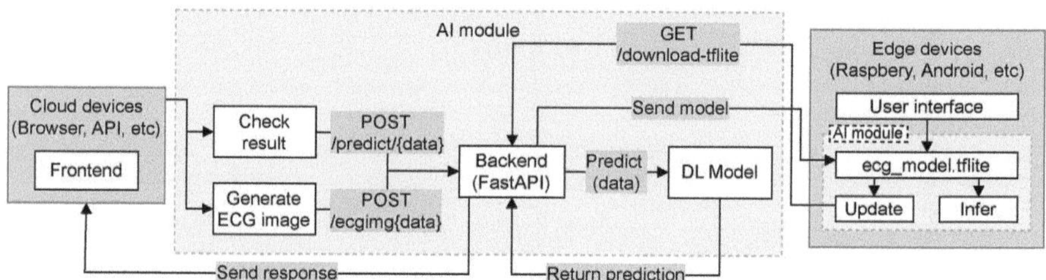

Fig. 2. ECGTwinMentor AI module

Key ECG Parameters. Evaluating ECG parameters in isolation can obscure important findings or cause misinterpretation [2, 11]. These parameters reflect the timing and shape of ECG waves and intervals, essential for diagnosing cardiac conditions. Table 1 presents typical values, normal ranges, and common alterations linked to specific cardiopathies [8]. Key parameters include HR (bpm), Rhythm (conduction pattern), PR (atrial to ventricular depolarization), QRS (ventricular depolarization), ST Segment (early repolarization), T Wave (final repolarization), and QTc (heart-rate–corrected repolarization interval).

Table 1. ECG Parameters with normal values and pathological variations

HR (bpm)	Rhythm	PR (ms)	QRS (ms)	ST Segment	T Wave	QTc (ms)
75	Sinus	160	90	Normal	Normal	400
45	Sinus Bradycardia	180	100	Normal	Normal	420
110	Sinus Tachycardia	140	80	Normal	Normal	390
90	Atrial Fibrillation	180	110	ST Depression	Inverted	450
85	Sinus	150	95	Elevated (2 mm)	Normal	410
72	1st Degree AV Block	220	100	Normal	Normal	420
80	Sinus	160	130	Normal	Normal	390
60	Sinus	140	90	Normal	Normal	400
95	Ventricular Tachycardia	–	160	ST Depression	Peaked	500
55	Sinus	170	110	Normal	Flattened	430

These parameters are used to illustrate how variations in key electrocardiographic parameters correspond to specific cardiac conditions. Each row reflects a distinct ECG profile with plausible values derived from clinical norms and known pathological deviations.

Dataset and Data Generation. The dataset used to train the Deep Learning model was generated synthetically based on the ECG parameters described above. A total of 3,000 samples were simulated, each containing controlled variations in key morphological and temporal features of the ECG waveform (e.g., P wave duration, PR interval, QRS width, QT interval). The generation process followed physiologically plausible ranges derived from clinical literature to ensure realism and internal consistency. To mitigate the risks of introducing unrealistic patterns, we applied rule-based validation checks on each sample, discarding those that violated known electrophysiological constraints or produced implausible waveforms. The exclusive use of synthetic data limits the immediate clinical applicability of the model, as it has not yet been validated on real-world ECGs. However, this approach aligns with the educational focus of the project, enabling reproducible, privacy-preserving training scenarios. Synthetic data also allows for the creation of diverse and balanced samples, which is often difficult to achieve with real patient data due to class imbalance and access restrictions.

Model Implementation and Evaluation Metrics. The DL model was implemented using Python and TensorFlow. The model is constructed using three hidden layers with 64, 32, and 16 neurons, respectively, each using ReLU activation. Training is conducted over 100 epochs with a batch size of 32. Throughout the process, training and validation metrics are tracked using the history object, which is useful for evaluating learning dynamics and detecting overfitting or underfitting. Algorithm 1 presents the pseudocode of the implementation of the DL model.

Algorithm 1: Pseudocode of ECGTwinMentor AI module

    Input: CSV file with simulated ECG parameters and diagnoses
    Output: Trained DL model capable of predicting cardiopathies
1 **Step 1:** Import required libraries (NumPy, Pandas, scikit-learn, Keras, etc.);
2 **Step 2:** Load ECG dataset from CSV;
3 **Step 3:** Encode categorical variables using `LabelEncoder`:;
4   Rhythm $\leftarrow$ Encode(Rhythm);
5   T_Wave $\leftarrow$ Encode(T_Wave);
6   Diagnosis $\leftarrow$ Encode(Diagnosis);
7 **Step 4:** Prepare dataset:;
8     $X \leftarrow$ All input features;
9     $y \leftarrow$ Encoded diagnosis labels;
10   Standardize $X \rightarrow X_{\text{scaled}}$;
11   Train/test split: $(X_{\text{train}}, X_{\text{test}}, y_{\text{train}}, y_{\text{test}})$;
12 **Step 5:** Apply SMOTE to balance training data:;
13    $(X_{\text{train}}^{\text{res}}, y_{\text{train}}^{\text{res}}) \leftarrow$ SMOTE$(X_{\text{train}}, y_{\text{train}})$;
14 **Step 6:** Define the neural network model:;
15   Input layer size = `len(features)`;
16   Dense(64, ReLU) $\rightarrow$ Dropout(0.3);
17   Dense(32, ReLU) $\rightarrow$ Dropout(0.3);
18   Dense(16, ReLU);
19   Output layer: Dense(number of classes, Softmax);
20 **Step 7:** Compile model with:;
21   Loss: sparse categorical crossentropy;
22   Optimizer: Adam;
23   Metrics: Accuracy;
24 **Step 8:** Train model with early stopping:;
25   Epochs = 100, Batch size = 32, Patience = 6;
26   Validation set: $(X_{\text{test}}, y_{\text{test}})$;
27 **Step 9:** Evaluate model:;
28   Predict $y_{\text{pred}} \leftarrow$ model(X_{test});
29   Compute classification report, MAE, R^2, and confusion matrix;
30 **Step 10:** Export model for edge deployment:;
31   Convert trained model to TensorFlow Lite format (TFLite);
32   Save model as `.tflite` file for use on Raspberry Pi and Android;

The dataset was divided into 80% for training and 20% for testing. The training subset was used to recognize relevant ECG patterns and associate them with potential cardiopathies, while the test set served to evaluate model performance and generalization capabilities within the simulated domain.

3.2   Web-Based Application: ECGTwinMentor

The ECGTwinMentor includes a web application designed to facilitate ECG interpretation and diagnosis for cardiology students. The application allows users to create their ECG simulations from customized parameters and, based on them, use the DL model to verify the diagnosis of their simulations.

Technologies and Features. ECGTwinMentor comprises a React.js frontend that enables a dynamic and user-friendly interface and a FastAPI backend. The application supports pre-defined training scenarios and provides diagnostic predictions. Figure 3 illustrates the main features of the application.

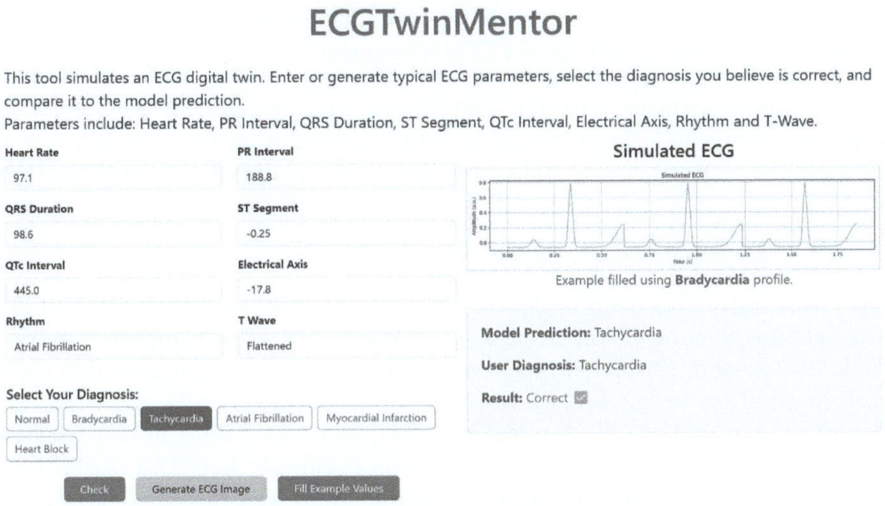

Fig. 3. ECGTwinMentor web user interface

Interactive Learning Tool. ECGTwinMentor provides ECG simulator functionality as an interactive tool. The simulator allows students to enter various ECG parameters, visualize the resulting ECG tracing, and make diagnoses based on the simulated data. This interactive module is essential for students to hone their ECG interpretation skills, allowing them to engage with the data and make informed decisions in a risk-free environment. By combining DL with a web-based platform and an interactive ECG simulator, the system provides a comprehensive, flexible, and accessible tool for cardiology students.

3.3   Security Enhancements

To ensure the secure handling of sensitive health-related data within the ECGTwinMentor, security measures were integrated into both the frontend and backend components of the system. These additions are intended to reduce the risk of unauthorized data access and to promote the integrity and confidentiality of transmitted information:

- **CORS**: a restrictive Cross-Origin Resource Sharing (CORS) policy has been implemented. This policy prevents unauthorized access from external origins.
- **Rate limiting**: to prevent abuse and mitigate the impact of potential denial-of-service (DoS) attempts, the API endpoints are protected using rate limiting based on client IP address, in our case, 100 requests per minute.
- **AES-Based data encryption**: the ECG input data is encrypted in the frontend using the AES algorithm (Advanced Encryption Standard) in CBC mode. The encrypted payload is then transmitted to the backend, where it is decrypted using a shared secret key and initialization vector (IV). This

mechanism ensures that sensitive data remains confidential during transport, even in the absence of TLS/HTTPS encryption.

These cybersecurity features collectively strengthen the reliability and robustness of the ECGTwinMentor system, making it suitable for educational scenarios where data privacy and system integrity are of paramount importance.

3.4   ECGTwinMentor in the Edge

ECGTwinMentor has been designed not only as a web-based educational platform but also with a vision toward integration with edge computing environments. The system can use its local model and update it from a remote server. Thus, in addition to ensuring data security, the system can be used in a non-networked environment. To demonstrate this, two edge-device implementations have been developed. These implementations exemplify how ECGTwinMentor can be extended beyond web interfaces to embedded and mobile systems.

Raspberry Pi Deployment. The first implementation targets a Raspberry Pi device, offering a minimal and cost-effective setup. A Python-based script executes ECG predictions using the TensorFlow Lite model. This implementation allows ECG parameters to be entered via command-line arguments, enabling efficient operation on low-resource devices. It performs on-device inference using the lightweight `tflite_runtime` interpreter, employing a classification logic that mirrors the behavior of the web-based model. Also, the implementation includes an update command to retrieve the latest model from a remote server. Listing 5.1 shows an example of the execution.

```
1  (venv) pi@raspberrypi:~/ECGVRDT $ python predict_ecg_edge.py predict
        --hr 69.8 --pr 172.8 --qrs 106.9 --st 0.81 --qtc 376.3 --axis 33.6
        --rhythm Bradycardia --t_wave Normal
2
3  - INFO: Created TensorFlow Lite XNNPACK delegate for CPU.
4  - Predicted class: Atrial Fibrillation
5  - Confidence: 96.9
6
7  (venv) pi@raspberrypi:~/ECGVRDT $ python predict_ecg_edge.py update --
        url http://localhost:8000/download-tflite
8
9  - Downloading updated model from http://localhost:8000/download-tflite
10 - Download complete. Validating model...
11 - Model successfully updated and saved to ./ECGVRDT
```

Listing 5.1. Python implementation for a Raspberry Pi in the Edge.

The Raspberry Pi used for testing was a Raspberry Pi 4 Model B, equipped with a quad-core ARM Cortex-A72 processor and 4 GB of LPDDR4 RAM. The device operated under a 64-bit Debian-based Raspberry Pi OS and utilized CPU-only inference with TensorFlow Lite. Despite its limited hardware, the Raspberry Pi achieved acceptable performance for real-time ECG predictions, with an average inference time below 500 ms.

Android Deployment. The second edge deployment is an Android application. This mobile version of ECGTwinMentor brings the system to smartphones and tablets, making it especially useful in educational settings or areas with limited infrastructure. The application integrates an embedded TensorFlow Lite model, enabling fast on-device predictions without the need for continuous server communication. The platform includes a self-assessment mechanism whereby users can select a suspected diagnosis and compare it against the model's prediction. Also, the system supports model updates of the TFLite model from a remote server, ensuring adaptability and continuous improvement in training accuracy (Fig. 4).

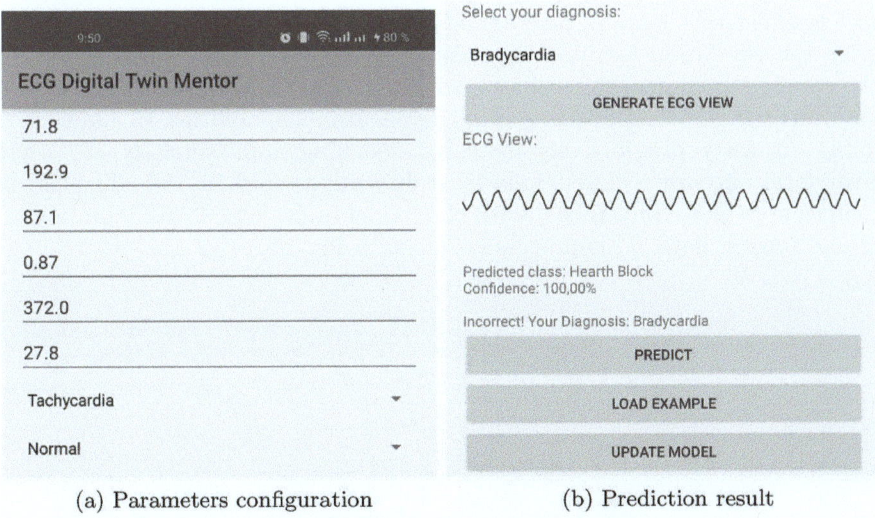

(a) Parameters configuration   (b) Prediction result

Fig. 4. ECGTwinMentor Android implementation.

For mobile deployment, the system was tested on a mid-range Android device, specifically a OnePlus 9, powered by a Qualcomm Snapdragon 888, 8 GB of RAM, an Adreno 660 GPU, and Android 14. The mobile version provided near-instantaneous inference, typically under 150 ms, enabling a smooth user experience without relying on cloud resources.

These scenarios highlight the flexibility of ECGTwinMentor and its potential to adapt to various platforms and scenarios, maintaining consistency in predictive capability and educational value. ECGTwinMentor is available in the following repository for the deep learning model, the web, and edge devices[1].

---

[1] https://github.com/dflores0806/ECGVRDT.

4   Results

This section presents the results obtained from the ECGTwinMentor system, focusing on the performance of the machine learning model, the evaluation of the ECG simulation, and the technical validation of the overall system. The results demonstrate the effectiveness of the model, the robustness of the web application, and the functionality of the ECG simulator, providing insight into the potential of ECGTwinMentor as a valuable tool for cardiology education.

4.1   Model Performance Evaluation

The training loss steadily decreases throughout the epochs, indicating that the model is effectively learning the underlying patterns in the data. As shown in Fig. 5a, the validation loss follows a similar trend with minor fluctuations, and both converge to comparable values below 0.6. This behavior suggests the model is not overfitting and maintains good generalization capabilities. In addition, the training accuracy progressively increases, reaching approximately 86%, while the validation accuracy closely follows, stabilizing around 70–75%. The learning dynamics appear well-balanced, with the model improving steadily on both the seen and unseen data. This process is shown in Fig. 5b.

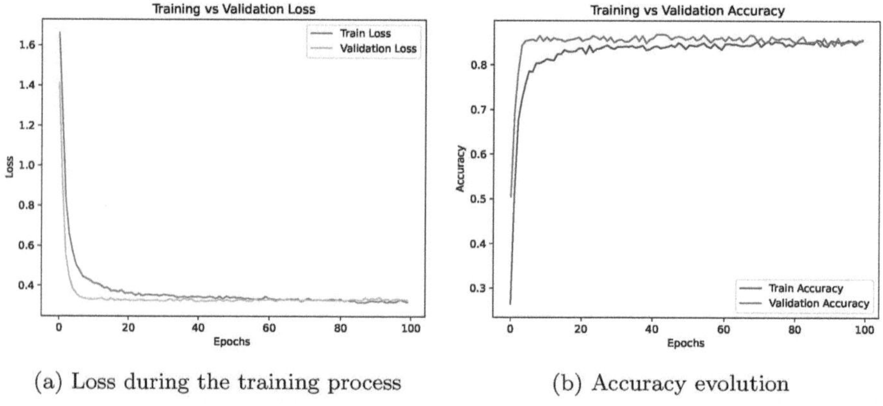

<table>
<tr><td>(a) Loss during the training process</td><td>(b) Accuracy evolution</td></tr>
</table>

Fig. 5. Model training details

The results highlight the effectiveness of the ECGTwinMentor in educational settings. The DL model demonstrated high accuracy in predicting various heart conditions based on ECG input data. Simulations were performed using parameter configurations corresponding to well-known cardiopathies, validating the system's predictive capabilities. The consistent behavior and reliable output across different ECG scenarios support its suitability as a digital educational tool, offering students the opportunity to explore and understand cardiac abnormalities interactively. ECGTwinMentor proves to be a valuable asset for personalized learning and the practical interpretation of electrocardiographic patterns. Also, the following evaluation metrics were used to assess the model's performance:

- **Accuracy:** the model achieved an accuracy of 92% on the test set, indicating strong performance in correctly classifying ECGs into their respective categories (normal vs. abnormal).
- **Mean absolute error (MAE):** the MAE was calculated to be 0.08, suggesting that the model's predictions are consistently close to the true values, with a low margin of error.
- **R-squared (R^2):** the model achieved an R^2 score of 0.85, indicating that 85% of the variance in cardiopathy prediction can be explained by the model, highlighting its predictive power.
- **Confusion matrix:** the confusion matrix was used to further analyze the classification performance of the model, showing high precision and recall for predicting both arrhythmias and ischemia. The model exhibited fewer false positives for arrhythmias, with a specificity of 94%.

The selected evaluation metrics—accuracy, MAE, R^2, and specificity—were chosen to assess both classification performance and numerical prediction quality. This combination ensures not only correct diagnostic categorization, but also precise estimation of parameter-based outcomes relevant to ECG interpretation.

Inference time was also evaluated across different platforms. On desktop environments, predictions were obtained in under 50 ms, while Raspberry Pi and Android devices maintained average inference times below 500 ms and 150 ms, respectively, enabling real-time interaction.

4.2 Performance of the Web-Based Application

The ECGTwinMentor web application was subjected to technical testing to ensure that it operates efficiently across various devices and network conditions. Several optimization techniques were applied:

- **Efficient data processing:** FastAPI was used for asynchronous processing, ensuring the application could handle multiple user requests concurrently.
- **Model optimization:** the model was optimized to reduce inference time, ensuring real-time predictions for students.
- **Responsive frontend:** React.js was used to build a responsive frontend, ensuring that the application is easy to navigate on various devices.

The results obtained from the ECGTwinMentor system demonstrate its effectiveness as a comprehensive educational tool for cardiology students. The machine learning model achieved high accuracy in predicting cardiopathies, while the ECG visualization and simulation tools provide students with a dynamic and interactive learning experience. The web application performed well across various devices and browsers, and the system's ability to generate a diverse set of simulated ECGs further enhances the educational value of the platform.

While ECGTwinMentor demonstrates strong potential as an educational tool, several aspects present opportunities for improvement. The use of synthetically generated ECG data—though effective for controlled experimentation and privacy preservation—may not capture the full complexity of real-world signals. However, this design choice aligns with the system's educational focus and lays the groundwork for future integration of real clinical datasets. Similarly, the edge deployment on devices such as Raspberry Pi and Android has proven technically feasible, yet further optimizations could enhance performance under more constrained hardware conditions. Additionally, current interactions are session-based; integrating long-term progress tracking and adaptive feedback mechanisms would further enrich the learning experience. These aspects define a clear path for the ongoing development and expansion of the system's capabilities.

The following section will discuss the conclusions drawn from the results and the potential for future development of the system.

5   Conclusions

The ECGTwinMentor system provides an innovative solution to the challenges of cardiology education. The ability to practice interpreting ECGs, simulate various heart conditions, and receive immediate feedback allows for effective and safe learning. ECGTwinMentor significantly enhances the learning experience for cardiology students by providing an interactive platform for ECG interpretation and diagnosis. The DL model embedded within the platform demonstrates strong performance in predicting cardiopathies with high accuracy and reliability. Also, the ECG simulator provides students with hands-on experience, helping them develop practical skills in ECG interpretation and diagnosis. Future work will focus on improving the model's accuracy, expanding the ECG database, including a 3D heart model, and incorporating virtual reality to further enhance the learning experience in a more inmersive environment.

Acknowledgement. This work was supported by the projects PID2021-124054OB-C31, TED2021-130913B-I00, PDC2022-133465-I00 (MCIU/AEI/FEDER, UE), by the Department of Economy, Science and Digital Agenda of the Government of Extremadura (GR21133 and IB20094), by the European Regional Development Fund, and by INCIBE and the "European Union NextGenerationEU/PRTR" (C110.23). All authors contributed equally. We thank the COMPUTAEX Foundation for allowing us to use the computational resources of the LUSITANIA supercomputer.

References

1. Alazab, M., et al.: Digital twins for healthcare 4.0—recent advances, architecture, and open challenges. IEEE Consum. Electron. Maga. **12**(6), 29–37 (2022)
2. Ali, O.M.A., Kareem, S.W., Mohammed, A.S.: Evaluation of electrocardiogram signals classification using CNN, SVM, and LSTM algorithm: a review. In: 2022 8th International Engineering Conference on Sustainable Technology and Development (IEC), pp. 185–191. IEEE (2022)

3. Breen, C., Kelly, G., Kernohan, W.: ECG interpretation skill acquisition: a review of learning, teaching and assessment. J. Electrocardiol. **73**, 125–128 (2022)
4. Chiu, T.K., Xia, Q., Zhou, X., Chai, C.S., Cheng, M.: Systematic literature review on opportunities, challenges, and future research recommendations of artificial intelligence in education. Comput. Educ. Artif. Intell. **4**, 100118 (2023)
5. Cluitmans, M.J., Plank, G., Heijman, J.: Digital twins for cardiac electrophysiology: state of the art and future challenges. Herzschrittmachertherapie+ Elektrophysiologie **35**(2), 118–123 (2024)
6. Flores-Martin, D., Laso, S., Berrocal, J., Murillo, J.M.: Towards digital health: integrating federated learning and crowdsensing through the contigo app. SoftwareX **28**, 101885 (2024)
7. Ko, Y., Issenberg, S.B., Roh, Y.S.: Effects of peer learning on nursing students' learning outcomes in electrocardiogram education. Nurse Educ. Today **108**, 105182 (2022)
8. Park, J., et al.: Study on the use of standard 12-lead ECG data for rhythm-type ECG classification problems. Comput. Methods Prog. Biomed. **214**, 106521 (2022)
9. Qi, W., Su, H.: A cybertwin based multimodal network for ECG patterns monitoring using deep learning. IEEE Trans. Ind. Inf. **18**(10), 6663–6670 (2022)
10. Rafie, N., Kashou, A.H., Noseworthy, P.A.: ECG interpretation: clinical relevance, challenges, and advances. Hearts **2**(4), 505–513 (2021)
11. Rijnbeek, P.R., et al.: Normal values of the electrocardiogram for ages 16–90 years. J. Electrocardiol. **47**(6), 914–921 (2014)
12. Shivashankara, K.K., Shervedani, A.M., Clifford, G.D., Reyna, M.A., Sameni, R., et al.: ECG-image-kit: a synthetic image generation toolbox to facilitate deep learning-based electrocardiogram digitization. Physiol. Meas. **45**(5), 055019 (2024)
13. Siontis, K.C., Noseworthy, P.A., Attia, Z.I., Friedman, P.A.: Artificial intelligence-enhanced electrocardiography in cardiovascular disease management. Nat. Rev. Cardiol. **18**(7), 465–478 (2021)
14. Somani, S., et al.: Deep learning and the electrocardiogram: review of the current state-of-the-art. EP Europace **23**(8), 1179–1191 (2021)
15. Stamate, E., et al.: Revolutionizing cardiology through artificial intelligence–big data from proactive prevention to precise diagnostics and cutting-edge treatment–a comprehensive review of the past 5 years. Diagnostics **14**(11), 1103 (2024)
16. Wen, H., et al.: Application of the BOPPPS-CBL model in electrocardiogram teaching for nursing students: a randomized comparison. BMC Med. Educ. **23**(1), 987 (2023)
17. Wu, H., et al.: A fully-automated paper ECG digitisation algorithm using deep learning. Sci. Rep. **12**(1), 20963 (2022)

PROPER-SDP: PROmpt-Based Project Evolution-awaRe Software Defect Prediction for Edge-Cloud Systems

Inseok Yeo[1], Sungu Lee[1], Duksan Ryu[2], and Jongmoon Baik[1]

[1] Korea Advanced Institute of Science and Technology, Daejeon, Republic of Korea
{yinseok38,sungu0027,jbaik}@kaist.ac.kr
[2] Jeonbuk National University, Jeonju, Republic of Korea
duksan.ryu@jbnu.ac.kr

Abstract. Edge-cloud systems, which bring computing, storage, and networking resources closer to end-users, offer significant advantages in reducing latency and enabling real-time data processing. Ensuring software reliability in these environments is critical, which has led to growing attention on Just-in-Time (JIT) defect prediction as an effective technique for prioritizing testing efforts by identifying code changes likely to introduce defects. However, edge-cloud systems often face challenges such as data scarcity, rapid project evolution, and limited historical defect information. These characteristics lead to the cold-start problem, where prediction models struggle to perform accurately on new or low-data projects due to the lack of training data.

In this paper, we propose a novel prompt-based approach that uses Large Language Models (LLMs) in a prompt-based framework. By incorporating project evolution data directly into prompts, our approach enables LLMs to effectively capture the contextual information essential for accurate JIT defect prediction. Evaluation results demonstrate that our method significantly improves prediction performance, surpassing baseline method by an average of 13% in F1 score. This approach offers a practical solution for achieving high-accuracy JIT defect prediction in resource-constrained, rapidly evolving edge-cloud environments.

Keywords: Just-in-time defect prediction · Large Language Model · Edge-cloud system

1 Introduction

An edge cloud system is a distributed computing architecture designed to bring cloud resources closer to end-users and devices by deploying computing, storage, and networking capabilities at the edge of the network. Unlike traditional cloud computing, which relies on centralized data centers, edge cloud systems process data locally, significantly reducing latency [15]. This has motivated extensive research on ensuring the software reliability of edge cloud systems [6,10,16].

Y.-C. Hsu et al. (Eds.): ICWE 2025, CCIS 2735, pp. 68–81, 2026.
https://doi.org/10.1007/978-3-032-11233-0_6

Among these, software defect prediction has emerged as a key technique to optimize testing strategies, enabling developers to prioritize the testing on defect-prone software components, ultimately reducing the cost of ensuring software reliability in edge-cloud environments.

Software Defect prediction (SDP) is a crucial aspect of software engineering that aims to identify defective code components before deployment, improving software quality and reducing maintenance costs [1,3]. Software defect prediction models predict potential defective software components [5]. The primary goal of SDP is to assist developers in prioritizing testing efforts, allocating resources efficiently, and mitigating risks associated with software failures [7]. Given the increasing complexity of modern software systems, accurate defect prediction models have gained significant attention, with researchers exploring various features, classifiers, and evaluation metrics to enhance predictive performance [11].

Just-in-Time (JIT) defect prediction is the task of predicting whether a code change (e.g., a commit or pull request) will introduce a defect, so that potential bugs can be caught early, just in time before integration [20]. Unlike traditional file-level or module-level defect prediction, JIT defect prediction operates at the change level, allowing developers to focus code review and testing efforts on the riskiest changes [4,20]. The advantage of JIT prediction has been highlighted in prior studies; by inspecting only a small fraction of commits (e.g., the top 20% most risky changes), it is possible to capture a significant portion (35%) of defects [8], enhancing the effectiveness of defect prediction.

Due to its advantages, JIT defect prediction has been applied in edge-cloud environments, where software is deployed across distributed edge devices and cloud backends. Testing resources and time are limited in edge-cloud environments [10], making it crucial to prioritize problematic commits. By directing scarce testing efforts to the most error-prone changes, JIT defect prediction significantly improves software reliability without requiring exhaustive testing of every modification.

However, building accurate JIT defect predictors for edge-cloud systems presents significant challenges. Training a defect prediction model requires a large amount of error data, but in real-world scenarios, machine learning models often struggle due to insufficient labeled defect data [18]. This challenge is even more pronounced in edge-cloud software projects, which are frequently new or rapidly evolving, making it difficult to collect enough labeled commit data for effective training.

To address the data scarcity problem, cross-project defect prediction (CPDP) was proposed, where a model trained on one set of projects is applied to a new project [14]. However, CPDP often suffers from poor performance due to dataset shifts [8,13]. Recent research on defect prediction in edge-cloud systems further highlights these challenges: while machine learning models perform well on the projects they were trained on, their effectiveness degrades significantly in cross-project scenarios [10]. In summary, existing JIT defect prediction methods for edge-cloud systems face two major limitations: they require impractically large labeled datasets for each project, and they struggle to maintain accuracy when applied across different projects.

In this paper, we propose PROPER-SDP, a novel approach of JIT defect prediction for edge-cloud services that leverages Large Language Models (LLMs) in a prompt-based manner, eliminating the need for extensive defect datasets or fine-tuning. By utilizing an LLMs which has been pre-trained on vast code and text corpora, we aim to harness its broad knowledge to generalize to new projects with minimal training data. PROPER-SDP enhances the LLM's predictions by incorporating the project's documentation and evolution data as contextual information concatenated to the defect prediction prompt. This enriched context allows the LLM to accurately capture project-specific nuances and evolution patterns, which are crucial for effective Just-in-Time defect prediction in software projects it has not been explicitly trained on. **As a result, PROPER-SDP enables high-performance JIT defect prediction for edge-cloud systems, outperforming baseline models by an average of 13% in F1 score, without requiring any training data.**

2   Background

2.1   Edge-Cloud System and Go Language

In recent years, the adoption of edge-cloud architectures has become increasingly prevalent in software systems requiring low latency, scalability, and efficient resource utilization [15]. Edge-cloud systems combine centralized cloud infrastructure with decentralized edge nodes, enabling data processing closer to the source while leveraging the computational power and storage of the cloud. This hybrid model supports applications ranging from real-time analytics to IoT and autonomous systems, where responsiveness and bandwidth optimization are critical.

Within this architectural shift, programming languages that support concurrency, performance, and portability have gained attention. The Go programming language, developed by Google, has emerged as a strong candidate for building edge-cloud services due to its lightweight runtime, efficient memory usage, and native support for concurrency. Go's simplicity and performance make it well-suited for implementing microservices, APIs, and lightweight daemons that can run reliably in both cloud servers and edge devices. Due to its popularity, Go is the main focus of this paper.

2.2   Software Defect Prediction and Just-in-Time Defect Prediction

The goal of Software Defect Prediction (SDP) is to aid developers find defects without testing. Traditional SDP techniques aim to identify defect-prone modules (files, classes, or functions) using static code metrics and historical defect data. These models are typically trained offline and used periodically during development to guide testing and code review efforts. While useful, conventional

SDP approaches often operate at coarse granularity and may struggle to provide timely insights during fast-paced development cycles.

In response to these limitations, researchers have introduced JIT defect prediction techniques, which aim to predict whether certain software change is likely to introduce defects. JIT SDP techniques leverage fine-grained features such as code churn, change history, developer activity, and social metrics, related to target software change, allowing for predictions to be made immediately when changes are submitted. This enables more targeted reviews and resource allocation at the commit level.

2.3   Large Language Models

Large Language Models (LLMs) are transformer-based deep neural networks pre-trained on vast corpora of natural language and source code. Their primary strength lies in learning generalized representations that enable zero-shot or few-shot performance on downstream tasks without requiring task-specific training [12,19]. Unlike traditional deep learning based methods that depend on large labeled datasets and fine-tuning, LLMs can make predictions through prompt-based interactions, significantly lowering the barrier for practical deployment in data-scarce environments.

Recent work has explored various ways to enhance LLM performance in software engineering tasks such as defect prediction, fault localization, and code summarization [2]. These include integrating external tools or providing additional context [9,17]. Such approaches have shown affectiveness in guiding LLMs toward more accurate and context-aware predictions across diverse downstream tasks.

3   Related Works

Kwon et al. [10] conducted one of the earliest studies on applying Just-In-Time software defect prediction to edge-cloud systems by leveraging pre-trained deep learning models. In their work, they collected a large-scale dataset from GitHub using a GitHub Pull Request (GHPR)-based method, which enables automated identification and labeling of defective and clean code at the function level. They focused on three popular transformer-based models—CodeBERT, GraphCode-BERT, and UniXcoder—evaluating their predictive performance under both within-project defect prediction (WPDP) and cross-project defect prediction (CPDP) settings.

Their results showed that UniXcoder generally performed best in the WPDP scenario, thanks to its abstract syntax tree-based representation learning. However, they also highlighted a key limitation: all three models exhibited poor generalization in CPDP scenarios, largely due to project-specific code characteristics and data distribution shifts, which hindered cross-project transferability.

Building upon this foundation, our work proposes PROPER-SDP, a novel LLM-based approach that addresses the data scarcity and cross-project generalization challenges. Instead of relying on model fine-tuning, we employ a prompt-based strategy using large language models (LLMs), enhanced with project evolution data such as README modifications and file structure changes. This approach enables effective zero-shot JIT defect prediction and reduces reliance on labeled training data, offering a practical and scalable solution for dynamic edge-cloud environments.

4   Methodology

In this section, we present PROPER-SDP. It leverages the predictive power of large language models incorporated with valuable project evolution data to assess software changes and identify potential defects at an early stage. We first outline the data preparation process that captures project evolution data, followed by a detailed overview of proposed approach. The detailed Overall Approach is illustrated in Fig. 2.

4.1   Data Preparation

Given a JIT defect dataset initially collected through GitHub Pull Requests (GHPR), we conducted an additional data preparation phase aimed at effectively integrating project evolution context into the Large Language Model (LLM). To accurately capture this evolutionary context, we specifically identified and analyzed the key differences between the current and previous software versions associated with each pull request.

We defined project evolution context using three criteria: changes in the main project README files, modifications to local README files, and adjustments to the local file structure. These were chosen because they are the key representative indicators of meaningful changes in project. The main README often reflects high-level updates to the system's functionality or architecture. Local README changes capture information closer to the target function, such as usage details or implementation notes, offering fine-grained context. File structure changes, including added or removed files in the same directory, may signal refactoring or feature updates that affect code behavior. Together, these elements provide both global and local context to support more accurate defect prediction.

Utilizing these criteria, we filtered the GHPR dataset to retain only entries that exhibited at least one form of evolutionary change. Subsequently, we addressed class imbalance by applying elimination-based data filtering. The resulting test dataset statistics are detailed in Table 1.

To systematically and efficiently assemble this enriched dataset, we leveraged the RESTful GitHub API, automating the identification and extraction of project evolution data. Consequently, the final dataset is enriched with comprehensive contextual details, including the target function's name and code,

---

Algorithm 1 Generate JIT Dataset

1: **function** GENERATE_JIT_DATASET
2:     $jit\_commits \leftarrow collect\_jit\_commits(ghpr\_data)$
3:     **for** each commit in $jit\_commits$ **do**
4:         $prev\_commit \leftarrow get\_previous\_commit(commit)$
5:         $cur\_readme \leftarrow get\_main\_readme(commit)$
6:         $prev\_readme \leftarrow get\_main\_readme(prev\_commit)$
7:         $l\_readme\_cur \leftarrow get\_local\_readme(commit)$
8:         $l_readme\_prev \leftarrow get\_local\_readme(prev\_commit)$
9:         $fs_current \leftarrow get\_file\_structure(commit)$
10:         $fs\_prev \leftarrow get\_file\_structure(prev\_commit)$
11:         $main\_readme\_change \leftarrow diff(prev\_readme, cur\_readme)$
12:         $l\_readme\_change \leftarrow diff(l\_readme\_prev, l\_readme\_cur)$
13:         $fs\_change \leftarrow diff(fs\_prev, fs\_current)$
14:
15:
            ###Checking if change data exists
16:         **if** $main\_readme\_change$ **or**
            $local\_readme\_change$ **or**
            $file\_structure\_change$ **then**
17:             $changes \leftarrow ($
                $main\_readme\_change,$
                $local\_readme\_change,$
                $file\_structure\_change)$
18:             Add $(commit, changes)$ to $enriched\_dataset$
19:         **end if**
20:     **end for**
21:
22:
        ###Data balancing
23:     **for** each entry in $enriched\_dataset$ **do**
24:         **if** entry contains evolutionary changes **then**
25:             Eliminate entry to balance dataset
26:         **end if**
27:     **end for**
28:     **return** $enriched\_dataset$
29: **end function**

Fig. 1. Dataset Collection Algorithm

pull request messages, main and local README modifications, and specific changes to the local file structure. This structured, context-rich dataset significantly enhances the capability of the LLM in accurately predicting defect-related changes within edge-cloud system projects.

The detailed algorithm used for data preparation is provided in Fig. 1.

4.2   Overview of PROPER-SDP

Following the data preparation phase, we conduct defect prediction by integrating both static code attributes and evolutionary project context to improve predictive accuracy. The defect prediction process consists of two stages: Change Analysis and Prompt Generation. In the Change Analysis stage, we extract information from the target commit that contains the function to be classified, as

Table 1. Comparison of Number of Bugs in Original and New Datasets

Project	Original	New
Edgeex	1148	869
Kube	1139	1132
Openshift	5541	3695
Traefik	1080	629

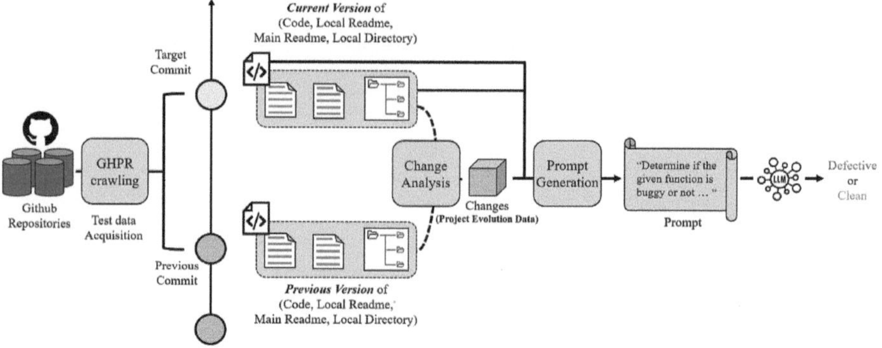

Fig. 2. Overall Approach of PROPER-SDP

well as from its immediately preceding commit. This allows us to capture both the current state and recent changes to the code. In the Prompt Generation stage, we construct a carefully organized prompt that conveys the most relevant information—highlighting both code differences and contextual evolution—to ensure the LLM receives the appropriate signals and nuance for accurate defect prediction.

Change Analysis. The first stage of PROPER-SDP involves analyzing the change between commits to extract all relevant information for defect prediction. Specifically, we identify the target commit, which includes the function whose defect status needs to be predicted, as well as its immediate preceding commit. From these two snapshots, we extract the function's source code before and after the change, its name, and its location in the project. We also gather metadata from the associated pull request, such as the title and description, which often reflect the developer's intent or rationale behind the change.

To provide additional context about how the project is evolving, we incorporate project evolution data across three dimensions: (1) modifications to the main project-level README file, (2) changes to local README files located in the same directory as the target function, and (3) structural changes in the local file system, such as added or removed files. For file structure changes, we list file names without including the full source code to keep the input compact. For README files, if no change is detected, we explicitly indicate this; otherwise,

```
"-Objective: Determine if the given function reflects the software state
before the pull request( Buggy) or After the pull request ( Non-buggy)


-Provided Information:
- **Project**:
{projects[index]}
- **Function Name**:
{function_name}
- **Source Code**:
{source_code}
- **PR Message**:
{PR_message}
- **PR Body**:
{PR_body}
- **README (Current)**:
{cur_main_readme}
- **README (Previous)**:
{'[No change]' if cur_main_readme == prev_main_readme
else prev_main_readme}
- **Deleted Files**:
{', '.join(deleted_files) if deleted_files else 'None'}
- **Added Files**:
{', '.join(added_files) if added_files else 'None'}
- **Local README (Current)**:
{cur_readme if cur_readme else 'None'}
- **Local README (Previous)**:
{'[No change]' if cur_readme == prev_readme
else prev_readme if prev_readme else 'None'}

-Task:
Predict the function's state relative to the PR:

Now, let's begin."
```

Fig. 3. Example Prompt for PROPER-SDP

we include both the full "before" and "after" versions rather than line-by-line diffs, allowing the model to capture broader semantic changes.

Prompt Generation. The prompt generation strategy is illustrated in Fig. 3. Once the change-related and contextual data have been collected, we proceed to the prompt generation stage. In this stage, the extracted information is organized into a structured, natural-language prompt designed to emphasize both static code features and the evolution context surrounding the target function. Each component—such as the pull request title, function path, before/after code, README changes, and file structure updates—is clearly labeled to help the LLM interpret the role and relevance of each element.

To conserve input space and focus on meaningful content, the main project-level README and local README files from the previous version are included only if changes are detected compared to the current version. If no differences are found, a brief note indicating "no change" is provided instead of repeating unchanged content.

This comprehensive prompt is then passed to the LLM, which performs a binary classification—predicting whether the target function is buggy (pre-change) or clean (post-change). The resulting predictions are stored and evaluated using standard classification metrics, primarily the F1-score.

5 Experimental Setup

5.1 Research Questions

We set the following research questions:

- **RQ1: What is the performance of PROPER-SDP compared to Learning based baselines?**
- **RQ2: What is the optimal LLM model for PROPER-SDP?**
- **RQ3: What is the effect of different model design choices on PROPER-SDP?**

5.2 Dataset

We utilized the GHPR edge-cloud defect dataset introduced by Kwon et al. [10]. From this dataset, we specifically selected entries containing at least one type of evolutionary context information. Detailed statistics of the resulting dataset are presented in Table 1. The final dataset encompasses data from four open-source edge-cloud projects.

5.3 Used Models and Evaluation Metrics

To determine the most optimal model for JIT defect prediction in edge-cloud systems, we evaluated multiple state-of-the-art Large Language Models (LLMs). Specifically, we compared the performance of GPT-3.5, GPT-4o-Mini, and Gemini-2-Flash, which are widely utilized in various natural language processing tasks. The experiments were conducted using their respective APIs to ensure a standardized evaluation framework.

For performance assessment, we primarily employed the F1-score, a widely recognized metric in defect prediction. Unlike learning-based models that may output probabilistic or multi-class predictions, PROPER-SDP strictly adheres to binary classification. The F1-score is particularly suitable in this context as it balances precision and recall, making it an effective metric for evaluating defect prediction accuracy.

5.4 Baselines

We compared PROPER-SDP with the learning-based defect prediction method proposed by Kwon et al. [10]. To effectively evaluate defect prediction performance in edge-cloud systems with limited training data, we compared our results with the cross-project defect prediction outcomes from that study.

The previous work evaluated defect prediction performance using three pre-trained models: CodeBERT, GraphCodeBERT, and UnixCoder. Each model was trained on three different source projects and tested on four target projects. The authors noted that they excluded Traefik as a source project due to differences such as project length and structural variations. However, for a fair evaluation of defect prediction in scenarios lacking test data, we included Traefik as a source project, training it on the CodeBERT model.

To simplify comparisons, we presented the previous work's results using both its best-performing scenario and its average performance. This approach ensures a more comprehensive evaluation of our defect prediction methodology.

6 Results

6.1 RQ1: JIT-SDP Performance of Proposed Approach

To evaluate the effectiveness of PROPER-SDP, we compared its defect prediction performance with cross-project defect prediction (CPDP) baselines, including the best-performing result and the average performance of various models. Table 2 presents the F1 scores for four edge-cloud projects: EdgeX, Kube, Openshift, and Traefik.

Table 2. F1 score comparison of PROPER-SDP and baselines

	PROPER-SDP	CPDP(best)	CPDP(average)
EdgeX	**0.679**	0.667	0.586
Kube	**0.695**	0.688	0.583
Openshift	**0.679**	0.666	0.594
Traefik	0.648	**0.667**	0.623

Across the evaluated projects, PROPER-SDP consistently achieved higher F1 scores than the CPDP average and outperformed the CPDP best in three out of four cases. Specifically, for the EdgeX, Kube, and Openshift projects, our approach surpassed the best-performing CPDP baseline, while achieving comparable performance on the Traefik project. Furthermore, it significantly outperformed the CPDP average across all projects, outperforming F1 score by 13% on average, demonstrating the effectiveness of prompt-based LLM defect prediction in data-scarce edge-cloud environments.

6.2 RQ2: JIT-SDP Performance of Different LLM Models

To identify the most effective large language model (LLM) for JIT defect prediction, we evaluated three commonly used LLMs: `gpt-3.5-turbo`, `gemini-2.0-flash`, and `gpt-4o-mini`. Table 3 presents the F1 scores for each model across the four target edge-cloud projects.

Table 3. F1 score comparison between different LLM models

	gpt-3.5-turbo	gemini 2.0 flash	gpt-4o-mini
EdgeX	**0.679**	0.551	0.619
Kube	**0.695**	0.576	0.545
Openshift	**0.679**	0.43	0.425
Traefik	**0.648**	0.537	0.529

Among the evaluated models, `gpt-3.5-turbo` consistently achieved the highest F1 scores across all projects, demonstrating superior capability in understanding code changes and contextual project evolution. The performance gap between `gpt-3.5-turbo` and the other models was especially prominent in the Openshift and Kube projects, where its F1 scores surpassed the others by more than 0.1 in some cases.

In addition to predictive accuracy, we also compared the inference cost and latency of each model. Table 4 summarizes the average monetary cost and response time per prediction.

Table 4. Cost comparison between different LLM models

Model	Money ($)	Time (s)
gpt-3.5-turbo	9.59	1.01
gemini-2.0-flash	2.11	1.13
gpt-4o-mini	2.31	0.87

The results indicate that `gpt-3.5-turbo` required the highest cost and was also among the slowest models in terms of execution time. In contrast, `gpt-4o-mini` had the best overall performance in the cost analysis, offering faster responses and lower cost. While `gpt-3.5-turbo` achieved the highest F1 scores across all projects, its higher resource usage may be a drawback in cost-sensitive environments. `gemini-2.0-flash` was the cheapest, but its predictive performance was the weakest. Considering both accuracy and efficiency, `gpt-4o-mini` can be a good alternative when budget and time are important.

Considering the trade-offs between accuracy, cost, and latency, `gpt-3.5-turbo` remains the most effective choice when predictive quality is the top priority. However, `gpt-4o-mini` could be a reasonable and cost-efficient alternative for scenarios where resources are limited or faster responses are required.

6.3   RQ3: Impact of Project Evolution Context Components

To understand the impact of different project evolution context components on performance, we performed an ablation study by removing one component at a time: main README changes, local README changes, and file structure changes. The results can be seen in Table 5, with the best-performing f1 scores shown in bold and the second-best f1 scores underlined.

The local README changes had the most significant impact on model performance. This suggests that local README files, which are typically situated closest to the target function, provide the most directly relevant context for defect prediction, making them a critical source of information. In contrast, changes to the main README had the smallest impact. This may be because the main README is often located farther from the specific code being modified, tends to contain high-level or general project information, and does not change frequently—reducing its value in predicting function-level defects.

These results suggest that combining both global (main README) and local (local README and file structure) context is important for effective LLM-based JIT defect prediction in edge-cloud systems.

Table 5. Ablation Study(f1 score)

	Original	No local RM	No File Structure	No Main RM
EdgeX	**0.679**	0.645	<u>0.655</u>	0.651
Kube	**0.695**	<u>0.678</u>	0.610	0.609
Openshift	**0.679**	0.642	<u>0.673</u>	0.654
Traefik	<u>0.648</u>	0.480	0.583	**0.657**

7 Threats to Validity

Internal Validity. The internal threat to validity is potential bias in the project evolution data extraction process. PROPER-SDP relies on automated retrieval of project-specific context, including README changes and file structure modifications. However, incomplete or erroneous extraction could introduce inconsistencies, affecting the model's defect prediction performance.

External Validity. LLMs used in our study are pre-trained on publicly available code, and their effectiveness in predicting defects for private or domain-specific projects, which may follow different coding standards, has not been assessed. Future studies should evaluate the generalizability of our method in broader software development contexts.

Construct Validity. We compared our method against baseline models trained with cross-project learning, differences in training data distributions may affect the fairness of comparisons. Further validation using industry benchmarks and real-world defect reports would provide a more comprehensive assessment of the model's effectiveness in just-in-time defect prediction in edge-cloud systems.

8   Conclusion

In this paper, we proposed a novel prompt-based approach to Just-in-Time (JIT) defect prediction for edge-cloud systems using Large Language Models. Our PROPER-SDP incorporates project-specific evolutionary context—such as changes to README files and file structures—into the input prompts, enabling accurate defect prediction without requiring extensive labeled datasets or model fine-tuning. Experimental results across four real-world edge-cloud projects demonstrate that PROPER-SDP consistently outperforms traditional cross-project learning methods in predictive accuracy, particularly when using GPT-3.5-turbo. Furthermore, our ablation study highlights the importance of contextual information, especially local README changes, in improving model performance. This study suggests that prompt-based LLMs provide a scalable and adaptable solution for enhancing software reliability in dynamic, data-scarce edge-cloud environments. Future work will explore the integration of domain-specific knowledge and the applicability of this approach in industrial and proprietary settings.

Acknowledgements. This work was supported by the IITP(Institute of Information & Communications Technology Planning & Evaluation)-ITRC(Information Technology Research Center) grant funded by the Korea government (Ministry of Science and ICT) (IITP-2025-RS-2020-II201795).

References

1. Akimova, E.N., et al.: A survey on software defect prediction using deep learning. Mathematics **9**(11), 1180 (2021)
2. Fan, A., et al.: Large language models for software engineering: survey and open problems. In: 2023 IEEE/ACM International Conference on Software Engineering: Future of Software Engineering (ICSE-FoSE), pp. 31–53 (2023). https://doi.org/10.1109/ICSE-FoSE59343.2023.00008
3. Giray, G., Bennin, K.E., Ömer Köksal, Önder Babur, Tekinerdogan, B.: On the use of deep learning in software defect prediction. arXiv:2210.02236 (2022)
4. Guo, Y., Gao, X., Jiang, B.: An empirical study on JIT defect prediction based on BERT-style model. arXiv preprint arXiv:2403.11158 (2024)
5. Hall, T., Beecham, S., Bowes, D., Gray, D., Counsell, S.: A systematic literature review on fault prediction performance in software engineering. IEEE Trans. Software Eng. **38**(6), 1276–1304 (2011)
6. Hong, H., Lee, S., Ryu, D., Baik, J.: Enhancing software defect prediction in ansible scripts using code-smell-guided prompting with large language models in edge-cloud infrastructures. In: International Conference on Web Engineering, pp. 30–42. Springer (2024). https://doi.org/10.1007/978-3-031-75110-3_3
7. Hosseini, S., Turhan, B., Gunarathna, D.: A systematic literature review and meta-analysis on cross project defect prediction. IEEE Trans. Software Eng. **45**(2), 111–147 (2017)
8. Kamei, Y., Fukushima, T., McIntosh, S., Yamashita, K., Ubayashi, N., Hassan, A.E.: Studying just-in-time defect prediction using cross-project models. Empir. Softw. Eng. **21**, 2072–2106 (2016)

9. Kang, S., An, G., Yoo, S.: A quantitative and qualitative evaluation of LLM-based explainable fault localization. Proc. ACM Softw. Eng. **1**(FSE) (2024). https://doi.org/10.1145/3660771
10. Kwon, S., Lee, S., Ryu, D., Baik, J.: Pre-trained model-based software defect prediction for edge-cloud systems. J. Web Eng. **22**(2), 255–278 (2023)
11. Malhotra, R.: A systematic review of machine learning techniques for software fault prediction. Appl. Soft Comput. **27**, 504–518 (2015)
12. Minaee, S., et al.: Large language models: a survey. arXiv:2402.06196 (2025)
13. Nam, J., Pan, S.J., Kim, S.: Transfer defect learning. In: 2013 35th International Conference on Software Engineering (ICSE), pp. 382–391 (2013). https://doi.org/10.1109/ICSE.2013.6606584
14. Pal, S., Sillitti, A.: Cross-project defect prediction: a literature review. IEEE Access **10**, 118697–118717 (2022)
15. Shi, W., Cao, J., Zhang, Q., Li, Y., Xu, L.: Edge computing: vision and challenges. IEEE Internet Things J. **3**(5), 637–646 (2016)
16. Soualhia, M., Fu, C., Khomh, F.: Infrastructure fault detection and prediction in edge cloud environments. In: Proceedings of the 4th ACM/IEEE Symposium on Edge Computing, pp. 222–235 (2019)
17. Yeo, I., Ryu, D., Baik, J.: Improving LLM-based fault localization with external memory and project context. arXiv preprint arXiv:2506.03585 (2025)
18. Z. Wan, X. Xia, A.E.H.D.L.J.Y., Yang, X.: Perceptions, expectations, and challenges in defect prediction (2020)
19. Zhao, W.X., et al.: A survey of large language models. arXiv:2303.18223 (2025)
20. Zhao, Y., Damevski, K., Chen, H.: A systematic survey of just-in-time software defect prediction. ACM Comput. Surv. **55**(10), 1–35 (2023)

3rd International Workshop on the Semantic Web of Everything (SWEET 2025)

Reasoning over Personal Health Knowledge Graph for Healthcare Monitoring on Apple Watch

Ivano Bilenchi[1], Agnese Pinto[1,2]($\boxtimes$), Grazia Mascellaro[1], Filippo Gramegna[1,2], Giuseppe Loseto[2,3], and Michele Ruta[1,2]

[1] Polytechnic University of Bari, via E. Orabona 4, Bari 70125, Italy
{ivano.bilenchi,agnese.pinto,grazia.mascellaro,filippo.gramegna,
michele.ruta}@poliba.it
[2] donkeyPower S.r.l., via E. Orabona 4, Bari 70125, Italy
{agnese.pinto,filippo.gramegna,giuseppe.loseto,
michele.ruta}@donkeypower.it
[3] LUM "G. Degennaro" University, S.S. 100 km 18, Casamassima (BA) 70010, Italy
loseto@lum.it

Abstract. Wearable devices are increasingly used for personal health monitoring. However, existing decision-making approaches often raise concerns related to outcome interpretability, context awareness and data privacy. This work proposes a novel knowledge-based framework for on-board health monitoring and inference on Apple Watch devices. HealthKit data are annotated as Description Logic concept expressions with respect to a reference ontology to produce a dynamic Personal Health Knowledge Graph. Then, by applying semantic inferences via an embedded reasoner, the framework enables local, explainable analysis of user health status without transmitting sensitive data to external devices or services. A case study focusing on asthma monitoring is presented, in which the severity of symptoms is estimated through locally available data and a custom ontology aligned with the Asthma Control Questionnaire (ACQ) clinical gold standard. A prototypical stand-alone watchOS application demonstrates the feasibility of the approach.

Keywords: Description Logics · Knowledge Representation and Reasoning · Wearable devices · Personal Health Knowledge Graph

1 Introduction

Wearable devices have seen growing adoption in recent years, particularly in domains such as fitness tracking, wellness monitoring, and personal healthcare. Among available devices, the Apple Watch stands out for its widespread usage and technical capabilities, including a rich set of onboard sensors and seamless integration with a range of health-related services and devices.

Machine Learning (ML) methods have been increasingly adopted to extract insights from wearable data [9,12,13]. However, their applicability in personal

Y.-C. Hsu et al. (Eds.): ICWE 2025, CCIS 2735, pp. 85–97, 2026.
https://doi.org/10.1007/978-3-032-11233-0_7

healthcare is constrained by several factors, including the lack of interpretability in predictive model outputs and the privacy risks associated with transmitting sensitive health data to external servers for inference. This is particularly problematic in scenarios requiring transparency, accountability, or real-time, offline decision-making. In contrast, Knowledge Representation and Reasoning (KRR) approaches provide logically grounded inferences inherently endowed with explicit symbolic explainability [30]. Furthermore, methods based on Knowledge Graphs (KGs) facilitate context-aware applications, by integrating annotations of sensor data with available context information on the user and the environment. For these reasons, Personal Health Knowledge Graph (PHKG) is a growing trend in ubiquitous healthcare [6,7,25]. Recent advances in embedded reasoning engines on KGs have enabled the execution of semantic inference tasks on constrained devices, as envisioned by the Semantic Web of Everything (SWoE) [21].

This paper introduces a PHKG-based framework for onboard healthcare reasoning on Apple Watch. By leveraging Apple HealthKit for data acquisition and a SWoE-oriented reasoning engine for semantic matchmaking, the system enables local, privacy-preserving inference on user health status. Health-related parameters are preprocessed and annotated as Web Ontology Language (OWL) 2 concept expressions, using lightweight ontologies aligned to gold-standard clinical questionnaires for disease activity monitoring, to model relevant biomedical knowledge. Inference outcomes are both machine-processable and human-understandable, supporting personalized context-aware recommendations and transparent decision-making.

To validate the feasibility and effectiveness of the approach, a case study is presented in the domain of asthma monitoring. A prototypical Apple Watch application estimates asthma symptom severity based on passively collected physiological data, using semantic matchmaking to emulate responses to the Asthma Control Questionnaire (ACQ) [11]. The watch app works in stand-alone mode, without resorting to a companion smartphone for processing tasks. The prototype demonstrates the applicability of the framework to real-world use cases on resource-constrained wearable devices.

The remainder of the paper is organized as follows: after related work in Sect. 2, Sect. 3 describes the proposed framework for PHKG creation and reasoning on Apple Watch in detail. Section 4 illustrates the aforementioned case study on asthma monitoring, describing the PHKG design, reasoning process, and the implementation of the Apple Watch application, before conclusions.

2   Related Work

The development of lightweight and stretchable sensors has significantly improved the portability and functionality of wearable devices for healthcare. By embedding heterogeneous sensors, continuous real-time monitoring of important physiological parameters is possible. This is fundamental for early diagnosis, chronic disease monitoring and the development of personalized treatment plans. Devices like smartwatches or fitness trackers often include biosensors to detect biological signals, such as heart rate, blood pressure levels or oxygen saturation [8]. Inertial sensors (accelerometers and gyroscopes) are also employed to monitor physical activity by tracking movement patterns and identifying anomalies that may indicate underlying health issues [15]. Environmental sensors can be used to monitor external conditions such as temperature and humidity, which may influence physiological responses and overall wellbeing [18].

The integration of ML algorithms into wearable devices further enhances their capabilities, enabling predictive analytics [12], personalized insights [9], and improved decision-making [13]. For example, models have been employed in wearable healthcare systems to: (i) perform classification tasks to detect abnormal heart rhythms or predicting disease onset [16]; (ii) analyze complex data patterns, such as those derived from ECG signals, to identify cardiovascular risks [28]; (iii) enable accurate health state assessments through multiclass classification [1].

The importance of integrating gold-standard clinical questionnaires into mobile applications, especially for self-management of chronic diseases, has been highlighted in [20]. To improve interoperability among heterogeneous health sensor data and to support onboard complex reasoning for decision-making, the exploitation of semantic technologies is a valuable solution. Authors in [2,10] combined multi-source sensing and machine learning algorithms with logical reasoning to improve health monitoring through wearable devices. A semantic-enhanced Decision Support System has been proposed in [14] to annotate medical data via Near-Field Communications (NFC) for therapy guidance in a rheumatology domain. In [4], a prototypical wearable system has been designed to support users in making informed choices based on explainable AI feedback. Apple platforms have been widely explored w.r.t. the integration of Semantic Web standards [22], reasoning tools [21,23], and benchmarking frameworks [24].

Unlike prior works relying on centralized processing or ML-based inference, this study employs local semantic reasoning on wearable devices to deliver explainable, user-specific health assessments. By leveraging lightweight ontologies and an embedded reasoner, it addresses key open issues such as data privacy, limited device resources, and the need for transparent, standards-aligned outputs.

3   Framework

The proposed framework adopts a two-phase process that enables automated onboard reasoning directly on Apple wearables. In the first step, health-related data is acquired through the *Apple HealthKit* (https://developer.apple.com/health-fitness/) framework and annotated into OWL 2 concept (a.k.a. class) expressions. In the second step, the *Tiny-ME* [21] SWoE-oriented reasoner is exploited to carry out inference, supporting context-aware decision-making. Other than being fully local and ensuring no sensitive data ever leaves the device, the framework is generic and domain-independent, allowing it to be applied across a wide spectrum of health monitoring scenarios, including but not limited to chronic disease assessment, wellness tracking, and personalized health recommendations.

3.1   Data Acquisition and Annotation

Apple HealthKit is a centralized framework that enables authorized applications to access health and fitness data from Apple devices such as the Apple Watch. It supports a wide range of numerical and categorical data, including values sensed by the watch, manually entered by the user, or aggregated from external health devices and systems.

To support automated inference, data retrieved from HealthKit is translated into OWL 2 [19] class expressions, and specifically into the fragment of OWL 2 corresponding to the Attributive Language with unqualified Number restrictions and concrete Domains ($\mathcal{ALN}$(D)) Description Logic (DL), which is particularly suitable for devices with limited memory and processing resources [21]. Data are annotated according to an ontology that encompasses the domain knowledge, thus enriching and updating the user's PHKG in real time. The specific mapping depends on the underlying data type of each measurement, as in what follows:

- **Primitive types and ranges:** primitive data types such as numeric measurements (e.g., heart rate, step counts), dates (e.g., date of birth), and strings, are directly mapped to OWL datatypes and related properties. For instance, an average heart rate between 60 and 80 BPM may be modeled as: `hasHeartRate only int[>=60,<=80]`.
- **Categorical types:** data such as blood type, body part or symptom severity level are instead encoded via OWL classes. For example, the HealthKit categorical data type `bloodType` with values like `aPositive`, `oNegative`, etc., can be represented in $\mathcal{ALN}$(D) through a hierarchy of classes starting from a `BloodType` parent class, branching into `BloodTypeA`, `BloodTypeB`, etc., with further branches for the Rhesus factor.
- **Boolean values:** information such as `wheelchairUse` or `isDiabetic` are modeled as a single class, which is included in the overall concept expression either in its atomic (*e.g.*, `Wheelchair`) or negated form (`not Wheelchair`) to encode their truth values.

3.2   Inference Procedure

In the proposed framework, the task at hand is reframed as a *semantic matchmaking* [21] problem, which involves identifying the most suitable *resource(s)* for a given *request*, where suitability is measured through a *semantic distance* metric. Within this framework, a request represents the user's query encoded through logical expressions, reflecting aspects such as the user's health profile, personalized health preferences, or specific medical constraints. Conversely, resources are formal logic-based representations of potential responses or recommendations, encompassing various possible health conditions, interventions, recommendations, or known medical scenarios taken from clinical best practices or health facility guidelines.

The system relies on a composition of monotonic and non-monotonic inference services, which is particularly valuable in healthcare scenarios: *monotonic inference services* provide consistent reasoning, where adding new information cannot invalidate previous conclusions, thus ensuring robust logical deductions. In personal healthcare settings, they are useful to ensure that inferred facts remain valid when additional health information is introduced. On the other hand, *non-monotonic inference services* enable reasoning in dynamic environments characterized by incomplete, evolving, or conflicting information, such as missing health parameters, changes in patient conditions, and contrasting medical indications or recommendations (*e.g.*, adverse effects of treatments).

Formally, a DL concept expression of the request R is compared to a set of available resources S by means of the *Concept Contraction* (CC) and *Concept Abduction* (CA) non-standard, non-monotonic reasoning services [21]. In case S and R contain clashing concepts, there is a *partial match* between them, and CC is applied to determine a pair $\langle G, K \rangle$ representing what has to be retracted G (for *Give-up*) and what can be kept K (for *Keep*) in R, in order for K to reach a *potential match* with S. Basically, G includes the elements of R conflicting with S, while K is the (best) contraction of R compatible with S. In case R and S are not conflicting, but S does not completely satisfy R, there is a *potential match*, and CA is applied to find the concept H (for *Hypothesis*) specifying what has to be hypothesized in S to reach a *full match* with R (or its contracted version K).

Semantic-based quantitative *penalty scores* are provided by both Concept Contraction and Concept Abduction [21], which can be combined via the following formula into a compound *distance metric*:

$$distance(R, S) = \frac{\alpha * penalty_c(R, S) + \beta * penalty_a(H, S)}{penalty_a(R, \top)}$$

where $penalty_a$ and $penalty_c$ measure the Abduction- and Contraction-induced semantic distances, respectively. Choosing $\alpha \geq 0$ and $\beta \geq 0$ such that $\alpha + \beta = 1$, and dividing by the penalty between R and the universal concept *Thing* (a.k.a. *Top*, $\top$), ensures that the distance falls in the $[0, 1]$ range.

The above procedure is repeated for all resources defined within the KG, comparing each one with the current request R, and the resource S with the lowest distance is selected. Hence, the adopted approach: (i) produces a fine-grained logic-based ranking identifying the most appropriate health recommendation or medical scenario; (ii) detects possible incompatibilities between the request (*i.e.*, the user's health profile or medical query) and resources (*i.e.*, known scenarios or health recommendations); (iii) provides outcomes that are both human- and machine-understandable, along with a logic-based explanation (provided by G and H), which is crucial for trustworthy health-related Artificial Intelligence applications.

4 Case Study: Monitoring Asthma on Board Apple Watch

Asthma is a chronic respiratory condition characterized by inflammation and narrowing of the airways, leading to episodes of wheezing, shortness of breath, chest tightness, and coughing [29]. Although asthma is not fully curable, international guidelines have been developed for its monitoring with the aim of reducing symptoms and bronchial restrictions. In this regard, the ACQ [11] is a clinical gold standard for assessing a subject's level of control over their asthma status. The questionnaire encompasses a series of inquiries designed to appraise various dimensions of the disease, including the frequency and intensity of the symptoms, the impact on daily functioning, and the use of bronchodilators.

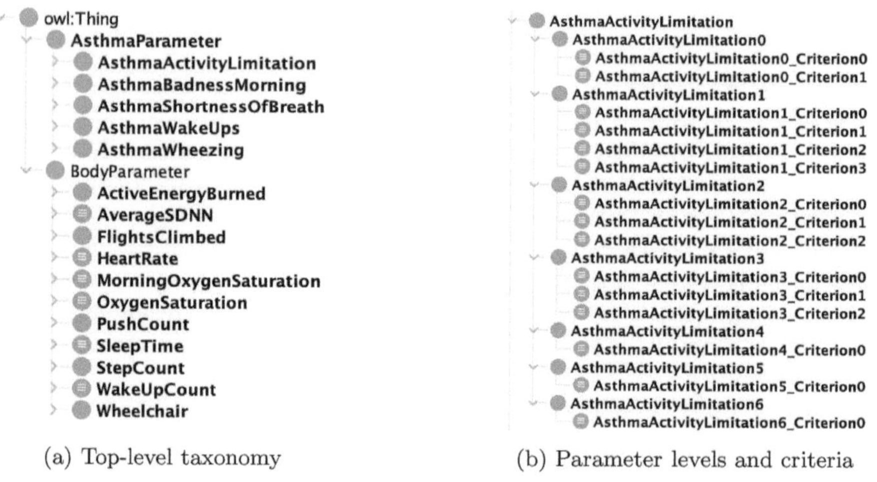

(a) Top-level taxonomy   (b) Parameter levels and criteria

Fig. 1. Excerpt of the asthma knowledge base.

To validate the applicability of the proposed framework, a case study has been conducted by developing an Apple Watch application prototype whose goal is to aid asthma patients track the severity of symptoms. According to well-known correlations [5,26,27,29], a subset of the answers to ACQ questions can be estimated without the need for user input: **i)** the frequency of **nighttime awakenings** due to asthma attacks is contingent upon the number of HealthKit `sleepAnalysis` samples that are designated as `awake` and that coincide with those categorized as `inBed`; **ii)** the **morning symptoms severity** is known to be positively correlated with the average heart rate and oxygen saturation one-to-two hours after waking up [27]; **iii) activity limitation** can be estimated from the mean values of the following variables: `activeEnergyBurned`, `stepCount`, `flightsClimbed` (or `pushCount` for wheelchair users), `heartRateVariabilitySDNN` [26], and total sleep hours; **iv)** the **dyspnea severity** is associated with the average weekly heartRateVariabilitySDNN [5], categorizing it into healthy, impaired, and unhealthy intervals [26]; **v)** the **number of wheezing episodes** is known to be correlated with the average weekly oxygenSaturation [29].

4.1 Semantic Data Annotation and Inference

An ontology concerning chronic asthma management has been developed by identifying and abstracting pertinent medical indicators, physiological traits, and contextual elements associated with the disease. The ontology was created in Protégé [17] with constructs limited to the $\mathcal{ALN}(\mathcal{D})$ DL. The overall class taxonomy, shown in Fig. 1a, has been organized into two primary branches: one centered on general physiological measurements (BodyParameter), and the other focusing on asthma symptoms (AsthmaParameter). Subclasses belonging to the first branch are used to construct a *user profile* concept expression, which aggregates user data, health parameters, and sensors readings from the HealthKit framework, translating them into relevant BodyParameter subclasses. Each subclass represents a specific physiological dimension and includes defined classes that describe severity levels based on medical thresholds. As an example, SevereOxygenSaturation, one of the child classes of OxygenSaturation, is defined as an oxygenation level falling within the range of 83% to 85%:

```
SevereOxygenSaturation ≡ OxygenSaturation and (hasOxygenSaturation only
float [>=83.0,<=85.0])
```

Activity-related parameters, such as StepCount or FlightsClimbed, are not modeled via static ranges but through mutually exclusive subclasses indicating whether a value is above or below the user's baseline, dynamically derived from historical averages. As an example, class expressions look like the following:

```
AboveAverageFlightsClimbed ≡ FlightsClimbed and (not
BelowAverageFlightsClimbed)
BelowAverageFlightsClimbed ≡ FlightsClimbed and (not
AboveAverageFlightsClimbed)
```

On the other hand, the AsthmaParameter branch of the taxonomy is used to model responses to ACQ questions, whose answers fall in the $[0, 6]$ range. Each ACQ item is thus abstracted as a class (e.g., AsthmaActivityLimitation) with one subclass for each possible answer (e.g., AsthmaActivityLimitation0, ..., AsthmaActivityLimitation6). Figure 1b illustrates this structure, focusing on the AsthmaActivityLimitation class. Each response is associated with an AsthmaParameterLevel, which can be used at runtime to retrieve the numerical score. As an example, the AsthmaActivityLimitation6 class is defined as follows:

```
AsthmaActivitylimitation6 ⊑ AsthmaActivityLimitation and
(hasAsthmaParameterLevel only int[>=6,<=6])
```

The leaf concepts are defined as conjunctions of multiple BodyParameter subclasses. For example, AsthmaActivityLimitation0_Criterion0 formalizes the ideal case (score 0) as a combination of AboveAverageActiveEnergyBurned, HighSleepTime, and absence of wheelchair use and it is defined as follows:

`AsthmaActivityLimitationO_CriterionO` $\equiv$ `AsthmaActivityLimitationO` and
`AboveAverageActiveEnergyBurned` and `AboveAverageFlightsClimbed` and
`AboveAverageStepCount` and `HighSleepTime` and `NormalAverageSDNN` and (`not`
`Wheelchair`)

Each such leaf class has been associated to a KG individual for use as a *resource* in the matchmaking framework described in Sect. 3.2. Answers to each ACQ question are estimated by running five separate semantic matchmaking procedures, comparing the annotation of the *user profile* concept expression with the subset of `AsthmaParameter` individuals related to the specific question. The `hasAsthmaParameterLevel` datatype property restriction of the best matching individual for each question carries the information concerning the inferred score.

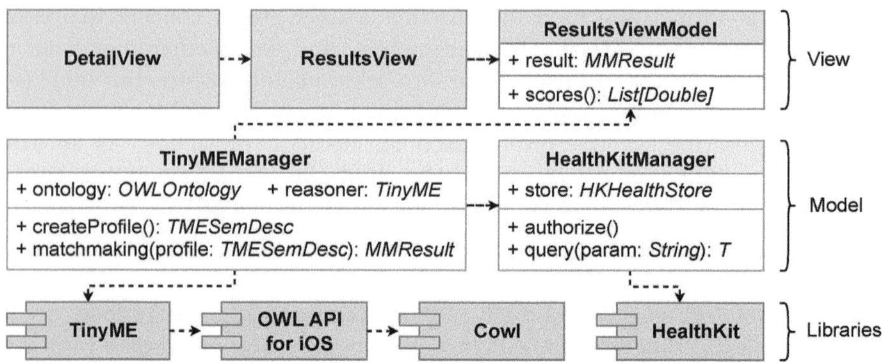

Fig. 2. UML class diagram

4.2 Apple Watch App

Figure 2 illustrates the main classes and methods that define the application architecture. The `HealthKitManager` and `TinyMEManager` *singleton* classes are responsible for managing the core business logic of the application. `HealthKitManager` leverages the methods provided by the HealthKit framework to interact with its health record database. The `authorize()` method is called as soon as the app is started, enabling users to grant permission in a granular and individualized manner for each type of data the application requires access to. Additionally, several query methods are implemented, allowing the retrieval of relevant samples from the HealthKit `store`.

Conversely, `TinyMEManager` is a facade for the Tiny-ME [21] and *OWL API for iOS* [22] APIs. The latter has been reworked to be an Objective-C wrapper for the Cowl library [3], iterating on its original feature set to support OWL 2 data ranges [19]. When initialized, `TinyMEManager` loads the domain ontology and instantiates the Tiny-ME reasoner. Additionally, the class implements the following facilities: `createProfile()` constructs an ontology-based annotation of the patient's health status by querying the HealthKit database through `HealthKitManager` methods; `matchmaking()` implements the inference procedure described in Sect. 3.2, and returns a `MMResult` aggregated object containing the outcomes of five inference procedures, one for each ACQ question.

The app design follows the Model-View-ViewModel (MVVM) pattern to separate the user interface representation logic from the view-related data processing flow. These two responsibilities are handled by the `ResultsView` and `ResultsViewModel` classes, respectively. The main screen of the app displays an overall health score for the patient, as shown in Fig. 3a, computed as the average of all ACQ question scores. `DetailView`, on the other hand, models the outcome of a single matchmaking operation. This view presents matchmaking outcomes with respect to a single ACQ parameter, such as the number of night awakenings or the limitation of the user's activity. As illustrated in Fig. 3b, `DetailView` displays a list comprising: (i) the semantic-based description that most closely explains the patient's current state; (ii) the semantic expressions for *Keep*, *Give up*, and *Hypothesis*, produced as output of Concept Contraction (CC) and Concept Abduction (CA) inference services; (iii) the penalty values computed for CC and CA.

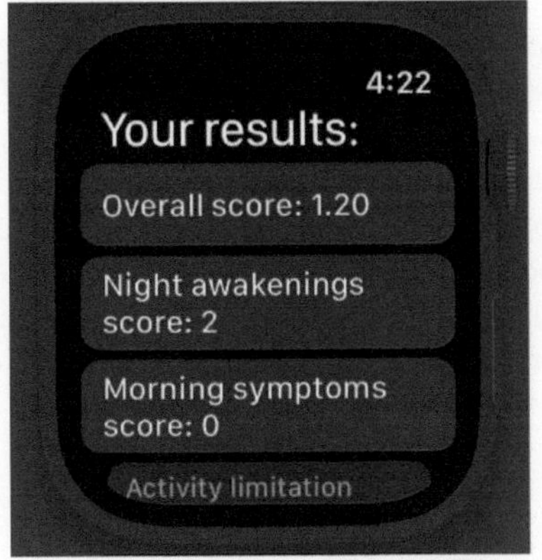

(a) Home screen of the app.

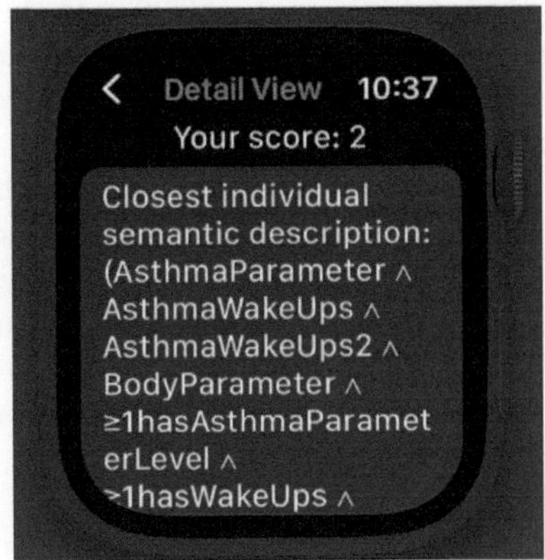

(b) Semantic-based score explanation.

Fig. 3. Views of the watchOS application.

4.3   Illustrative Example

As an example, let us consider the following user profile annotation, derived from the data annotation process described in Sect. 4.1:

```
User_Profile: AverageActiveEnergyBurned and AverageFlightsClimbed and
AverageStepCount and (not Wheelchair) and (hasHeartRate only
int[>=80,<=80]) and (hasMorningOxygenSaturation only
float[>=95.0,<=95.0]) and (hasOxygenSaturation only float[>=90.0,<=90.0])
and (hasSDNN only int[>=105,<=105]) and (hasSleepTime only
float[>=42.0,<=42.0]) and (hasWakeUps only int[>=8,<=8])
```

A semantic matchmaking process is initiated for each ACQ question, considering only the relevant subset of individuals representing match criteria for each score level. The following individuals match the above user profile:

```
AsthmaWakeUps2_Criterion0: (hasAsthmaParameterLevel only int[>=2,<=2])
and
(hasWakeUps min 1) and (hasWakeUps only int[>=6,<=10])
AsthmaBadnessMorning0_Criterion0: (hasAsthmaParameterLevel only
int[>=0,<=0]) and (hasHeartRate min 1) and (hasHeartRate only
float[<90.0]) and (hasMorningOxygenSaturation min 1) and
(hasMorningOxygenSaturation only float[>=93.0])
AsthmaActivityLimitation2_Criterion2: (hasAsthmaParameterLevel only
int[>=2,<=2]) and BelowAverageStepCount and (not Wheelchair) and (hasSDNN
min 1) and (hasSleepTime min 1) and (hasSDNN only int[>=100]) and
(hasSleepTime only int[>=42,<=48])
AsthmaShortnessOfBreath0_Criterion0: (hasAsthmaParameterLevel only
int[>=0,<=0]) and (hasSDNN min 1) and (hasSDNN only int[>=100])
AsthmaWheezing2_Criterion0: (hasAsthmaParameterLevel only int[>=2,<=2])
and (hasOxygenSaturation min 1) and (hasOxygenSaturation only
float[>=89.0,<=91.0])
```

Note how each individual has a `hasAsthmaParameterLevel` datatype restriction, whose value represents the exact score for the corresponding ACQ question. Due to the above matches, the reasoning process results in the following scores: night awakenings - 2; morning symptoms - 0; activity limitation - 2; shortness of breath - 0; wheezing - 2. The overall score is 1.2, indicating a low level of incidence of (*i.e.*, a good level of control on) the disease.

5   Conclusion

This paper has presented a novel PHKG-based framework for performing automated, explainable health monitoring on Apple Watch devices. By integrating HealthKit for data acquisition, PHKG annotation and a lightweight OWL 2 reasoning engine, the system enables local, privacy-preserving inference over user health information. The proposed approach supports transparent and context-aware decision-making, without relying on remote computation or opaque machine learning models. A case study on asthma monitoring has demonstrated the applicability of the framework through a prototype watchOS app that infers asthma symptom severity scores from passively collected data, leveraging a domain-specific ontology modeled on the basis of a gold-standard clinical questionnaire, and a well-established semantic matchmaking framework.

Future work will focus on thorough performance evaluation to demonstrate the computational sustainability of on-device reasoning. The user interface will be enhanced by introducing semantic visual elements such as icons and color-coded explanations to improve clarity and usability. Additionally, support for continuous background monitoring and event-driven notifications is planned, including secure storage of the PHKG by leveraging watchOS data protection APIs. Acceptability tests with users and clinical evaluations with physicians will be carried out to guarantee the usefulness of the proposal. Finally, the framework will be extended to cover a broader set of health domains, including sleep quality assessment, stress monitoring, and cardiovascular risk evaluation, leveraging tailored KG modelings for each application.

Acknowledgments. The research was supported by the cascade call project *SHIELD (Securing Decentralized Finance and Remote Healthcare Systems)* –project code B53C22003990006– of the *SERICS (SEcurity and RIghts in CyberSpace)* Extended Partnership (project code PE_00000014), funded by the Italian National Recovery and Resilience Plan (NRRP) of the NextGenerationEU program, and by the *xTech NextHub: Competence Center for Innovative Solutions Development* grant (grant number VTOIFW0), co-funded by Deloitte NextHub S.r.l. S.B. and the European Regional Development Fund for Apulia Region 2014/2020 Operating Program.

Disclosure of Interests. The authors have no competing interests to declare that are relevant to the content of this article.

References

1. Abu-Samah, A., et al.: Deployment of TinyML-based stress classification using computational constrained health wearable. Electronics **14**(4), 687 (2025)
2. Alsaadi, M., et al.: Logical reasoning for human activity recognition based on multisource data from wearable device. Sci. Rep. **15**(1), 380 (2025)
3. Bilenchi, I., Gramegna, F., Loseto, G., Ieva, S., Scioscia, F., Ruta, M.: Cowl: pushing OWL 2 over the Edge. Internet Things **29**, 101439 (2025)
4. Danry, V., Pataranutaporn, P., Mao, Y., Maes, P.: Wearable reasoner: towards enhanced human rationality through a wearable device with an explainable AI assistant. In: Proceedings of the Augmented Humans International Conference. ACM, New York (2020)
5. Giardino, N.D., Chan, L., Borson, S.: Combined heart rate variability and pulse oximetry biofeedback for chronic obstructive pulmonary disease: preliminary findings. Appl. Psychophysiol. Biofeedback **29**, 121–133 (2004)
6. Gyrard, A., Gaur, M., Shekarpour, S., Thirunarayan, K., Sheth, A.: Personalized health knowledge graph. In: Joint Proceedings of the International Workshops on Contextualized Knowledge Graphs, and Semantic Statistics. CEUR Workshop Proceedings, vol. 2317, p. 5 (2018)
7. Hendawi, R., Li, J.: Comprehensive personal health knowledge graph for effective management and utilization of personal health data. In: 2024 IEEE First International Conference on Artificial Intelligence for Medicine, Health and Care, pp. 92–100. IEEE (2024)

8. Huang, J.D., Wang, J., Ramsey, E., Leavey, G., Chico, T.J.A., Condell, J.: Applying artificial intelligence to wearable sensor data to diagnose and predict cardiovascular disease: a review. Sensors **22**(20), 8002 (2022)

9. Huang, W., Pang, I., Bai, J., Cui, B., Qi, X., Zhang, S.: Artificial intelligence-enhanced, closed-loop wearable systems toward next-generation diabetes management. advanced intelligent systems (2400822) (2025)

10. Joshi, S., Murugan, R., Balaji, N., Chandrakala, P., Deshmukh, G.B., Mathur, M.: Bridging automated reasoning and machine learning for information analysis. In: 2nd International Conference on Futuristic Technologies (INCOFT), pp. 1–6 (2023)

11. Juniper, E., O'Byrne, P., Guyatt, G., Ferrie, P., King, D.: Development and validation of a questionnaire to measure asthma control. Eur. Respir. J. **14**(4), 902–907 (1999)

12. Kajornkasirat, S., Sawangwong, C., Puangsuwan, K., Chanapai, N., Phutthamongkhon, W., Puttinaovarat, S.: Integrating AI-driven predictive analytics in wearable iot for real-time health monitoring in smart healthcare systems. Appl. Sci. **15**(8), 4400 (2025)

13. Kumaran, S., Princy, I.E., Agnes, J.: Smart healthcare: machine learning enabled wban for early detection of chronic diseases. In: 2nd International Conference on Sustainable Computing and Smart Systems, pp. 998–1003 (2024)

14. Loseto, G., et al.: Knowledge-based decision support in healthcare via near field communication. Sensors **20**(17), 4923 (2020)

15. Manimegalai, D., Gunasekari, R., Sujatha, S., Karthikeyan, M., Umasankar, A.: AIoT-powered intelligent remote patient activity tracking and comprehensive vital sign analysis system for enhanced healthcare. In: Technologies for Sustainable Healthcare Development, pp. 147–173. IGI Global, Hershey, PA (2024)

16. Muhammad Arslan, M., Yang, X., Zhang, Z., Ur Rahman, S., Ullah, M., Abbasi, Q.H.: Advancing healthcare monitoring: integrating machine learning with innovative wearable and wireless systems for comprehensive patient care. IEEE Sens. J. **24**(18), 29199–29210 (2024)

17. Musen, M.A.: The Protégé project: a look back and a look forward. AI Matters **1**(4), 4–12 (2015)

18. Nong, H., et al.: Intelligent sensing technologies based on flexible wearable sensors: a review. IEEE Sens. J. **24**(14), 22197–22217 (2024)

19. Parsia, B., Motik, B., Patel-Schneider, P.: OWL 2 Web Ontology Language Structural Specification and Functional-Style Syntax (Second Edition). Recommendation, W3C (2012). http://www.w3.org/TR/owl2-syntax/

20. Praino, E., et al.: SScEntry: a personal disease diary app for systemic sclerosis patients. Ann. Rheum. Dis. **79**, 558–559 (2020)

21. Ruta, M., et al.: A multiplatform reasoning engine for the semantic web of everything. J. Web Semant. **73**, 100709 (2022)

22. Ruta, M., Scioscia, F., Di Sciascio, E., Bilenchi, I.: OWL API for iOS: early implementation and results. In: 13th OWL: Experiences and Directions Workshop and 5th OWL Reasoner Evaluation Workshop. LNCS, vol. 10161, pp. 141–152. Springer (2016)

23. Ruta, M., Scioscia, F., Gramegna, F., Bilenchi, I., Di Sciascio, E.: Mini-ME Swift: the first OWL reasoner for iOS. In: 16th Extended Semantic Web Conference (ESWC 2019), pp. 298–313. Springer (2019). https://doi.org/10.1007/978-3-030-21348-0_20

24. Scioscia, F., Bilenchi, I., Ruta, M., Gramegna, F., Loconte, D.: A multiplatform energy-aware OWL reasoner benchmarking framework. J. Web Semant. **72**, 100694 (2022)
25. Seneviratne, O., Harris, J., Chen, C.H., McGuinness, D.L.: Personal health knowledge graph for clinically relevant diet recommendations. In: Workshop on Personal Knowledge Graphs (2021)
26. Shaffer, F., Ginsberg, J.P.: An overview of heart rate variability metrics and norms. Front. Public Health **5**, 258 (2017)
27. Siddiqui, T., Morshed, B.I.: Severity classification of chronic obstructive pulmonary disease and asthma with heart rate and SpO2 sensors. In: 40th Annual International Conference of the IEEE Engineering in Medicine and Biology Society, pp. 2929–2932. IEEE (2018)
28. Siontis, K.C., Noseworthy, P.A., Attia, Z.I., Friedman, P.A.: Artificial intelligence-enhanced electrocardiography in cardiovascular disease management. Nat. Rev. Cardiol. **18**(7), 465–478 (2021)
29. Sundbom, F., Janson, C., Ljunggren, M., Lindberg, E.: Asthma and asthma-related comorbidity: effects on nocturnal oxygen saturation. J. Clin. Sleep Med. **18**(11), 2635–2641 (2022)
30. Van Woensel, W., et al.: Explainable clinical decision support: towards patient-facing explanations for education and long-term behavior change. In: International Conference on Artificial Intelligence in Medicine, pp. 57–62. Springer (2022). https://doi.org/10.1007/978-3-031-09342-5_6

Annotating 3D Scenes with Knowledge Graphs for Smart Infrastructure Digital Twins

Saverio Ieva[1,2], Davide Loconte[1], Francesco De Feudis[1],
Valerio Di Ceglie[1], and Floriano Scioscia[1,2(✉)]

[1] Polytechnic University of Bari, via E. Orabona 4, Bari 70125, Italy
{saverio.ieva,davide.loconte,francesco.defeudis,
valerio.diceglie,floriano.scioscia}@poliba.it
[2] donkeyPower S.r.l., via E. Orabona 4, Bari 70125, Italy
{saverio.ieva,floriano.scioscia}@donkeypower.it

Abstract. The accurate semantic representation of 3D assets is increasingly crucial for the development of Digital Twins (DTs) in smart infrastructure scenarios. Although standard formats like Universal Scene Description (USD) provide a robust framework for modeling and composing large-scale 3D environments, they lack native support for expressing ontology-based semantics. This paper introduces a lightweight ontology-agnostic framework to embed annotations based on Web Ontology Language (OWL) directly within USD scenes. The proposed approach enables the association of OWL individuals, class expressions, and property assertions with scene primitives, supporting reasoning and integration with knowledge graphs without altering geometric or rendering behavior. The framework is designed to be modular and general-purpose, enabling deployment across authoring pipelines and visualization platforms. A prototypical implementation in the Unity engine demonstrates the feasibility of the approach and highlights its potential to enrich smart infrastructure DT representations with machine-understandable semantics.

Keywords: Smart Infrastructures · Digital Twin · 3D Scenes · Universal Scene Description · Web Ontology Language · Knowledge Graph

1 Introduction

Digital representation of physical assets has become crucial in the design, operation and management of complex systems, especially in the context of Smart Infrastructures. Among them, the Digital Twin (DT) paradigm is increasingly being adopted to mirror, monitor, and simulate real-world entities. A DT encompasses both the 3D structural information of a system and the knowledge needed to reason about its operational semantics, contextual state, and lifecycle processes.

Y.-C. Hsu et al. (Eds.): ICWE 2025, CCIS 2735, pp. 98–109, 2026.
https://doi.org/10.1007/978-3-032-11233-0_8

The expressivity and machine-understandability of such digital abstractions are key requirements for enabling automated decision-making, configuration, and integration into heterogeneous workflows. This is evident in smart building scenarios, where a wide range of sensing and actuation devices must be orchestrated in response to contextual changes, user preferences, or strategic goals. As highlighted in [15], Home and Building Automation (HBA) systems are often lacking in terms of flexibility and interoperability. Semantic technologies offer a viable solution and enable devices to interact as autonomous agents, using formal ontologies to describe capabilities, goals, and context. The emerging fusion of the Social Internet of Things (SIoT) [3] and Semantic Web of Everything (SWoE) [14] paradigms further emphasizes the value of knowledge-based device cooperation, enabled through high-level semantic models. This is exemplified by recent advances in enabling smart objects with ontology-based social capabilities, allowing them to engage in context-aware interactions and collaborative behavior [16].

The *Universal Scene Description (USD)* (https://openusd.org/) format, originally developed by Pixar, has emerged as a *de-facto* open standard for information interchange across 3D computer graphics tools, supporting both individual asset models and hierarchical scene descriptions. It allows associating metadata to 3D primitives, attributes and objects. Meanwhile, the Web Ontology Language (OWL) [12] provides logic-based semantics for Web resource metadata, enabling knowledge modeling as well as inference across distributed systems. Leveraging these two widely-adopted standards, this work proposes a formal specification for the semantic annotation of 3D digital assets. The goal is to enable embedding OWL ontology-based statements within the metadata layer of USD 3D scenes, in a way that preserves the semantics while retaining compatibility with existing rendering and authoring tools. The proposed approach supports multiple ontology scopes, modular annotation fragments, and both forward and backward mapping between scene primitives and semantic entities.

The main contributions of the work are: (i) a formal API specification for managing OWL annotations in USD scenes; (ii) a conceptual alignment with smart infrastructure and building automation needs; (iii) a prototype integrating the *Cowl* [5] OWL engine within the *Unity* platform. The remainder of the paper is structured as follows. Section 2 surveys the existing approaches to semantic enrichment of 3D models. Section 3 presents the conceptual architecture of the proposed annotation framework. Section 4 describes a reference implementation that demonstrates its applicability. Finally, Sect. 5 describes future research directions.

2 Background

2.1 Basics of Knowledge Graphs and 3D Scene Description

The OWL is a World Wide Web Consortium (W3C) standard for expressing ontologies and Knowledge Graphs (KGs), semantically grounded in the Description Logics (DLs) family of logical languages. An OWL KG consists of a set of entities uniquely identified by Internationalized Resource Identifiers (IRIs). Classes and datatypes define abstract collections of individuals and data values, respectively. Individuals represent domain entity instances, whereas literals denote data values (*e.g.* strings or numerical values). Individuals make up the so-called Assertion Box (ABox), while classes, properties, and their logical relationships form the Terminological Box (TBox) a.k.a. ontology.

The level of expressiveness in an OWL KG depends on the subset of DL logical constructs that are used, and it determines the reasoning complexity. OWL supports automated deductive reasoning, allowing to infer implicit knowledge from explicitly asserted axioms. More expressive DLs allow to model more complex domains while requiring more resources for reasoning. In order to balance expressivity and decidability, OWL language subsets, known as *profiles*, have been defined, which target specific application requirements and reasoning performance.

USD is an open-source, extensible framework and format for representing three-dimensional computer graphics scenes. It allows the composition and rendering of Virtual Environments (VEs). The base data structure of USD is the *scenegraph*, which encodes the primary attributes of the scene's assets. The core abstraction, the *stage*, comprises an assembly of scenegraph nodes, known in USD as *prims*. USD provides flexibility for handling dynamic scene definitions, encoding both temporal changes in scene parameters and alterations to assets. It identifies and organizes objects using namespaces and property paths.

USD adopts an extensible schema model. This approach allows for the incorporation of domain-specific metadata directly within *prims*, either through user-defined custom attributes or via the application of standardized Application Programming Interface (API) schemas. This characteristic inherently enables interoperability with external semantic frameworks, like ontologies or knowledge graphs, but requires the explicit definition and mapping of identifiers and type information within the scene's definition.

2.2   Related Work

Smart building systems can rely on semantic models to interpret and manage system data automatically. Key standardization efforts include ontologies like Brick [4], BOT [13], and ASHRAE 223P [1], providing base vocabularies to express and identify building elements and sensor data. A framework has been proposed that leverages Shapes Constraint Language (SHACL) [7] and template modeling patterns to efficiently generate ontologies tailored to application requirements [6]. Practical deployment in sensor networks is enabled by SWoE tools such as Cowl [5], which provides efficient OWL 2 implementation. This characteristic is key to enable real-time reasoning and ontology manipulation directly on resource-constrained embedded platforms prevalent in building environments.

To support advanced capabilities in navigation, manipulation, and interaction, effective semantic scene modeling requires rich, machine-interpretable representations of physical space and objects. In addition to DT for Smart Infrastructures, Robotics is a major application area. The 3D Scene Graph [2] approach defines a structured, multi-layer model that integrates semantic information at object, room, and building levels with underlying spatial and visual data. This proposal allows the semi-automatic annotation of 3D reconstructions with semantic attributes by leveraging techniques such as multi-view consistency and object detection methods, thereby supporting complex spatial reasoning. In [11] a pipeline is proposed to translate USD scene graphs into OWL KGs for robotic environment modeling. The approach incorporates a semantic tagging mechanism using USD API schemas, grounded in a formal ontology aligned with DOLCE+DnS Ultra-lite. This enables logical querying and dynamic state updates during task execution. Experimental results demonstrate successful integration of semantic reasoning and control in a robotic box-unpacking scenario.

Analogously, autonomous driving systems benefit from annotated 3D representations for perception and decision-making. SSCBench [9] offers large-scale benchmarks that combine Light Detection and Ranging (LiDAR) inputs, camera data, and semantic labels to support Semantic Scene Completion (SSC). Both semantic and non-semantic approaches are employed: the former involve ontology-informed labeling and semantic segmentation, while the latter use volumetric or graph-based models to represent geometry and occupancy.

In [8] an object-level 3D semantic mapping system is proposed, which combines RGB-D smart sensors with Convolutional Neural Networks (CNNs) to construct object-centric semantic maps. It employs keypoint-based pose estimation and point cloud fusion, enabling real-time tracking of dynamic objects. The earlier *AnnoSceneBased* proposal [10] operates on scene trees, using ontology-based reasoning to infer semantics for unannotated models based on their annotated neighbors. The algorithm propagates semantic labels through relationships within the scene, achieving higher precision and recall compared to traditional content-based approaches.

Table 1. Comparative overview of semantic modeling approaches for smart environments and 3D scenes

Proposed approach	Modeling Scope	Semantic formalism	Symbolic reasoning	Real-time feasibility
[6]	Building metadata	SHACL, OWL	✓	✗
[11]	Robotic environment	OWL, RDF	✓	✓
[9]	Autonomous driving	N/A	✗	✓
[8]	Object-level 3D mapping	N/A	✗	✓
[10]	Scene-based 3D annotation	OWL	✓	✗
Ours	Multi-domain semantic embedding in 3D Scenes	OWL 2	✓	✓

This paper is complementary to the majority of the aforementioned works (Table 1), as it focuses on embedding semantics from heterogeneous domains into

3D scenes, rather than defining specific ontologies to model geometric elements semantically.

3   Proposed Approach

```
def Mesh "Room101"
{
    custom string semantic:annotation:building_manual = """
    Individual: ex:Room101
        Types:
            ex:Room and
            ex:hasPart only (
                ex:LightSensor and
                ex:OccupancyDetector and
                (
                    ex:TemperatureSensor and
                    ex:connectedTo only ex:SetPoint and
                    ex:monitors only ex:Environment and
                    ex:isComponentOf only ex:HVAC
                )
            )
    """

    custom string semantic:ontologyIRI:building_manual =
        "http://example.org/building#"
}
```

Fig. 1. Example of annotated USD.

This section presents an approach for the semantic annotation of 3D scenes encoded in the USD format by leveraging formal ontologies expressed in OWL. The main objective is to embed machine-interpretable metadata directly within USD files, thereby enabling formal reasoning and improving interoperability across diverse platforms, tools and applications.

A 3D scene is represented as a scene graph $\mathcal{G} = (V, E)$, where V denotes the set of scene primitives (nodes) and E represents the spatial and hierarchical relationships among them as edges in the graph. The USD format permits parallel edges, allowing for the representation of multiple relationships between the same nodes. The proposed methodology annotates these primitives with semantic metadata structured according to a knowledge representation formalism, typically an ontology $\mathcal{O}$.

Each primitive $p \in V$ is associated with a set of semantic annotations $\mathcal{A}_p = \{(k_i, v_i)\}_{i=1}^{n}$, where each (k_i, v_i) is a key-value pair describing a semantic attribute. An annotation function $\alpha : V \to \mathcal{P}(K \times V)$ maps each primitive to its set of annotations. These annotations are embedded directly within the

USD file using a dual-attribute scheme: one attribute encodes a serialized fragment of semantic content (e.g., an OWL snippet), and the other specifies a reference to the corresponding ontology $\mathcal{O}$. This design supports the coexistence of multiple, potentially overlapping semantic annotations for a single primitive. Listing 1 shows a semantically annotated USD primitive representing a mesh named `Room101`. The annotation, written in Manchester OWL syntax, describes `ex:Room101` as an instance of `ex:Room`, composed of several sensor elements including a temperature sensor linked to a set point, monitoring an environmental quantity, and being part of an HVAC subsystem.

To address structural mismatches between the USD scene graph and external domain models (e.g., simulations, control systems, or DTs) these semantic annotations act as a formal intermediate layer enabling consistent interpretation and integration. In this work, Unity's object hierarchy is used as reference, but the approach generalizes to other frameworks.

Given Unity's object tree $\mathcal{H}_U$, the mapping function $\mu : \mathcal{H}_U \to V$ identifies the most suitable USD primitive corresponding to a given Unity hierarchy path $h \in \mathcal{H}_U$, based on a path similarity metric $\sigma(h, v)$. The semantic content associated with a primitive can be formalized using a triple generation function $\gamma : V \times \mathcal{A}_p \to \mathcal{T}$, which produces a set $\mathcal{T}$ of Resource Description Framework (RDF)/OWL triples. These triples establish links between the USD scene content and semantic individuals defined in the ontology $\mathcal{O}$. The overall transformation procedure for Unity scenes is formalized as the function:

$$\mathcal{F} : \mathcal{M} \times \mathcal{H}_U \times \mathcal{A} \to \mathcal{M}' \cup \mathcal{T}$$

which takes as input an unlabeled USD scene $\mathcal{M}$, an external hierarchy $\mathcal{H}_U$, and a set of semantic annotations $\mathcal{A}$. The output consists of an updated USD scene $\mathcal{M}'$ with embedded semantic metadata and a corresponding KG $\mathcal{T}$ (Fig. 1).

3.1 Knowledge Graph Annotation Format for Universal Scene Description 3D Scenes

The proposed method embeds the KG, in the form of OWL/RDF triples, directly into the USD file using custom attributes associated with primitives, without breaking compatibility with existing implementations.

The core of the format relies on a dual-attribute scheme applied to each USD primitive p intended for annotation:

1. `semantic:annotation:<key>` : this attribute stores the primary annotation content. The value is a string containing the serialized OWL/RDF fragment that describes the semantic annotation of the primitive.
2. `semantic:ontologyIRI:<key>` : this attribute stores an IRI identifying an OWL ontology, which is treated as the reference vocabulary for the corresponding `semantic:annotation:<key>` attribute having matching `<key>`.

These attributes are also visible in the Listing 1 example. The `<key>` component in both attribute names serves as a symbolic identifier for a specific annotation instance tied to a primitive. This allows a single primitive to hold multiple, potentially overlapping, distinct semantic annotations, that can be also expressed using different ontologies. The proposed annotation methodology uses the following key convention:

$$\texttt{<ontologyPrefix>\_<annotationType>}$$

where `<ontologyPrefix>` is a short, human-readable prefix representing the ontology namespace (*e.g.*, `building` for `http://example.org/ontologies/-building#`), and `<annotationType>` is a term denoting the nature or origin of the annotation (*e.g.*, `manual`, `autogen`, `derived`).

3.2 Annotation Application Programming Interface

To manage semantic annotations within USD files according to the described format, a formal, abstract API is proposed. It provides a simplified, unified interface that abstracts the underlying complexities of the annotation subsystem. These complexities include navigating the USD scene graph, mapping application-level identifiers to primitive paths (via the μ function), managing specifically formatted USD attributes (`Annotation:<key>`, `ontologyIRI:<key>`), handling OWL/RDF serialization, and associating annotations with ontology IRIs.

The workflow begins with loading a USD scene using `LoadScene(file-path)`. Subsequently, `SelectPrimitive(path)` establishes the necessary context by identifying the target primitive within the loaded scene, upon which subsequent annotation operations will act. This stateful dependency is central to the API's interaction model.

Once a primitive is selected, the API offers operations that closely mirror Create, Read, Update, and Delete (CRUD) functionalities for managing the collection of semantic annotations associated with that primitive.

- **Create** and **Update**: The `Annotate(individualIRI, ontologyIRI, content, format)` operation handles both the creation of new annotations and the update (by replacement) of existing ones. If the specified key does not exist for the selected primitive, a new annotation is created; if it does exist, it is overwritten.
- **Read**: Reading is supported by `ListAnnotations()`, which retrieves the keys of all annotations present on the selected primitive, and `GetAnnotation(key)`, which fetches the specified content and format of a single annotation identified by its key.
- **Delete**: Finally, `DeleteAnnotation(key)` removes a specific annotation, identified by its key, from the selected primitive.

4 Case Study: Unity Editor for Annotating USD Scenes in OWL

To demonstrate the practical applicability of the proposed annotation API for 3D digital assets, an early implementation has been developed in accordance with the conceptual model presented in Sect. 3. This prototype provides an interactive environment for visually constructing semantic annotations over mesh elements, using OWL 2 ontologies. While generic and editor-agnostic by design, the implementation is extensible and can be integrated into toolchains that support USD 3D content.

The system is implemented as a custom editor plug-in within the Unity platform (version 6000.27f1). It introduces a dedicated panel accessible from the Unity Editor interface, offering both scene interaction and ontology-driven semantic modeling capabilities.

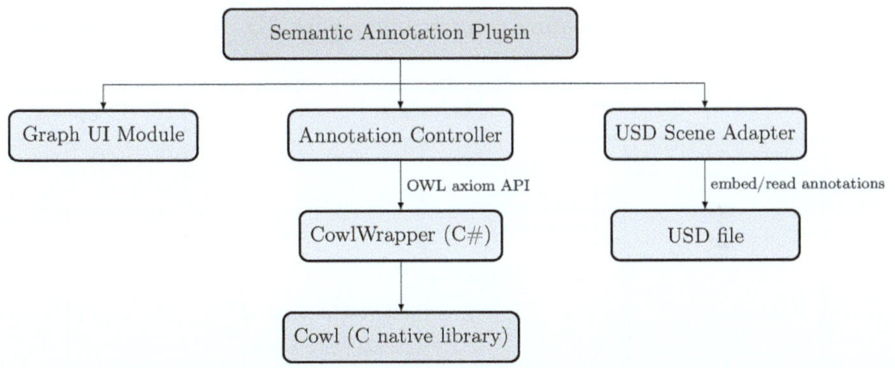

Fig. 2. Component diagram of the semantic annotation tool.

Figure 2 illustrates the high-level architecture of the semantic annotation tool. The system is organized as a modular plug-in comprising three main components: a Graph User Interface (UI) Module for ontology-driven visual modeling; an Annotation Controller that coordinates internal logic and user interactions; and a USD Scene Adapter that interfaces with the 3D scene structure to read and write metadata. At the backend, semantic operations are delegated to *Cowl-Wrapper*, a C# library that wraps the native *Cowl* OWL manipulation engine [5]. Designed for performance-constrained environments, *Cowl* implements a profile of the OWL 2 structural specification and supports both stream- and store-based workflows. It focuses solely on syntactic manipulation and does not provide reasoning capabilities such as classification or consistency checking. The wrapper exposes high-level methods to: (i) declare individuals and associate them with complex class expressions using existential or universal quantification; (ii) assert object and data properties; (iii) serialize ontologies or axiom fragments and embed them into scene metadata using the proposed approach described in Sect. 3.

To enable interoperability with USD assets within the Unity environment, the implementation leverages the official Unity USD package `com.unity.usd.core` (https://docs.unity3d.com/Packages/com.unity.usd.core@1.0). This package provides native support for importing, visualizing, and editing USD files

–including `.usda`, `.usdc`, and `.usdz` formats– within the Unity Editor. It allows seamless access to mesh data and scene graph structures, which is essential for resolving primitive paths and embedding semantic annotations as metadata. The package also ensures compatibility with the USD stage abstraction, facilitating direct manipulation of scene elements at runtime or in editor mode.

Annotations are represented as complete OWL axioms. Multiple annotations can be attached to the same scene element, each scoped to a distinct ontology namespace, thus supporting cross-ontology modeling. The annotation layer remains decoupled from rendering and simulation components, and adheres to the OWL 2 structural specification without imposing a specific serialization syntax. This design choice enables interoperability with KGs and automated reasoning engines, while maintaining compatibility with 3D modeling pipelines.

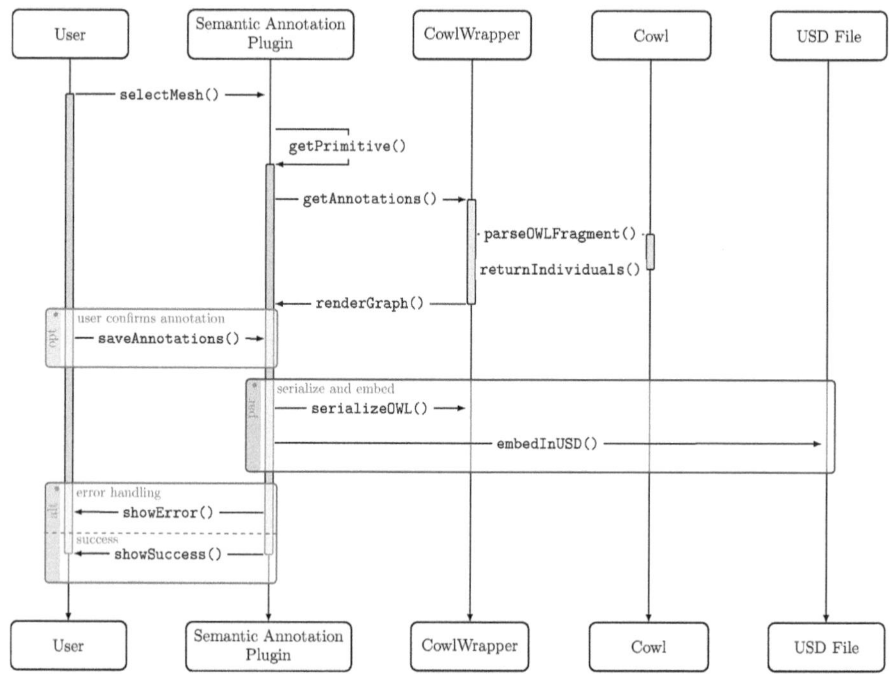

Fig. 3. Sequence diagram of the semantic annotation interaction flow.

Figure 3 outlines the workflow for annotating a 3D scene element. Upon mesh selection, the plug-in resolves the corresponding USD primitive and retrieves any existing OWL annotations via the `CowlWrapper`, which interfaces with the `Cowl` library. Parsed individuals are rendered in the graph editor. When the user confirms the annotation, the plug-in serializes the OWL content and embeds it into the USD file. Basic feedback mechanisms handle success or error reporting.

Figure 4 illustrates the graphical user interface of the proposed semantic annotation framework. The tool provides the following key features:

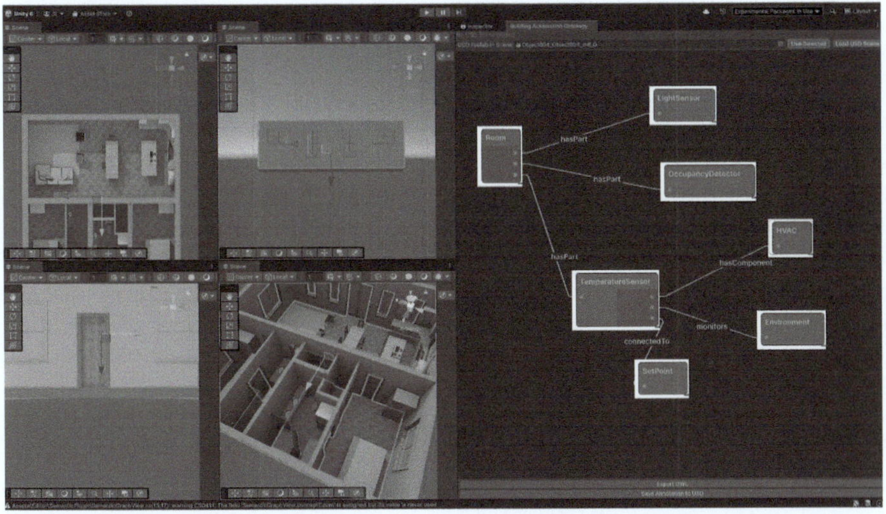

Fig. 4. Semantic annotation prototype in Unity.

- browsing and loading 3D scenes from supported formats;
- inspecting individual mesh elements and dynamically retrieving their associated OWL annotations, previously embedded as metadata within the scene graph;
- visually creating OWL individuals and complex class expressions that reference selected mesh elements via named object properties;
- exporting annotations to standard OWL serialization formats or embedding them directly into the corresponding digital asset.

The left portion of the interface displays a multi-view layout of a smart building interior, composed of structured architectural meshes. The selected element corresponds to a single room instance, imported from a USD prefab and highlighted on different camera views for inspection. On the right, a semantic graph editor is embedded into a custom plug-in panel. Users can instantiate ontology-derived concepts, such as `Room`, `LightSensor`, `TemperatureSensor`, and `HVAC`, and connect them through predefined object properties including `hasPart`, `monitors`, and `connectedTo`. These visual elements correspond to OWL individuals and property assertions, enabling the user to construct domain-specific axioms through an interactive interface. Graphs can be constructed by means of drag-and-drop interactions: nodes representing classes or individuals can be inserted and freely positioned within the canvas, while semantic relations are established via contextual menus. For example, the `Room` node in the figure is semantically composed of multiple sensors, each defined by a typed link and placed to reflect its logical role in the system. Upon selecting a mesh in the 3D scene, such as the room object shown, its corresponding USD primitive is resolved, and any existing semantic annotations stored as metadata are automatically retrieved and rendered in the graph. If no annotations are found, a new configuration can be authored and embedded into the scene using the *Save Annotation to USD* button.

5   Conclusion

This paper has introduced a procedure to embed OWL-based semantic annotations directly into USD digital assets. While the method is general-purpose, the work targets the needs of smart infrastructure and DT applications. By formalizing a lightweight annotation API and providing a prototype implementation within a Unity plug-in, the approach demonstrates the feasibility of bridging 3D scene definition and knowledge representation. The proposed solution is ontology-agnostic and compatible with existing rendering and simulation pipelines, while enabling reasoning workflows through the integration of OWL 2 semantics. Annotations are stored in the USD metadata and allow multiple, scoped assertions to coexist within the same scene. The Unity prototype presented in this work demonstrates the practicality of the approach through a visual interface that supports drag-and-drop graph editing, scene inspection, and round-trip annotation persistence.

Future work will focus on two directions. First, reasoning capabilities will be integrated to enable real-time inference over annotated USD scenes. This will allow the system to validate consistency, infer implicit knowledge, retrieve specific individuals and support context-aware behaviors directly within 3D environments. This will involve integrating a lightweight reasoning engine, such as Tiny-ME [14], which supports OWL 2. Its real-time performance and suitability for resource-constrained environments make it a viable addition to the annotation stack, enabling inference over OWL 2 axioms embedded in USD metadata. Second, collaborative editing features will be introduced to support distributed semantic modeling sessions. This includes mechanisms for conflict resolution, ontology versioning, and multi-user synchronization—extending the framework toward shared semantic authoring in DT infrastructures.

Acknowledgments. The research was supported by *xTech NextHub: Competence Center for Innovative Solutions Development* grant (grant number VTOIFW0), co-funded by Deloitte NextHub S.r.l. S.B. and the European Regional Development Fund for Apulia Region 2014/2020 Operating Program.

Disclosure of Interests. The authors have no competing interests to declare that are relevant to the content of this article.

References

1. ASHRAE Standard 223P, Designation and classification of semantic tags for building data. Proposed Standard, ASHRAE. https://docs.open223.info/intro.html
2. Armeni, I., et al.: 3D scene graph: a structure for unified semantics, 3D space, and camera. In: Proceedings of the IEEE/CVF International Conference on Computer Vision, pp. 5664–5673 (2019)

3. Atzori, L., Iera, A., Morabito, G., Nitti, M.: The Social Internet of Things (SIoT)-when social networks meet the internet of things: concept. Architect. Netw. Characterization. Comput. Netw. **56**(16), 3594–3608 (2012)
4. Balaji, B., et al.: Brick: metadata schema for portable smart building applications. Appl. Energy **226**, 1273–1292 (2018). https://doi.org/10.1016/j.apenergy.2018.02.091
5. Bilenchi, I., Gramegna, F., Loseto, G., Ieva, S., Scioscia, F., Ruta, M.: Cowl: pushing OWL 2 over the Edge. Elsevier Internet Things J. **29**(101439), 1–20 (2025)
6. Fierro, G., Saha, A., Shapinsky, T., Steen, M., Eslinger, H.: Application-driven creation of building metadata models with semantic sufficiency. In: Proceedings of the 9th ACM International Conference on Systems for Energy-Efficient Buildings, Cities, and Transportation, pp. 228–237 (2022)
7. Gayo, J.E.L., Prud'hommeaux, E., Boneva, I., Kontokostas, D.: SHACL. In: Validating RDF Data, pp. 119–194. Springer (2018). https://doi.org/10.1007/978-3-031-79478-0
8. Hau, J., Bultmann, S., Behnke, S.: Object-level 3D semantic mapping using a network of smart edge sensors. In: 2022 Sixth IEEE International Conference on Robotic Computing (IRC), pp. 198–206. IEEE (2022)
9. Li, Y., et al.: SSCBench: a large-scale 3D semantic scene completion benchmark for autonomous driving. In: 2024 IEEE/RSJ International Conference on Intelligent Robots and Systems (IROS), pp. 13333–13340. IEEE (2024)
10. Liu, J., Su, W., Sun, Y.: 3D model semantic automatic annotation based on X3D scene. In: 2013 International Conference on Computational and Information Sciences, pp. 282–285. IEEE (2013)
11. Nguyen, G.H., Beßler, D., Stelter, S., Pomarlan, M., Beetz, M.: Translating universal scene descriptions into knowledge graphs for robotic environment. In: 2024 IEEE International Conference on Robotics and Automation (ICRA), pp. 9389–9395. IEEE (2024)
12. Parsia, B., Rudolph, S., Krötzsch, M., Patel-Schneider, P., Hitzler, P.: OWL 2 web ontology language primer (Second Edition). In: Recommendation, W3C (2012). http://www.w3.org/TR/owl2-primer
13. Rasmussen, M.H., Lefrançois, M., Schneider, G.F., Pauwels, P.: BOT: the building topology ontology of the W3C linked building data group. Semant. Web **12**(1), 143–161 (2020)
14. Ruta, M., et al.: A multiplatform reasoning engine for the semantic web of everything. J. Web Semant. **73**, 100709 (2022)
15. Ruta, M., et al.: Social internet of things for domotics: a knowledge-based approach over LDP-CoAP. Semant. Web **9**(6), 781–802 (2018)
16. Ruta, M., et al.: Internet of conscious things: ontology-based social capabilities for smart objects. Future Internet **16**(9), 327 (2024)

Semantic Search Engine for Technology Scouting in a Digital Innovation Platform

Corrado Fasciano[1] , Filippo Gramegna[1,2(✉)] , Federico Capello[3],
and Margherita Vitucci[4]

[1] Polytechnic University of Bari, via E. Orabona 4, 70125 Bari, Italy
`{corrado.fasciano,filippo.gramegna}@poliba.it`
[2] donkeyPower S.r.l., via E. Orabona 4, 70125 Bari, Italy
`filippo.gramegna@donkeypower.it`
[3] Deloitte Officine Innovazione S.r.l., Via Santa Sofia 28, 20122 Milan, Italy
`fcapello@deloitte.it`
[4] Deloitte NextHub S.r.l. S.B., Via Santa Sofia 28, 20122 Milan, Italy
`mvitucci@deloitte.it`

Abstract. In the context of open innovation, technology scouting has become a critical activity for identifying strategic partnerships and emerging technological solutions. Conventional keyword-based search mechanisms used in most digital innovation platforms are inherently limited in their ability to capture the semantic complexity of innovation needs and offerings. This paper presents a semantic search engine integrated within a Digital Innovation Platform to support intelligent technology scouting and recommendation tasks. The proposed approach leverages transformer-based language models to encode natural language descriptions of corporate initiatives and innovation profiles into dense semantic embeddings to enable retrieval based on contextual similarity rather than lexical overlap. A case study in the domain of application modernization demonstrates the effectiveness of the semantic matchmaking engine in generating accurate and strategically valuable recommendations.

Keywords: Semantic Search · Technology Scouting · Sentence Embeddings · Innovation Platforms · Intelligent Matchmaking

1   Introduction

In the contemporary innovation ecosystem, effective technology scouting has become a strategic priority for corporations and institutions seeking to remain competitive in fast-evolving markets. The increasing complexity and interdisciplinarity of technological domains has made the identification of relevant entities – *e.g.*, startups, Small and Medium-sized Enterprises (SMEs), business ideas, research projects – an inherently difficult task. Despite the widespread digitization of business information, most existing platforms still rely on rigid keyword-based search mechanisms that fail to capture the nuanced semantics of innovation

Y.-C. Hsu et al. (Eds.): ICWE 2025, CCIS 2735, pp. 110–121, 2026.
https://doi.org/10.1007/978-3-032-11233-0_9

needs and offerings [22]. This limitation significantly reduces the possibility of discovering potential partners or solutions which may use different terminologies to describe overlapping capabilities, thereby hindering unexpected connections and cross-domain fertilization. To overcome the shortcomings of syntactic approaches in technology scouting, there is a growing need for systems capable of capturing the underlying semantics of innovation profiles and corporate needs. The complexity of innovation-related content requires a shift from rigid keyword matching to more expressive models of similarity. Traditional search mechanisms are inherently limited in their ability to detect conceptual relationships between differently worded but semantically equivalent descriptions. Advances in Natural Language Processing (NLP) have introduced a new paradigm for intelligent information retrieval, enabling the transition from syntactic search to semantic search. In particular, embedding techniques based on transformer architectures allow unstructured textual descriptions to be encoded into dense, high-dimensional vectors that capture semantic nuances and contextual meaning [7]. In this vector space, the proximity between representations reflects conceptual similarity rather than surface-level lexical overlap, thus allowing the comparison of heterogeneous inputs expressed in different terminologies.

This paper presents the design and implementation of a semantic matchmaking engine integrated within the NextHub Digital Innovation Platform, which aims to support intelligent technology scouting and strategic matchmaking among innovation actors. The proposed solution leverages transformer-based language models, particularly those from the *SentenceTransformers* library [21], to embed textual descriptions of corporate initiatives and innovation profiles into dense semantic vectors. Once generated, these representations are indexed within high-performance vector databases that support scalable and approximate similarity search grounded in contextual semantics. By enabling retrieval based on conceptual proximity rather than lexical correspondence, the proposed method is designed to improve the relevance and inclusivity of discovered matches by leveraging semantic representations that capture contextual meaning beyond surface-level lexical similarity. The main contributions of the work are summarized as follows:

1. the conceptualization of a modular architecture for semantic matchmaking within a digital innovation platform;
2. the description of a robust data preparation pipeline that ensures high-quality semantic representations of heterogeneous entities;
3. the validation of the approach through a real-world case study in the domain of application modernization.

The remainder of the paper is as follows: Section 2 describes the architecture and core functionalities of the NextHub platform. Section 3 details the design of the semantic matchmaking engine, including its data preparation, reasoning, and interaction layers. Section 4 presents a case study in the application modernization domain. Section 5 discusses related work, and Sect. 6 concludes with perspectives for future research.

2   The NextHub Digital Innovation Platform

The NextHub Digital Innovation Platform is conceived as a cloud-native system deployed in a Software-as-a-Service (SaaS) model on Amazon Web Services (AWS)[1], designed to support the end-to-end innovation lifecycle through semantic scouting, intelligent matchmaking, and business intelligence services. Its architecture enables the acquisition, integration, and analysis of data pertaining to startups, SMEs, research projects, and corporate innovation initiatives, with the goal of identifying strategic complementarities and fostering high-impact technological synergies. A foundational component of the platform is a centralized and continuously evolving repository that consolidates rich, multi-source data on *entities* within the innovation ecosystem. This encompasses business ideas, ongoing research activities and detailed profiles of startups and SMEs. The data model also supports the creation and management of *initiatives*, defined as structured expressions of specific innovation needs issued by corporates or other actors in the ecosystem. Such demands can concern emerging technological trends, vertical sector requirements, or targeted problem-solving objectives. The platform enables the identification of potential matches between initiatives and entities from the innovation ecosystem, supported by a hybrid process that integrates algorithmic recommendations with human expert-driven validation. The matchmaking mechanism utilizes NLP techniques and semantic similarity models to compute compatibility scores between entities and innovation needs. These scores serve as an initial ranking layer, facilitating the human-in-the-loop validation and refinement process. In addition, the platform supports the inclusion of related innovation artefacts such as scientific publications and patents, thereby enriching the contextual background of each entity.

From a technical standpoint, the platform is deployed within a dedicated Virtual Private Cloud (VPC) in the AWS Ireland region, and relies on Amazon Relational Database Service (RDS)[2] configured with MariaDB[3] as the primary database engine. The infrastructure ensures compliance with the ISO/IEC 27001 security standard and General Data Protection Regulation (GDPR), while adhering to enterprise-grade governance and operations management policies. The system architecture allows for the integration of external data sources such as Crunchbase[4] and national business registries, providing a broader view of the innovation landscape. The scouting and recommendation pipeline integrates a hybrid approach that combines semantic analysis of textual descriptions with user-driven pre-filtering functionalities. Expert users can refine their searches in advance by specifying multiple criteria, such as technological domain, business model typology, funding stage, geographical scope, Technology Readiness Level (TRL), maturity stage, and target market descriptors. The accuracy of the suggestion results is improved by this layered filtering method. Furthermore, the

---

[1] https://aws.amazon.com/.

[2] https://aws.amazon.com/rds/.

[3] https://mariadb.org/.

[4] https://www.crunchbase.com/.

platform facilitates the human integration of externally found candidate solutions, adding expert-driven insight to the algorithmic discovery process.

The output of the scouting process includes the automatic generation of summary reports in multiple standard formats – Portable Document Format (PDF), Office Open XML Document (DOCX), Office Open XML Presentation (PPTX) – as well as an advanced analytics dashboard implemented using *Amazon QuickSight*[5]. Key performance indicators (KPIs) are visualized in real time. They include the percentage of initiatives that match, the average processing time, the number of candidates assessed for each initiative, and the distribution of technological domains throughout the innovation landscape. The insights generated are used to support both operational monitoring and strategic assessment, while also feeding back into the continuous improvement cycle of the Artificial Intelligence (AI)-based recommendation framework.

3 Semantic Matchmaking for Intelligent Search and Recommendation

The increasing interdisciplinarity of technological innovation has made it essential to adopt intelligent tools for identifying and connecting relevant actors within the innovation ecosystem. In the NextHub Digital Innovation Platform, the semantic matchmaking engine serves as a core component for enabling intelligent technology scouting by matching corporate project briefs with the most semantically aligned startups. This component leverages advanced NLP techniques and vector-based retrieval mechanisms to provide meaningful, context-aware recommendations. Semantic search enables the transformation of traditional, manual, and keyword-based scouting workflows into automated, scalable processes. The core innovation lies in embedding textual descriptions into a high-dimensional semantic space, where conceptually similar entities are placed in close proximity. This allows for the identification of relevant matches even when descriptions use different terminologies or writing styles.

The architecture of the semantic matchmaking engine reflects a modular and layered design aimed at ensuring robustness, scalability, and interpretability. It is composed of three core layers, each responsible for a distinct stage in the processing pipeline, from initial data ingestion to AI-powered semantic inference and user-facing service delivery. This layered structure allows for a clear separation of concerns, facilitating both system maintainability and future extensibility.

An overview of the architectural pipeline is depicted in Fig. 1, which illustrates the end-to-end flow of data between components. In this architecture:

- Data Preparation Layer focuses on the acquisition, cleansing, and transformation of unstructured or semi-structured textual data into formats suitable for semantic embedding.
- Semantic Reasoning Layer is responsible for encoding inputs into dense vectors, storing them in a scalable vector database, and performing similarity-based retrieval using advanced AI techniques.

---

[5] https://aws.amazon.com/quicksight/.

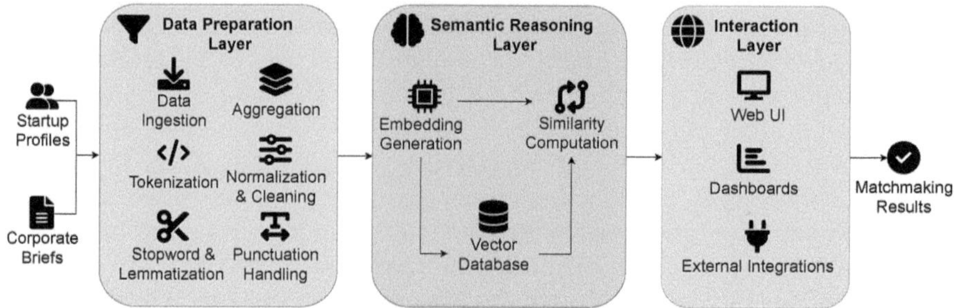

Fig. 1. Workflow of the matchmaking process.

– Interaction Layer offers Application Programming Interface (API) and visual tools to expose matchmaking results to users and enable real-time exploration and feedback.

This structure not only supports the modular development of each functional block but also ensures the scalability of the system as data volumes and user demands increase. The functionality of each layer is described in detail in the following subsections.

3.1 Data Preparation Layer

The Data Preparation Layer is the foundation of the semantic matchmaking pipeline, which is responsible for transforming raw textual data into structured, coherent inputs suitable for semantic vectorization. It operates on structured records originating from corporates and startups, such as project briefs, company descriptions, and innovation profiles, with the aim of producing clean, unified textual representations that effectively capture the semantic essence of each entity. The process begins with the aggregation of selected fields from the platform's data models. Informative elements –such as technology domains, customer segments, value propositions, market objectives, and application scenarios– are concatenated into a single textual representation. The selected fields are prioritized based on their semantic density and strategic relevance to innovation characterization. This consolidation step is crucial for preserving the multidimensional characteristics of each actor in the innovation ecosystem and ensuring that relevant contextual information is retained for subsequently processing. Following aggregation, the textual content undergoes a sequence of normalization and cleaning operations. Standard NLP preprocessing techniques are applied, including lowercasing, unicode normalization, and the correction of abnormal delimiters or excessive white-space. Spelling correction routines are applied where appropriate, particularly in user-generated content or in multilingual contexts, to enhance textual consistency. Proper tokenization is essential at this stage to ensure that the syntactic and semantic structure of the input is preserved across different linguistic configurations [6].

Noise reduction and lexical normalization are addressed through stopword removal and lemmatization. Non-informative words (*e.g.*, "the", "with", "of") are excluded from the text, while morphological variations are reduced to their base forms through lemmatization. These steps are intended to reduce lexical redundancy and improve the coherence of the input text. Lastly, the text is passed through a punctuation and special character handling module. In this phase, inconsistent punctuation is normalized, and non-informative symbols are removed.

The combined effect of these preprocessing activities is a refined input that is both semantically rich and structurally consistent. Careful text preparation can contribute to more consistent and interpretable semantic representations, although its impact on downstream retrieval accuracy is influenced by multiple factors and is not assessed in isolation in this work.

3.2   Semantic Reasoning Layer

At the core of the semantic matchmaking pipeline lies the Semantic Reasoning Layer, where natural language descriptions are converted into dense, context-aware vector representations, and semantic similarity is computed to enable intelligent retrieval. The computational process is organized around two primary modules: the *Embedding Generation Module* and the *Semantic Retrieval Module*.
Embedding Generation Module. Semantic representations are derived using transformer-based language models trained on large-scale corpora capable of encoding contextual meaning at both the word and sentence level. Within the NextHub platform, widely adopted models from the *SentenceTransformers*[6] library are employed. They produce dense embeddings that reflect the semantic structure of input text, mapping conceptually similar documents to proximate points in a high-dimensional space [21]. Each project brief or startup profile is encoded once into a fixed-length vector, depending on the model architecture. Embeddings are generated offline and updated periodically as new data becomes available. Domain-specific fine-tuning is not currently applied, but may be considered in future work to enhance retrieval performance on innovation-related content.
Semantic Retrieval Module. Once generated, embeddings are stored in dedicated *Vector Databases* (VDBs) designed for scalable, high-dimensional similarity search. Among the most widely adopted systems for this purpose there are *Pinecone*[7], *Weaviate*[8], and *Qdrant*[9]. These databases offer optimized indexing structures, metadata filtering, and distributed search capabilities, making them well-suited for large-scale semantic search applications. To identify relevant entities for a given query, vector semantic similarity is computed using standard distance metrics such as *cosine similarity* – which evaluates the angle between vectors and captures relative orientation independently of magnitude

---

[6] https://www.sbert.net.
[7] https://www.pinecone.io.
[8] https://weaviate.io.
[9] https://qdrant.tech.

– or *Euclidean distance*, which reflects absolute geometric proximity in vector space. Both metrics provide a meaningful approximation of conceptual relatedness across lexically dissimilar inputs, and the choice between them may depend on the specific characteristics of the embedding space and retrieval requirements.

In scenarios involving high-dimensional vectors and extensive datasets, exact similarity computation can become a performance bottleneck. As a potential enhancement, the adoption of *Approximate Nearest Neighbor* (ANN) algorithms has been considered [10]. Techniques such as *Locality-Sensitive Hashing* (LSH), *Hierarchical Navigable Small World* (HNSW) graphs [15], or product quantization could be integrated into the semantic matchmaking engine in future developments. These approaches offer sublinear-time retrieval and maintain competitive levels of precision, making them suitable for real-time semantic search applications at scale.

3.3   Interaction Layer

The Interaction Layer defines how users and external components interface with the semantic matchmaking engine, enabling transparent access to intelligent search functionalities and supporting seamless integration within the NextHub Digital Innovation Platform. The overall architecture of the matchmaking system has been modularized, allowing the semantic engine to operate as an external AI-powered service that exposes its capabilities through well-defined interfaces. At the core of this integration strategy lies a collection of RESTful APIs, designed to handle natural language search queries, manage entity-level retrieval, and return structured responses enriched with semantic similarity scores and contextual metadata. These API serve both the front-end of the platform and other internal modules, offering standard endpoints for invoking semantic search, applying filters, and accessing ranked results. The semantic search engine is accessible through an interactive Web interface integrated into the NextHub platform, where users can submit free-text queries and receive ranked results enriched with relevance scores and metadata; advanced dashboards and exploratory tools support filtering, comparison, and iterative refinement of search outcomes. The modular design of the Interaction Layer separates user-facing functionalities from backend retrieval logic. Such architectural separation simplifies maintenance, promotes reuse across different use cases, and allows the semantic matchmaking engine to operate as an independent microservice within the broader technological architecture of the NextHub platform. As a result, matchmaking capabilities remain adaptable and applicable across multiple application scenarios, increasing the overall value delivered by the AI infrastructure.

4   Case Study: Technology Scouting for Startups and Corporates

This section presents a real-world application of the semantic matchmaking engine described in Sect. 3, within a structured technology scouting initiative aimed at supporting application modernization [4]. The activity has been conducted in response to a request by an Open Innovation (OI) unit seeking to identify emerging solutions capable of enhancing the resilience, scalability, and maintainability of enterprise software systems. Application modernization refers to the strategic transformation of legacy software assets through the adoption of enabling technologies such as microservice architectures [12], containerization [14], DevOps automation, AI, and advanced compliance and security frameworks. These interventions often involve code refactoring, architectural redesign, and migration to cloud-native platforms. Additionally, modernization initiatives frequently encompass post-deployment support and integration mechanisms to ensure the long-term evolution of deployed solutions. In this context, a dedicated *initiative* has been formalized and recorded in the NextHub platform as a structured expression of a specific innovation need, with the objective of scouting European startups and SMEs offering modular and cloud-native platforms for modernizing legacy enterprise applications. The request has included the following key elements:

- **Objective:** Identify software solutions that support the transformation of monolithic legacy systems into scalable and maintainable architectures.
- **Technological focus:** Microservices orchestration, automated code refactoring, and cloud-readiness assessment.
- **Functional requirements:** Support for major programming languages (Java, .NET, Python), integration with DevOps toolchains and Integrated Development Environments (IDEs), generation of code-level metrics, and use of AI for pattern recognition and refactoring suggestions.
- **Preferred characteristics:** European-based companies; production-ready platforms; support for deployment in containerized or serverless environments.

The platform stores the new initiative after encoding it into a natural language input description. Next, by calculating semantic similarity scores between the initiative and existing innovation profiles, the semantic matchmaking engine produces an initial collection of candidate *entities*. The embedded semantic space created by the pipeline described in Sect. 3 is used to calculate the semantic similarity scores, together with a set of pre-filtering parameters pertaining to maturity level, technological domain, and geography. As a result of the overall process, eleven solutions have been shortlisted. Among them, three have been prioritized as top recommendations based on their semantic alignment with the initiative query, technical relevance, and potential for integration into modernization initiatives. The descriptions provided below have been anonymized for confidentiality reasons and focus on the salient technical features of the selected platforms:

- **Solution A**: Offers a platform for comprehensive source code analysis available in both on-premise and SaaS configurations. Key strengths include integration with industry-standard IDEs, multi-language compatibility (Java, Python, C#), and specialized modules for identifying code ownership and facilitating migration from monolithic to microservices architectures. A notable feature is the use of a proprietary Large Language Model (LLM) which delivers automated refactoring recommendations with high precision (98.7%) for specific languages.

- **Solution B**: Includes an AI-driven analytics engine for comprehensive assessment of application portfolios. The system enables architectural analysis of software components, dependency mapping, and cloud-migration readiness scoring. It supports modern deployment paradigms (*e.g.*, containers, serverless, WebAssembly) and offers automated refactoring suggestions. Language coverage includes Java, .NET, PHP, Ruby, and Python.
- **Solution C**: Delivers static code analysis tools focused on extracting metrics for maintainability and change risk. The platform computes cost estimations and technical debt indicators and integrates natively into DevOps pipelines. Supported languages include Java, C++, C, C#, and Python.

The outcome of the semantic matchmaking process demonstrates a high degree of alignment between the formulated initiative and the top-ranked results. The three prioritized solutions are not only technologically coherent with the functional profile specified in the query, but they also exhibit complementary characteristics that cover key dimensions of the modernization lifecycle: analysis, transformation, and evaluation. Overall, Solution A has been preferred over B and C as it offers the most comprehensive alignment with the initiative's goals, combining automated code refactoring via a proprietary LLM, broad language support, and integration with standard development environments. Unlike B and C, which focus respectively on infrastructure assessment and maintenance analytics, Solution A directly supports core transformation activities with a higher degree of automation and technical maturity.

5   Related Work

Matchmaking refers to the process of establishing meaningful connections between heterogeneous entities. Due to its inherent complexity, advanced AI technologies have proven effective in addressing this challenge both efficiently and accurately [20]. In the business domain, recommender systems constitute a fundamental component for supporting matchmaking processes, enabling the analysis of large amounts of user data to predict and suggest significant matches. Recommender systems can be categorized based on their underlying techniques and objectives [8,11]. Content-based systems suggest items by analyzing their attributes in relation to user preferences [13]. They are particularly effective when historical user data is limited, as they rely on explicit item features rather than patterns of user preferences. In Business-to-Business (B2B) matchmaking, such systems may recommend business partners with similar company demographics or industry focus [2,3]. Collaborative filtering systems exploit the collective behavior of users to generate recommendations [19], and can be useful for identifying potential business partners by analyzing co-occurrence patterns in past collaborations or transactions [23]. However, these systems are affected by the well-known *cold start* problem, which arises when new users or items lack sufficient historical data [5]. Environmental or situational factors – such as location, time, or market trends – can also be incorporated into context-aware systems to provide tailored recommendations [16]. In business matchmaking scenarios, such information can be valuable for suggesting partners bases on dynamic market conditions or geographic proximity [1]. To overcome the limitations of individual approaches, hybrid systems that combine two or more recommendation techniques have been propesed. In [18] a hybrid algorithm integrating collaborative filtering with content-based methods exploits both user behavior and item attributes to enhance recommendation accuracy and robustness.

In addition to traditional approaches, heterogeneous novel solutions for matchmaking have been proposed in recent years. For instance, explicit knowledge can be modeled within recommender systems to generate targeted suggestions. Knowledge-based systems may embed domain-specific rules and constraints to recommend suitable partners [25]. Furthermore, graph-based representations of knowledge can be exploited to improve the precision, reliability, and explainability of recommendations [24]. The use of Deep Learning (DL) models has also been proposed to enhance the accuracy and scalability of recommender systems [26], by virtue of their ability to capture complex patterns in user behavior and item attributes. Semantic search techniques employing vector databases and embeddings have been effectively applied to matchmaking tasks across various domains. The solution proposed in [17] addresses semantic gaps and high-dimensionality issues, significantly improving retrieval precision in large-scale tasks through multi-vector operations and language model encoding. Additional semantic-based matchmaking strategies have been explored and classified in [9]. Although such techniques enhance the accuracy and relevance of search results, several challenges remain to be addressed, including data sparsity, scalability, fairness, and high computational costs.

6   Conclusion and Future Work

This paper has presented the design of a semantic search engine integrated within the NextHub Digital Innovation Platform to support intelligent technology scouting and strategic matchmaking across heterogeneous innovation actors. Positioned within the broader context of digital platforms for open innovation, the proposed solution addresses key limitations of conventional keyword-based search tools by leveraging transformer-based language models and vector space representations to perform semantically grounded retrieval of relevant startup and SMEs profiles. The proposed layered architecture incorporates dedicated modules for data preparation, semantic reasoning, and user interaction, thereby supporting robustness, scalability, and extensibility in practical deployments. The case study in the application modernization domain has validated and clarified the ability of the proposed approach to generate relevant and contextually aligned recommendations, demonstrating the effectiveness of semantic similarity in capturing complex innovation requirements.

Future research will focus on the execution of an extensive experimental campaign involving large-scale, multi-sector datasets to empirically evaluate retrieval performance under diverse conditions. Additional efforts will be directed toward the full integration of the semantic search engine into platform workflows, ensuring seamless interoperability with other innovation intelligence services. Moreover, to enhance transparency and trust in recommendation results, the adoption of explainable artificial intelligence (XAI) techniques will be explored, with the objective of improving interpretability and user understanding of the semantic matching process and outcomes.

Acknowledgments. The research was supported by *xTech NextHub: Competence Center for Innovative Solutions Development* grant (grant number VTOIFW0), co-funded by Deloitte NextHub S.r.l. S.B. and the European Regional Development Fund for Apulia Region 2014/2020 Operating Program.

Disclosure of Interests. The authors have no competing interests to declare that are relevant to the content of this article.

References

1. Addagarla, S.K., Amalanathan, A.: A survey on comprehensive trends in recommendation systems & applications. Int. J. Electron. Commer. Stud. **10**(1), 65–88 (2019)
2. Adde, W.M., Rao, K.V.: A comprehensive study on recommender systems for e-commerce applications. Int. J. Emerg. Technol. Innovative Res. **7**(9), 948–957 (2020)
3. Aeron, P.: Content and context-aware recommender systems for business. In: Wang, J. (ed.) Encyclopedia of Data Science and Machine Learning, pp. 2763–2780. IGI Global, Hershey, PA (2023)
4. Assunção, W.K.G., Marchezan, L., Arkoh, L., Egyed, A., Ramler, R.: Contemporary software modernization: strategies, driving forces, and research opportunities. ACM Trans. Software Eng. Methodol. (2024)
5. Bali, N., Singh, K., Dhawan, S.: A survey and comparative analysis of relevant approaches of recommendation system. In: 2023 6th International Conference on Contemporary Computing and Informatics (IC3I), vol. 6, pp. 750–755 (2023)
6. Bird, S., Klein, E., Loper, E.: Natural Language Processing with Python: Analyzing Text with the Natural Language Toolkit. O'Reilly Media, Inc. (2009)
7. Devlin, J., Chang, M.W., Lee, K., Toutanova, K.: Bert: pre-training of deep bidirectional transformers for language understanding. In: Proceedings of the 2019 Conference of the North American Chapter of the Association for Computational Linguistics: Human Language Technologies, pp. 4171–4186 (2019)
8. Jia, L., Jia, L., Feng, L.: A survey of the state-of-the-art and some extensions of recommender system based on big data. In: Tian, Y., Ma, T., Jiang, Q., Liu, Q., Khan, M.K. (eds.) Big Data and Security, pp. 155–171. Springer, Singapore (2023). https://doi.org/10.1007/978-981-99-3300-6_12
9. Karabulut, E., Sofia, R.C.: An analysis of machine learning-based semantic matchmaking. IEEE Access **11**, 27829–27842 (2023)

10. Li, W., et al.: Approximate nearest neighbor search on high dimensional data–experiments, analyses, and improvement. IEEE Trans. Knowl. Data Eng. **32**(8), 1475–1488 (2019)
11. Li, Y., Liu, K., Satapathy, R., Wang, S., Cambria, E.: Recent developments in recommender systems: a survey. IEEE Comput. Intell. Mag. **19**(2), 78–95 (2024)
12. Loconte, D., et al.: Serverless microservice architecture for cloud-edge intelligence in sensor networks. IEEE Sens. J. **25**(5), 7875–7885 (2025)
13. Lops, P., de Gemmis, M., Semeraro, G.: Content-based recommender systems: state of the art and trends. In: Ricci, F., Rokach, L., Shapira, B., Kantor, P.B. (eds.) Recommender Systems Handbook, pp. 73–105. Springer, Boston, MA (2011). https://doi.org/10.1007/978-0-387-85820-3_3
14. Loseto, G., et al.: Osmotic cloud-edge intelligence for IoT-based cyber-physical systems. Sensors **22**(6), 2166 (2022)
15. Malkov, Y.A., Yashunin, D.A.: Efficient and robust approximate nearest neighbor search using hierarchical navigable small world graphs. IEEE Trans. Pattern Anal. Mach. Intell. **42**(4), 824–836 (2020)
16. Mateos, P., Bellogín, A.: A systematic literature review of recent advances on context-aware recommender systems. Artif. Intell. Rev. **58**(1), 20 (2024)
17. Monir, S.S., Lau, I., Yang, S., Zhao, D.: VectorSearch: enhancing document retrieval with semantic embeddings and optimized search (2024)
18. Pande, C., Witschel, H.F., Martin, A.: New hybrid techniques for business recommender systems. Appl. Sci. **12**(10) (2022)
19. Papadakis, H., Papagrigoriou, A., Panagiotakis, C., Kosmas, E., Fragopoulou, P.: Collaborative Filtering Recommender Systems Taxonomy. Knowl. Inf. Syst. **64**(1), 35–74 (2022)
20. Paul, A., Ahmed, S.: Computed compatibility: examining user perceptions of AI and matchmaking algorithms. Behav. Inf. Technol. **43**(5), 1002–1015 (2024)
21. Reimers, N., Gurevych, I.: Sentence-Bert: Sentence embeddings using Siamese Bert-networks. In: Proceedings of the 2019 Conference on Empirical Methods in Natural Language Processing. Association for Computational Linguistics (2019)
22. Ruta, M., et al.: A multiplatform reasoning engine for the Semantic Web of Everything. J. Web Semanti. **73**, 100709 (2022)
23. Sabbani, A., Haddadi, A.E., Routaib, H.: An efficient collaborative filtering and graph approach for business-matching systems. In: Ben Ahmed, M., et al. (eds.) SCA 2020. LNNS, vol. 183, pp. 700–713. Springer, Cham (2021). https://doi.org/10.1007/978-3-030-66840-2_53
24. Wang, S., et al.: Graph learning based recommender systems: a review. In: International Joint Conference on Artificial Intelligence (2021)
25. Wong, A.N., Raheem, M.: An appraisal on the methods and techniques of recommender models for personalised marketing campaigns. J. Phys. Conf. Ser. **1712**(1), 012043 (2020)
26. Zhang, S., Yao, L., Sun, A., Tay, Y.: Deep learning based recommender system: a survey and new perspectives. ACM Comput. Surv. **52**(1) (2019)

Distributed Ledger Technology Architecture for Private Event Tracking in Supply Chains

Arnaldo Tomasino[1] , Corrado Fasciano[1] , and Michele Ruta[1,2]([✉])

[1] Polytechnic University of Bari, via E. Orabona 4, 70125 Bari, Italy
{arnaldo.tomasino,corrado.fasciano,michele.ruta}@poliba.it
[2] donkeyPower S.r.l., via E. Orabona 4, 70125 Bari, Italy
ruta.michele@donkeypower.it

Abstract. Supply chain processes and logistics require both data interoperability and tamper-resistant long-term information storage for accountability. Fragmented data formats and limited trust between stakeholders still hinder end-to-end traceability in modern supply chains integrated with the Internet of Things. For this purpose, the GS1 Electronic Product Code Information Services (EPCIS) 2.0 standard aims to standardize event semantics. By itself, however, it cannot guarantee data security or fine-grained sharing across organizational boundaries. Here, we propose a lightweight architecture that integrates EPCIS 2.0 with the feeless IOTA distributed ledger, based on directed acyclic graph. A Ledger Gateway component exposes a RESTful Application Programming Interface to enable supply chain data management for involved parties, while a Data Standardization Service (DSS) handles bidirectional conversion between arbitrary JavaScript Object Notation (JSON) payloads and EPCIS documents via configurable mappings. This combination preserves interoperability, ensures tamper-proof storage, and remains suitable for resource-constrained IoT devices. An experimental campaign, based on a prototype relying on a private IOTA network, confirms the technical viability of the approach.

Keywords: Supply chain · Distributed ledger · EPCIS · Business event processing · Internet of Things

1 Introduction

In recent years, the domains of supply chain management and logistics increasingly need technological solutions to guarantee data integrity and immutability. To this end, Distributed Ledger Technologies (DLTs) are increasingly adopted to enable full auditability and to foster mutual trust among participants. Besides blockchain platforms, innovative proposals are based on Directed Acyclic Graph (DAG) DLTs granting more lightweight transaction validation, with the aim of facilitating applications in pervasive Internet of Things (IoT) environments,

Y.-C. Hsu et al. (Eds.): ICWE 2025, CCIS 2735, pp. 122–134, 2026.
https://doi.org/10.1007/978-3-032-11233-0_10

which are typical in the explored domains. However, one of the main issues in supply chains concerns the severe semantic fragmentation caused by the lack of adoption of interoperable standards for product tracking and logistics [13], which, in turn, increases the costs associated with data sharing [3]. For this purpose, the GS1 organization (https://www.gs1.org/) spearheads the Electronic Product Code Information Services (EPCIS) standard for real-time tracking of product-related events and processes and seamless information exchange among supply chain stakeholders. EPCIS latest version (2.0) [1] includes support for IoT industrial process monitoring and data capture, definitions of all event data fields and classes in JavaScript Object Notation (JSON)/JavaScript Object Notation for Linked Data (JSON-LD) syntax along with standards for implementing architectural components for storage and user interaction, including a REpresentational State Transfer (REST) Application Programming Interface (API) for streamlined event data integration.

Though promising proposals to address interoperability and scalability issues, EPCIS-based systems could still show vulnerabilities related to data tampering and unauthorized information disclosure [4]. For this reason, the integration of standards with DLTs can foster collaboration among all parties involved in logistics-related processes, while ensuring tamper-proof and auditable logging of information. In such a perspective, this paper introduces a platform for archiving supply chain events in EPCIS 2.0 format using the IOTA DAG-based distributed ledger. It features a REST API to handle private channels via the IOTA Streams framework, data insertion and retrieval. A translation module ensures non-standard data is converted to EPCIS 2.0-compliant JSON before being stored on the dedicated channels.

The remainder of the paper is as follows. Section 2 provides an overview of related works concerning DLTs in supply chains, then Sect. 3 describes in detail the proposed framework. An implemented prototype and early performance analysis are reported in Sect. 4, before conclusion.

2 Related Work

As highlighted in [9], many blockchain-based architectures have been proposed to track supply chain events in a wide variety of domains. Several studies [3,4,7,12] highlight the importance of traceability, accountability and transparency in supply chain and logistics, as well as the need for an accurate and standardized record of all events to enforce interoperability and stakeholders' trust. In these scenarios, data concerning products and materials typically originate from IoT-based environments. Furthermore, blockchain can also contribute to enhance existing industry standards, such as in the case of EPCIS. For instance, in [13] a system based on EPCIS enables authenticated users to register logistics and supply chain events through Near-Field Communication (NFC), Quick-Response (QR) codes and barcodes. The implemented platform supports event capture and storage, enriched with IoT sensory data, as well as product information querying and discovery. Blockchain can also effectively assist in advanced procedures of registration and discovery of information, as an example of Service Oriented Architecture (SOA) ([8]) to bring its advantages in IoT and resource-constrained environments. An interesting approach is presented in [10], where EPCIS events are mapped to operations on Non-Fungible Tokens (NFTs), ultimately treating products as NFTs. The system leverages *Hyperledger Fabric*[1] to restrict participation only to authorized parties. Hyperledger Fabric is also used in [3], where smart contracts define the operational logic and data models behind supply chain events, following the EPCIS 1.2 specification. The ledger stores data instances conforming to a defined EPCIS model, including hashes and non-sensitive information, while sensitive data remains off-chain. However, the system does not employ blockchain-specific mechanism for privacy and no conversion is performed, as incoming data is already formatted in EPCIS. On the other hand, the work in [12] emphazises the necessity of interoperability in supply chain also considering the proliferation of different standards. The main feature of the proposed system regards translation of IoT-acquired data in the entity-based context-oriented Next Generation Service Interfaces - Linked Data (NGSI-LD) format into the event-based EPCIS standard via a gateway component. Although sharing similar objectives with this paper, that approach only targets two predefined standards, whereas this proposal involves translation from a generic data format into EPCIS. Similarly, in an Ethereum-based system for the food supply chain [4], data captured via Radio-Frequency IDentification (RFID) in Binary JSON (BSON) format is converted to EPCIS JSON and stored off-chain. Smart contracts verify event information and register associated hash values to provide authenticity. Nevertheless, the use of Ethereum smart contracts implies considerations about transactions fees, that hinder their full applicability. Moreover, traditional blockchain technologies often encounter performance and scalability issues in IoT applications. This has led to the developement of platforms based on DAG data structures. Several recent proposals ([2,5] and [6]) leverage the IOTA DAG DLT framework in Cyber-Physical Systems (CPSs) to store supply chain related data produced by sensors and devices. Here, the DAG-based ledger stores hashes of off-chain data, ensuring verifiability and immutability of registered information.

3   Industrial Private Event Tracking

The main features and functional requirements of the proposed system are as follows:

- the platform must support the archival of information related to events corresponding to a wide variety of IoT-generated business processes in supply chain and logistics, mapped to the appropriate (sub)set of *EPCIS 2.0* constructs;

---

[1] https://github.com/hyperledger/fabric.

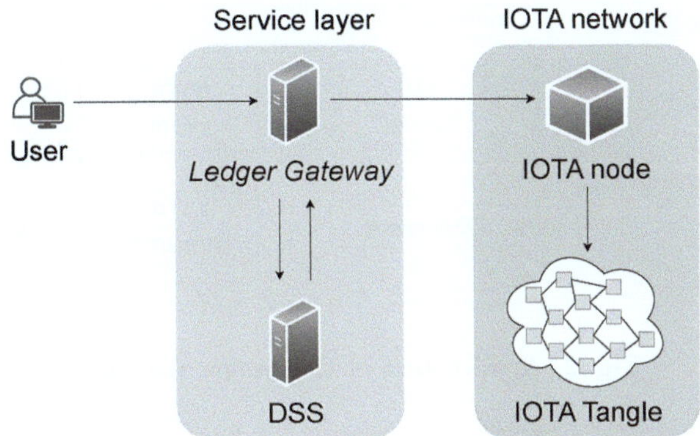

Fig. 1. Proposed architecture

- users and/or devices must be able to upload supply chain data in a format different from *EPCIS 2.0*, *e.g.*, supported by a third-party application. The system will convert this information internally to create or update the correct *EPCIS 2.0* documents;
- users must be able to retrieve documents stored in the system. These documents must be returned in the format supported by the application that requests them, despite being stored as *EPCIS 2.0* documents;
- data must be stored in a DAG-type DLT. Specifically, the proposed system employs the IOTA distributed ledger, chosen because of its lightweight implementation, which is better suited to IoT-based scenarios.

Moreover, it is assumed that users and/or devices will interact with the system through an additional dedicated client, which will perform client-side validation before actually transmitting data to the endpoints defined in the system. This approach helps reducing system complexity and server load by offloading those tasks to external components.

Based on the defined functionalities, the system architecture consists of two groups of core components, as shown in Fig. 1: (i) a service layer, including a Data Standardization Service (DSS) and a *Ledger Gateway* component; (ii) the IOTA network, comprising the nodes that manage the *Tangle* [11] data structure for document handling and storage.

3.1   Private Document Tracking

The main access point to the platform for external users is represented by the REST API of the *Ledger Gateway* component. For this purpose, the *Ledger Gateway* is further subdivided into the following components (Fig. 2):

- **controller**: it defines the endpoints for handling requests from external applications and invokes the appropriate services defined by other components. It incorporates (i) an *API server*, which exposes endpoints for requests from

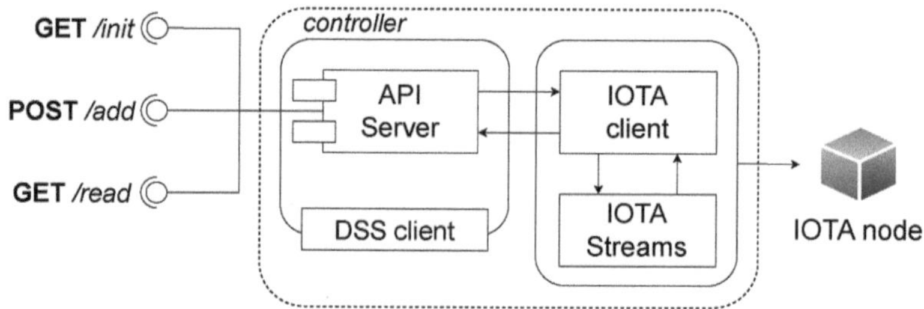

Fig. 2. Architecture of the *Ledger Gateway*

proprietary applications and (ii) a client for the DSS, which connects to request bidirectional document translation;

- **IOTA Client**: it interfaces with the IOTA network for document tracking. It utilizes the *IOTA Streams*[2] library to manage private **channels**, *i.e.*, secure communication pathway established on the Tangle. On an IOTA Streams channel, a user having the role of **author** can publish authenticated messages, that an authorized **subscriber** can access and read.

The *Ledger Gateway* exposes the following endpoints:

1. `/init`: an HTTP GET request. Input parameters include the number of authors and subscribers to istantiate. Each author is defined by a public identifier and is associated with exactly one corresponding IOTA Streams channel, where it has permission to write. Subscribers can read any channel, but cannot write data. Upon successful completion of channel and subscriber creation, a confirmation message is returned;

2. `/add`: an HTTP POST request to insert data into the system. It requires two parameters, (i) `author_id`, the public identifier of the user with the role of author in the system, used here to determine the channel on which the document will be published, and (ii) `message_id`, a public identifier for the message sent. The data to be stored must be included in the request body. As a response, the user receives a confirmation message acknowledging receipt of the document, *i.e.*, the successful insertion into the IOTA Tangle after a successful translation to *EPCIS 2.0* documents;

3. `/read`: an HTTP GET request to retrieve documents from the system. It requires the `subscriber_id` parameter, which identifies the subscriber fetching the message, the `channel` identifier, to specify the IOTA channel from which the message will be extracted, and the `message_id`, representing the packet containing the requested document. The response contains the requested document in the format supported by the third-party application.

The *IOTA node*, depicted in Fig. 2, represents the connection point between the *Ledger Gateway* component and the IOTA network. This node can be deployed as a peer connecting to one of the official IOTA networks such as the *Public Testnet* or the *Mainnet*, as well as a network managing a private Tangle.

---

[2] https://github.com/iotaledger-archive/streams.

Table 1. Modeled EPCIS events

Event	EPCIS event type	Action	Other fields	Fields (what)	Fields (when)	Fields (where)	Fields (why)
Insertion		ADD			EventTime		
Deletion	Object	DELETE	EventId	epcList quantityList	EventTime- ZoneOffset	bizLocation	bizStep disposition
Observation		OBSERVE					

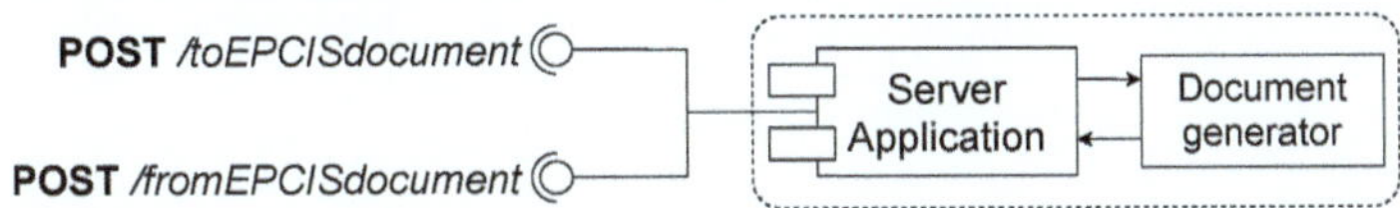

Fig. 3. Structure of the Data Standardization Service

3.2 Data Standardization

For the reference implementation, a subset of *EPCIS 2.0* data structure elements has been considered, as illustrated in Table 1. In this way, the system is able to keep track of the corresponding supply chain events.

The DSS is responsible for translating documents to and from the *EPCIS 2.0* standard document structure. As illustrated in Fig. 3, it defines two endpoints:

- `/toEPCISDocument`: a POST HTTP request. The request body contains data in `application/json`, which is provided in a format handled by the external application invoking the service. The returned response is a JSON document compliant with the EPCIS 2.0 standard;
- `/fromEPCISDocument`: similar to the previous one, it is an HTTP POST request that accepts `application/json` content in EPCIS 2.0 format and returns a response in pre-defined third-party format.

Internally, the *Document Generator* component handles the translation of the input document into the *EPCIS 2.0* data structure leveraging two JSON mapping files. The first includes keys representing field names from the third-party document format and respective values corresponding to the field names compliant with the EPCIS standard; the second defines the key-value mapping between EPCIS fields and their corresponding proprietary format fields. By customizing these mappings, the service can efficiently align external application formats with the EPCIS 2.0 standard. This involves adapting the respective data fields in the two JSON mapping files and providing them to the *Data Standardization Service*. In this way, the platform can interact with multiple third-party systems, adapt to diverse data structures, and ultimately enhance interoperability.

3.3 Components Interaction Flow

All interactions among components are designed to be asynchronous, allowing the *Ledger Gateway* controller to process new incoming requests, without waiting for the completion of each subsequent step of a previous request.

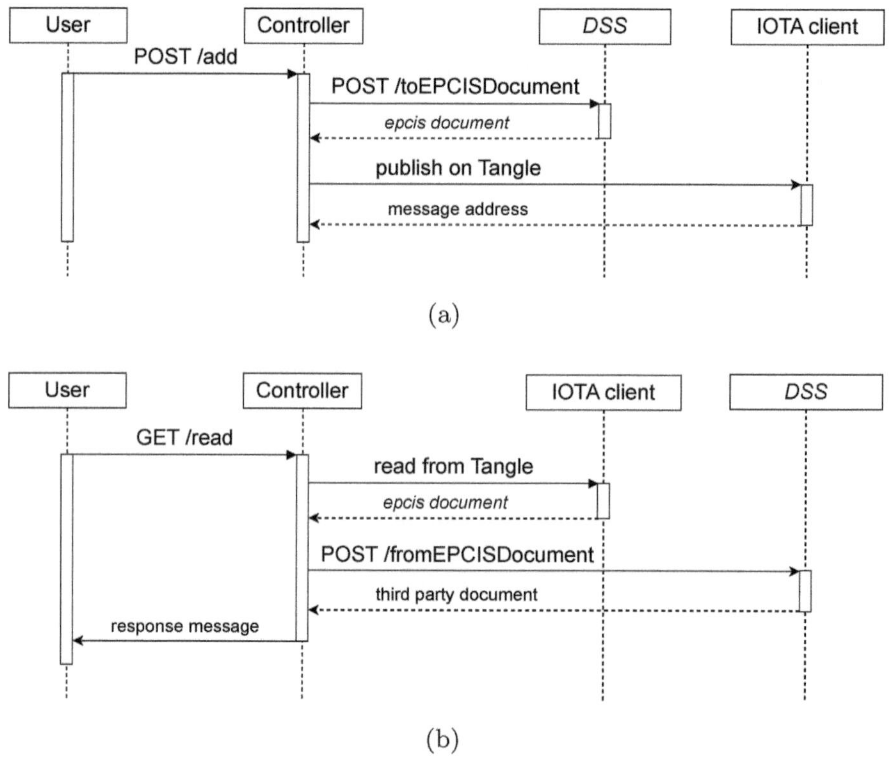

Fig. 4. Sequence diagrams of the (a) write and (b) read operations

Figure 4(a) illustrates the interactions for data insertion into the system. First, the user sends a request to the Ledger Gateway controller, which, in turn, passes it to the DSS. Then, the internal task of converting the document into the *EPCIS* standard starts and the translation result is encapsulated in the response to the POST request, sent back to the controller. Afterwards, the internal IOTA client service is invoked to publish the message into the DAG-based distributed ledger.

As shown in Fig. 4(a), when a user sends a request to read a previously stored message, the controller passes the request information to the IOTA client, which retrieves the relevant messages from the Tangle. The IOTA Client returns the message to the controller, which forwards it to the DSS. The message is translated into the format supported by the third-party platform and the result is encapsulated in the response. The controller, in turn, includes this document in the body of the HTTP response returned to the user.

4 Experiments

4.1 Testbed Setup and Deployment

For testing purposes, the proposed platform has been deployed leveraging a local private IOTA network managing a dedicated Tangle-based ledger. This setup has allowed to evaluate load requirements and performance under controlled conditions, w.r.t. an approach making use of a public IOTA test network. Both the *Ledger Gateway* and the DSS components (described in Sect. 3) were deployed as *Docker*[3] containers, as for the additional components to operate and maintain the private IOTA network. As illustrated in Fig. 5, all Docker components rely on specific exposed ports for communication.

According to the guidelines provided by the official repositories of the IOTA Foundation[4], the test environment is based on the IOTA official Go-based *Hornet* full node implementation[5]. Figure 5 shows the components that make up the test environment, including:

- *Hornet node*: the main IOTA node to which clients can connect, serving as a transport layer for submitting transactions to the private Tangle;
- *autopeering node*: it facilitates automatic peer discovery among network nodes, enabling seamless communication between Hornet nodes;
- *spammer node*: a Hornet node that continuously issues transactions at a predefined frequency to sustain a minimum network load;
- *coordinator node*: a specialized Hornet node responsible for periodically issuing milestones, which validate the transactions attached to them;
- *Explorer Web App*: a Web-based interface allowing users to query the Tangle, particularly by searching for transactions using their respective addresses;
- *Explorer API*: an intermediary service that interacts with the Hornet node to retrieve and expose Tangle-related information for visualization in the Web app.

This setup enables comprehensive testing of the private IOTA network under various load conditions while ensuring alignment with IOTA's official infrastructure specifications.

4.2 Performance Evaluation

This section examines the behavior of a locally deployed private IOTA Tangle when subjected to a series of consecutive requests. *Apache JMeter*[6] has been used to organize the test plan configuration reported in Table 2, simulating a flow of write and read interactions using the REST API endpoints of the Ledger Gateway with a given number of previously instantiated channels and subscribers and with predefined settings w.r.t. test duration and request rate. Metrics have

---

[3] https://www.docker.com/.
[4] https://github.com/iotaledger/one-click-tangle.
[5] https://wiki.iota.org/hornet/welcome/.
[6] https://jmeter.apache.org/.

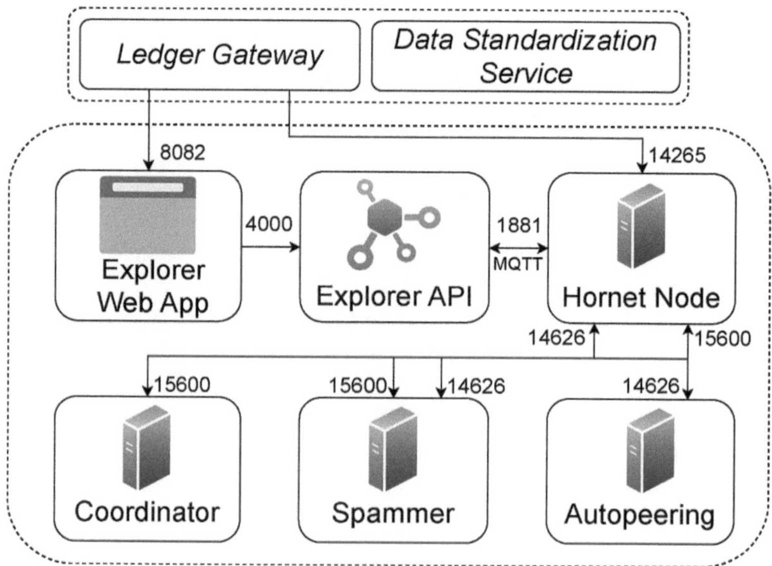

Fig. 5. Container-based testbed leveraging the IOTA private network

Table 2. Test configurations for evaluating the private IOTA Tangle

Test Case	Read	Write
Duration (minutes)	2	11
Request Type	/read	/add
Number of Channels	5	5
Subscribers per Channel	10	10
Configuration (req/min)	25	5

been gathered using the following components, packaged as an additional set of containers in the Docker environment:

- *cAdvisor*[7], to collect performance data from Docker containers;
- *Prometheus*[8], a time-series DataBase Management System (DBMS) to store metrics gathered with *cAdvisor*;
- *Grafana*[9], a dashboarding platform connecting to *Prometheus* to retrieve data for visualization.

The test results show that for a total of 50 /add requests sent, a total of 14 messages have published after 13 minutes Specifically, Fig. 6 and Fig. 7 respectively show the CPU and memory usage of the deployed containers through-

---

[7] https://github.com/google/cadvisor.
[8] https://prometheus.io/.
[9] https://grafana.com/.

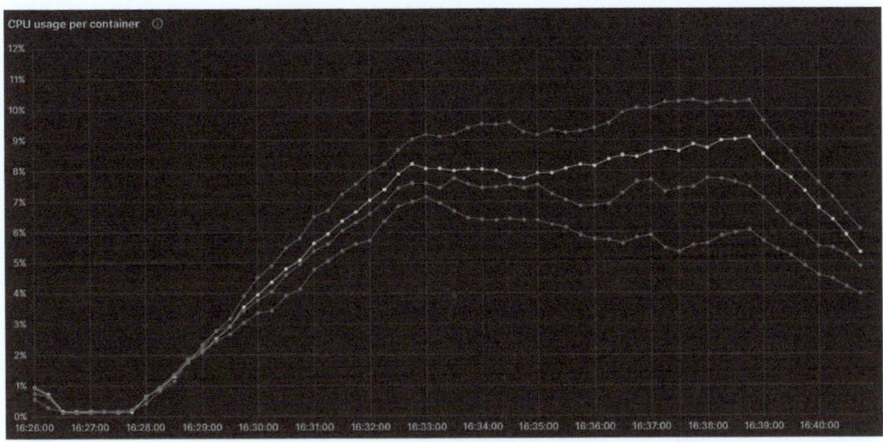

Fig. 6. CPU usage of Hornet node

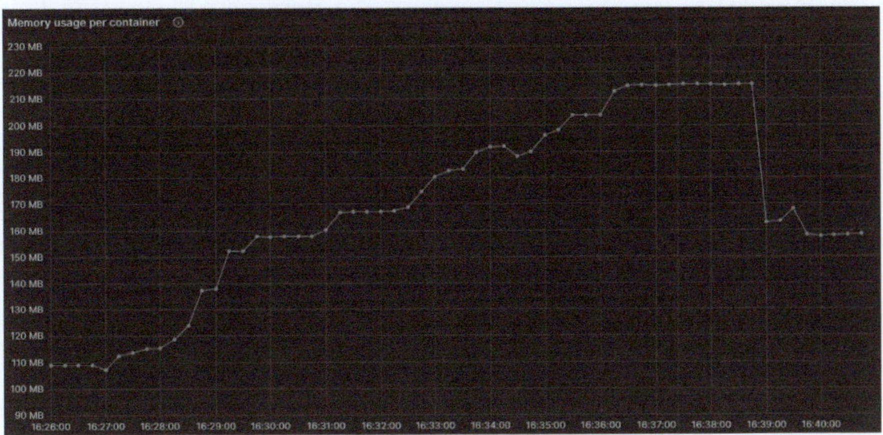

Fig. 7. Memory usage of Hornet node

out the test duration involving the writing and reading phases, while Fig. 8 presents the message traffic in the network. Figure 6 shows an important CPU load increase for the monitored containers. This is caused by the substantial CPU demand that the Hornet node requires to perform Proof of Work (PoW) which serves as the main anti-spam mechanism for the IOTA network. This high computational overhead could prevents the network from functioning correctly, as the Spammer node fails to publish transactions at a sufficient rate to sustain the minimum required load for transaction approval. This limitation is particularly evident in Fig. 8, which shows that no messages have been published throughout the entire test period. This suggests that excessive computational requirements for PoW can critically impact the performance of a private IOTA network, hindering its ability to process transactions efficiently. PoW execution

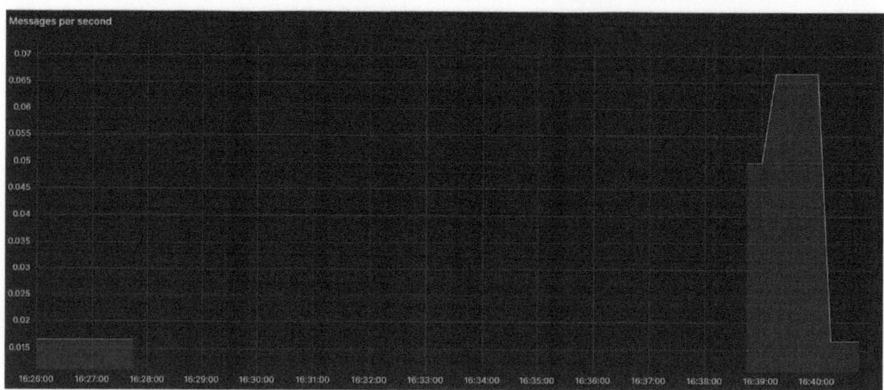

Fig. 8. Messages per second sent to the Tangle

can be offloaded to the local client invoking the Hornet node (*i.e.*, the *Ledger Gateway*), though this may degrade the performance of a lightweight component. This result highlights the need to design the infrastructure managing the IOTA node for optimal operational efficiency and functionality.

5 Conclusion

This paper has presented a prototype implementation of a platform for the archiving of EPCIS 2.0 formatted events related to supply chain operations. The proposal aims to integrate the lightweight and fee-less IOTA DLT platform in IoT-driven supply chain scenarios to enhance traceability and interoperability. The proposed system implements a REST API that allows users to initialize the IOTA-based substrate with the required number of private channels and related subscribers, insert new data and retrieve existing information. In order to support business applications where the incoming data is not formatted in a standardized data model, a dedicated module is responsible for translating it into EPCIS 2.0 formatted JSON documents, which are then inserted into the corresponding IOTA Streams private channels, interacting with the appropriate clients and nodes. A performance evaluation of the prototype implementation, based on a private Tangle ledger, has been carried out to investigate its behaviour in terms of computational load and network traffic. However, for large-scale deployments on public networks, scalability challenges such as increased network latency, variable transaction confirmation times, and dependence on public node stability must be considered as well.

Future work include extending the set of supported EPCIS data structure elements and events, considering not only generic events, but also operations such as the aggregation of multiple different products or the transformation of a set of tracked materials into new products. Furthermore, additional mechanisms to manage restricted IOTA Streams channels (as opposed to the publicly readable channels included in this prototype) will be considered, in order to allow access only to a set of subscribers authorized by the channel authors. Finally, performance optimizations will be needed and large-scale tests in open environments will be carried out to assess scalability.

Acknowledgments. The research was supported by the *Digital Enterprise* grant (code NIL6S28), co-funded by Lutech S.p.A. and European Regional Development Fund for Apulia Region 2014/2020 Operating Program, and by project *EmotIKON* (Emotional Inferences through Knowledge-based biO-signal miNing), funded by Cascade Call of Spoke 6 on "Symbiotic AI" of the Extended Partnership for Future Artificial Intelligence Research (FAIR), under the Italian National Recovery and Resilience Plan (NRRP) of the Italian Ministry of University and Research (MUR) funded by the NextGenerationEU program.

Disclosure of Interests. The authors have no competing interests to declare that are relevant to the content of this article.

References

1. Devins, C., et al.: EPCIS Standard. Release 2.0. Technical report, GS1 (2022). https://ref.gs1.org/standards/epcis/
2. Gligoric, N., Escuín, D., Polo, L., Amditis, A., Georgakopoulos, T., Fraile, A.: Iota-based distributed ledger in the mining industry: efficiency, sustainability and transparency. Sensors **24**(3) (2024)
3. Li, L., et al.: A blockchain-based product traceability system with off-chain EPCIS and IoT device authentication. Sensors **22**(22) (2022)
4. Lin, Q., Wang, H., Pei, X., Wang, J.: Food safety traceability system based on blockchain and EPCIS. IEEE Access **7**, 20698–20707 (2019)
5. Pullo, S., Pareschi, R., Piantadosi, V., Salzano, F., Carlini, R.: Integrating IOTA's tangle with the internet of things for sustainable agriculture: a proof-of-concept study on rice cultivation. Informatics **11**(1) (2024)
6. Raman, S.E., Venkatramaraju, D.: Secured and transparent transactions using iota tangle distributed ledger technology in dairy supply chains. In: 2024 International Conference on E-mobility, Power Control and Smart Systems (ICEMPS), pp. 1–6 (2024)
7. Ruta, M., Scioscia, F., Ieva, S., Capurso, G., Di Sciascio, E.: Supply chain object discovery with semantic-enhanced blockchain. In: Proceedings of the 15th ACM Conference on Embedded Network Sensor System, pp. 60:1–2 (11 2017)
8. Ruta, M., Scioscia, F., Ieva, S., Loseto, G., Pinto, A., Tomasino, A.: Blockchain and knowledge representation for service-oriented smart mobility platforms. Blockchain Res. Appl. (2025, in press). https://doi.org/10.1016/j.bcra.2025.100335
9. Sharabati, A.A.A., Jreisat, E.R.: Blockchain technology implementation in supply chain management: a literature review. Sustainability **16**(7) (2024)
10. da Silva Vanin, F.N., Tolcha, Y.K., da Rosa Righi, R., André da Costa, C., Kim, D.: Decentralized ledger technology for EPCIS 2.0: utilizing NFTS for enhanced product traceability. In: 2024 IEEE International Conference on Blockchain, pp. 64–71 (2024)
11. Silvano, W.F., Marcelino, R.: Iota tangle: a cryptocurrency to communicate internet-of-things data. Futur. Gener. Comput. Syst. **112**, 307–319 (2020)

12. Tolcha, Y., et al.: Towards interoperability of entity-based and event-based IoT platforms: the case of NGSI and EPCIS standards. IEEE Access **9**, 49868–49880 (2021)
13. Zervoudakis, P., Plevraki, M., Plevridi, E., Fragkiadakis, A.: SmartProduct: a prototype platform for product monitoring-as-a-service, leveraging IoT technologies and the EPCIS standard (2022). https://arxiv.org/abs/2210.09140

A Cloud-Edge Framework Combining AI, IoT and Blockchain for Smart Farming and Agrifood Traceability

Saverio Ieva[1,2(✉)] , Luigi Pio Battista[1] , Daniele Capriuolo[1] ,
Armando Ciardiello[3] , Simona Petrone[4], Gennaro Pio Auricchio[3],
and Luigi Uccello[3]

[1] Polytechnic University of Bari, via E. Orabona 4, 70125 Bari, Italy
{saverio.ieva,luigipio.battista,daniele.capriuolo}@poliba.it
[2] donkeyPower S.r.l., via E. Orabona 4, 70125 Bari, Italy
saverio.ieva@donkeypower.it
[3] Deloitte Consulting SRL SB, Via Santa Sofia 28, Milan, Italy
{aciardiello,gauricchio,luccello}@deloitte.it
[4] Deloitte NextHub SRL SB, Via Santa Sofia 28, Milan, Italy
spetrone@deloitte.it

Abstract. The growing need for process visibility, sustainability and responsiveness in the agrifood sector spurs the adoption of digital technologies throughout the value chain. This paper introduces a unified cloud-edge architecture combining Internet of Things, Artificial Intelligence and Blockchain technologies to support Smart Farming and end-to-end Product Traceability Management. In contrast to existing frameworks limited to specific value chain segments, the proposed architecture enables end-to-end process integration and technological convergence within a unified digital ecosystem. It is designed to be modular, interoperable and scalable, enabling data-driven monitoring, decision-making and secure certification of agricultural practices. A real-world use case focused on olive and grape cultivation in the Apulia region demonstrates the applicability of the architecture. The use case highlights the integration of multispectral imaging on tractors, edge-side inference for crop disease detection, microservice-based orchestration in the cloud, and blockchain-backed traceability, also considering interoperability with national registries.

Keywords: Smart Farming · Cloud-Edge Intelligence · Internet of Things · Blockchain · Architecture Design

1 Introduction and Motivation

Agrifood supply chains are vital to the global economy, but face mounting challenges due to population growth, environmental stressors and climate change, which threaten the sustainability and efficiency of traditional agricultural systems [2,3]. In response, the sector is embracing digital transformation through

Y.-C. Hsu et al. (Eds.): ICWE 2025, CCIS 2735, pp. 135–146, 2026.
https://doi.org/10.1007/978-3-032-11233-0_11

Smart Farming (SF), a paradigm that integrates advanced Information and Communication Technologies (ICTs), including Internet of Things (IoT), Artificial Intelligence (AI), robotics and cloud computing, across the agricultural value chain [15]. This shift enables data-driven, connected ecosystems that enhance decision-making and promote sustainable practices. A key component of this evolution is Precision Agriculture (PA), which leverages spatial and temporal data to optimize site-specific interventions, allowing for the precise management of resources like water and fertilizers. Together, these approaches aim to improve productivity, reduce waste, and ensure long-term resilience in agricultural operations.

The successful realization of SF and PA depends on the convergence of several enabling technologies: IoT for real-time environmental monitoring [6], Edge and Cloud Computing for distributed data management [5], AI for intelligent decision support [12], and Blockchain for secure, auditable traceability [11]. This technological stack provides a foundation for end-to-end digitalization across the agricultural supply chain.

Despite a growing number of solutions addressing operational challenges in heterogeneous and connectivity-limited environments [1], many existing frameworks remain dependent on centralized infrastructures [9]. Such designs often suffer from high latency, lack of responsiveness for real-time decisions (e.g., irrigation or disease alerts) and limited interoperability with external systems like national agricultural registries. Traceability mechanisms also tend to fall short in meeting transparency and auditability requirements.

To address these gaps, this paper proposes a unified and modular architecture integrating IoT sensing and edge-cloud architecture with data-driven analytics into a cohesive framework, also including blockchain technologies to ensure a complete resource traceability. The proposed solution supports low-latency field operations, scalable analytics and secure data management, while enabling compliance and integration with external platforms. Designed to be adaptable and interoperable, it targets both small-scale farms and complex industrial operations.

The remainder of the paper is organized as follows. Section 2 presents related work on cloud-edge architectures, AI/IoT-based monitoring, and blockchain for certification. Section 3 introduces the proposed framework and its components, whereas Sect. 4 details a real-world deployment in Apulian viticulture and olive farming. Finally, Sect. 5 concludes the paper and outlines future research directions.

2   Related Work

This section reviews recent key contributions from the literature, focusing on three core domains: distributed computing for responsiveness and data privacy; intelligent sensing and analytics for automation and decision support; secure and transparent systems for agrifood supply chain traceability.

Cloud-edge architectures have been widely explored in PA to address the latency and connectivity limitations of cloud-only solutions. Increasingly, studies highlight their synergy with AI to enhance responsiveness and decision-making capabilities. Kum *et al.* [4] propose a scalable framework for orchestrating AI services in smart agriculture. The system, tested in a strawberry greenhouse, uses a rail-mounted camera to monitor crop status and detect ripeness, diseases and anomalies. Edge-side processing minimizes data transmission and ensures responsiveness. Similarly, Sarantakos *et al.* [14] introduce a distributed system for detecting olive leaf infections using drone images. The solution achieves high accuracy while reducing latency, costs, and privacy risks through edge-based inference. In another study, Marković *et al.* [8] leverage fog computing to optimize image analysis on low-power devices, processing data close to the source in order to reduce network load and latency.

Blockchain has emerged as a promising tool for improving transparency and trust in agrifood systems. Its integration with IoT and cloud-edge architectures enables automated, secure, and immutable event data handling. Sakthi *et al.* [13] present a decentralized platform combining edge computing and blockchain for agricultural knowledge management. Data collected from IoT sensors (for example, humidity, temperature, presence of pests) are preprocessed locally and analyzed in the cloud using Machine Learning (ML). The multi-layer architecture (physical, edge, fog, cloud, interface, blockchain) enables real-time personalized insights and secure data records. Similarly, Ting *et al.* [16] propose an automated irrigation system that integrates IoT sensing, fuzzy logic and blockchain. Local inference determines water needs and triggers pumps, while blockchain ensures secure access to decision logs. Using low-cost hardware, the system demonstrates accurate irrigation control and sustainable water usage.

These studies demonstrate the potential of emerging technologies to improve agricultural practices. However, most of the existing approaches are still limited to partial integrations and lack a cohesive architectural vision. In response, the following section introduces a comprehensive framework that unifies IoT-based sensing, edge and cloud computing, AI-driven analytics and blockchain-enabled traceability in a single, interoperable architecture.

3   Proposed Framework

This section introduces a modular and scalable framework for IoT-based systems, detailing its layered architecture, the core services and functional modules that enable sensing, processing, orchestration, and traceability, as well as the interoperability strategies adopted to ensure integration across heterogeneous devices and platforms.

3.1   System-Level Architecture Overview

The proposed framework adopts the multi-tier architecture shown in Fig. 1, which spans sensing, edge, and cloud computing components, supported by transversal layers for traceability, persistence, and integration. It is designed to manage the complete IoT data lifecycle, from acquisition to decision-making and certification, while ensuring modularity, scalability and interoperability.

Sensing Layer: Distributed IoT devices acquire environmental, operational, and agronomic data using standard protocols, as described in Sect. 3.2. Devices may include embedded systems, sensors, and actuators with autonomous capabilities for time-stamping, data compression, simple pre-processing and supporting efficient data collection even in constrained network environments.

Edge Computing Layer: Embedded devices—including both standard and AI-capable edge nodes—perform tasks such as data preprocessing (e.g., normalization, aggregation) and, where applicable, local machine learning inference to detect anomalies or classify events. This layer enables low-latency decision-making in time-sensitive scenarios and reduces reliance on cloud connectivity.

Cloud Layer: Built on cloud native platforms, this layer hosts containerized microservices to orchestrate data workflows, manage model lifecycles, execute analytics pipelines and provide dashboards or APIs. ML models trained in the cloud are compiled and deployed to edge devices for near-real-time operation.

Three additional transversal layers extend across these tiers to enhance security, interoperability, and system coherence:

Traceability and Trust Layer: provides secure operation across the system via identity and access management, encryption, and tamper-proof logging. Blockchain-based components enable the certification and auditability of key actions, improving transparency and compliance with Product Traceability Management (PTM) requirements.

Persistence Layer: Manages structured, semi-structured, and unstructured data across layers using hybrid storage solutions, supporting policies for retention, replication and partitioning to satisfy consistency, availability, and scalability requirements.

Integration Layer: Enables interoperability among internal components and external systems. It includes Application Programming Interface (API) management services, message brokers and protocol adapters tailored for industrial and sector-specific standards.

Building on this architectural foundation, the following describes the core services and functional modules that implement the system's capabilities across each layer, enabling data acquisition, edge/cloud processing, orchestration and secure traceability throughout the platform. Figure 1 presents how these modules interact within the different layers.

In the Sensing Layer, the ***Data Acquisition Module*** is responsible for collecting data from heterogeneous sources, including local and remote sensors, using context-specific communication protocols.

The Edge Computing Layer hosts two key modules: the ***Edge Data Processing Module***, which performs data cleaning, normalization, and aggregation to reduce redundancy and transmission overhead; the ***Local Inference Module***, which executes pre-trained ML models or domain-specific rules to enable

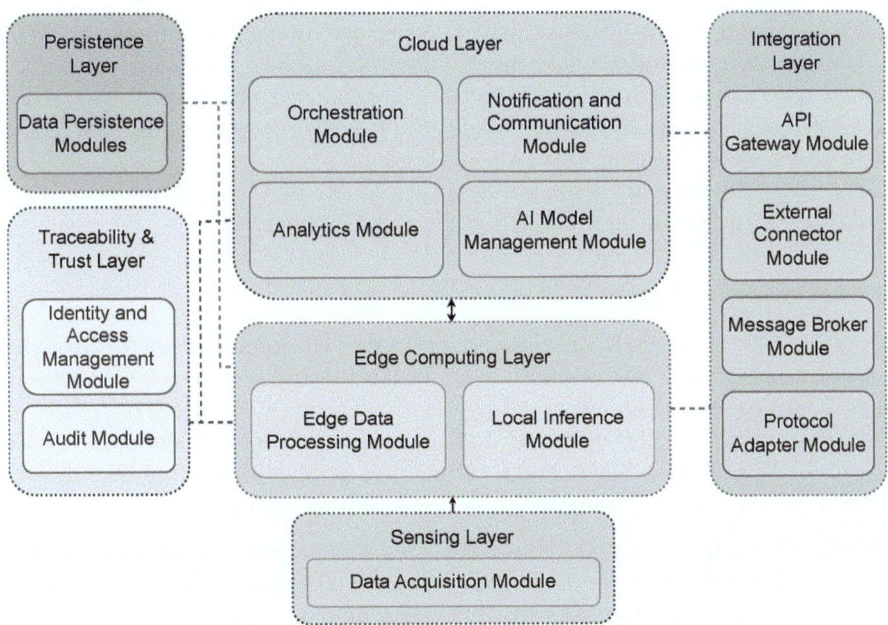

Fig. 1. Reference architecture of the proposed framework.

real-time event detection and localized decision-making, even in conditions of poor connectivity.

Within the Cloud Layer, the architecture includes an ***AI Model Management Module*** that oversees the training, optimization, and deployment of AI models; an ***Analytics Module*** for Key Performance Indicator (KPI) computation, dashboard generation and strategic insight extraction; an ***Orchestration Module*** to coordinate the execution and interaction of the different modules and services across the platform, ensuring the coherence of workflows and the correct sequencing of operations; and a ***Notification and Communication Module*** that ensures the delivery of alerts and operational messages through secure, redundant channels.

The Traceability & Trust Layer enforces security and transparency via an ***Identity and Access Management Module***, implementing role-based access control, authentication and session management and credential management policies, and a ***Traceability and Audit Module***, which ensures immutable recording of system events for compliance and certification.

In the Persistence Layer, ***Data Persistence Modules*** manage storage and retrieval for both structured and unstructured data across relational and NoSQL databases, applying data access abstraction mechanisms such as Data Access Object (DAO) to separate application logic from backend systems.

Lastly, the Integration Layer enables interoperability through an ***API Gateway Module*** that serves as the central entry point for routing incoming API requests exposed by the system to the appropriate internal resources, an ***External Connector Module*** that supports integration with third-party services not directly, a ***Protocol Adapter Module*** for normalizing heterogeneous protocols into common formats, and a ***Message Broker Module*** that enables reliable edge-cloud messaging using pub/sub patterns.

Together, these modules form a flexible and extensible architecture that can be adapted to different domains and operational scenarios.

3.2 Interoperability and Standards

Interoperability is a critical enabler in cloud–edge AI architectures for SF, where heterogeneous devices and services must reliably exchange data across multiple layers. The proposed framework addresses this through standardized communication protocols, open data formats and semantic models that promote modularity, scalability and long-term integration across diverse platforms. The proposal includes three primary communication flows, as reported below.

- **Sensor-to-edge**: is prevalent in PA scenarios, where IoT sensor data are processed locally by edge nodes using lightweight protocols such as Message Queuing Telemetry Transport (MQTT) secured with Transport Layer Security (TLS) and Constrained Application Protocol (CoAP) with Observe in constrained environments.
- **Edge-to-edge**: enables distributed coordination and shared inference among edge devices, supporting latency-sensitive operations without relying on constant cloud connectivity.
- **Edge-to-cloud**: handles the transmission of aggregated telemetry, inference results, and model updates using MQTT or Representational State Transfer (REST) APIs, enabling scalable integration with cloud-based orchestration and analytics services.

To ensure both **syntactic and semantic interoperability**, data is serialized in standard formats such as JavaScript Object Notation (JSON) facilitating exchange among heterogeneous components. At the semantic level, the architecture supports annotations using lightweight ontologies like Semantic Sensor Network (SSN) [10], which provide formal descriptions of sensor types, observations and context. These ontologies are leveraged to annotate raw sensor data or image-based detections produced during the field monitoring pipeline (Sect. 4), enabling consistent classification, traceability and integration with institutional systems.

Overall, this approach enables a robust and interoperable SF ecosystem, connecting edge intelligence, cloud orchestration and regulatory integration into a cohesive architecture.

4 Use Case: Smart Farming for Apulian Local Products

This section applies the proposed architecture to a real-world agricultural context in Apulia, southern Italy, focusing on olive and grape production—key regional assets increasingly exposed to climate variability, plant diseases (e.g., *Xylella fastidiosa*), and growing regulatory demands for transparency and sustainability. Unlike various fragmented digital approaches currently adopted, the proposed framework enables an end-to-end solution by integrating field sensing, edge-local AI inference, cloud orchestration, and blockchain-based traceability.

The deployment model is tailored to this domain, aligning with the multilayered architecture and functional modules described in Sect. 3.1. The next sections highlight two core capabilities: Sect. 4.2 presents edge-assisted detection of leaf disease using multispectral imaging for on-device inference; Sect. 4.3 describes how field events are captured, certified, and logged via blockchain to ensure traceability and compliance across the production lifecycle.

4.1 Scenario and Architecture Deployment

The architecture adopts a cloud-native microservice model in the cloud and distributed, AI-enabled processing at the edge, supporting local decision-making and seamless integration across layers. The proposed deployment is based on Amazon Web Services (AWS), though the design remains provider-agnostic. Figure 2 presents the overall deployment model.

At the core of the cloud layer, a collection of domain-specific microservices is deployed using either serverless functions or container orchestration services. Each service operates independently, managing its own persistence via relational databases or object storage systems. System APIs are exposed through a managed API gateway, handling authentication, throttling, and routing. An **External APIs Connector** module connects with external data providers, *e.g. EOSDA* (https://eos.com/) or *Open Meteo* (https://open-meteo.com/), to ingest satellite imagery and weather data into the system. An **Identity and Access Management** module manages user roles, *JSON Web Token (JWT)*-based authentication, and integrates with federated identity providers for Single Sign-On (SSO) and Multi-Factor Authentication (MFA). Complex inter-service workflows are orchestrated using *Apache Airflow* (https://airflow.apache.org/), leveraging *Apache Kafka* (https://kafka.apache.org/) for reliable, asynchronous messaging. Traceability and Trust are achieved via managed monitoring and logging services for system observability and blockchain-based notarization mechanisms for immutable traceability, as detailed in Sect. 4.3.

Core microservices include:

- **Cultivation**: handles agronomic task planning and monitoring (e.g. irrigation and phenological tracking).
- **Transformation**: oversees olive and grape processing (delivery, production, warehouse, register, quality tracking).
- **Sales & Administration**: manages reviews, products, bottle tracking, reporting and cost and revenue calculations. It also invokes serverless AI functions triggered by Kafka to analyze customer reviews and provide insights.
- **AI Model Management**: manages AI tasks such as keyword extraction, sentiment analysis, and object detection. The object detection model

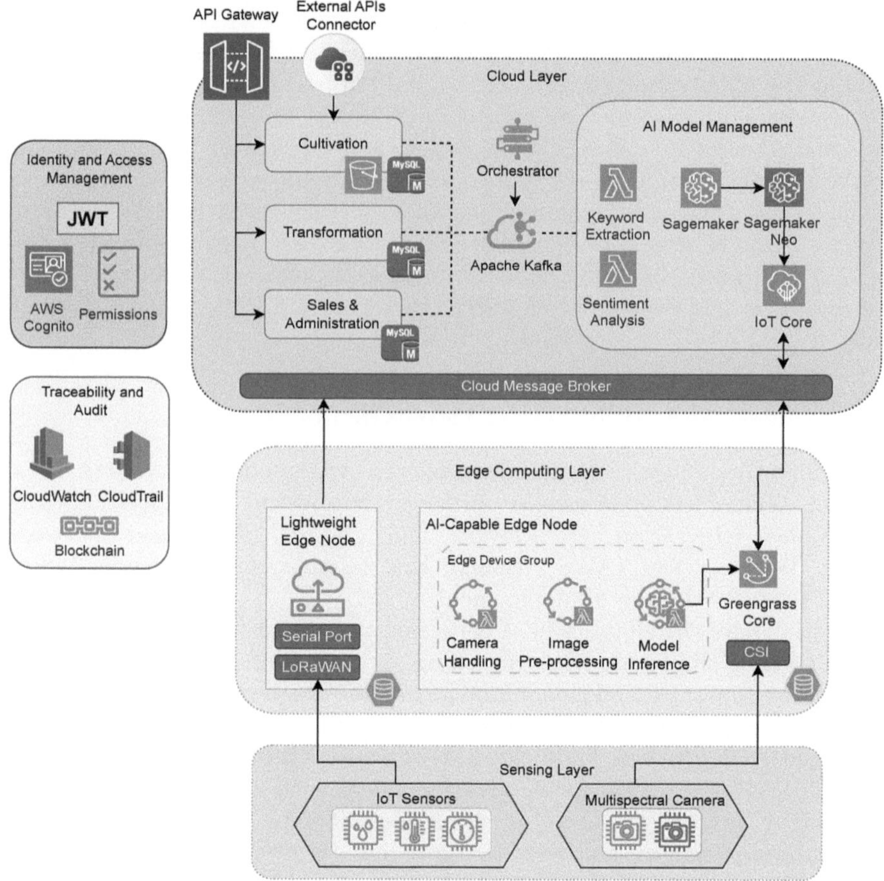

Fig. 2. Deployment model of the proposed architecture for the Apulian use case.

is trained and optimized with SageMaker's (https://aws.amazon.com/sagemaker/) infrastructure and its automatic hyperparameter tuning. It is then compiled for edge deployment by means of *SageMaker Neo* (https://docs.aws.amazon.com/sagemaker/latest/dg/neo.html), producing a device-specific binary optimized for edge nodes (e.g., Raspberry Pi or NVIDIA Jetson Nano). The model is deployed to edge nodes through *AWS IoT Greengrass* (https://aws.amazon.com/iot-greengrass/), with communication and cloud-edge integration handled through a cloud-based IoT core.

The edge layer includes two classes of nodes:

- **Lightweight Edge Nodes**, such as industrial weather stations, primarily responsible for sensor integration and data forwarding to the cloud via MQTT over Narrowband Internet of Things (NB-IoT) or Category M1 LTE (Cat-

M1) cellular networks. Without onboard AI, these nodes serve as transparent gateways.

- **AI-Capable Edge Nodes**—implemented with single-board computer devices like Jetson Nano[1] or Raspberry Pi with Coral Tensor Processing Unit (TPU)[2]—host the AWS Greengrass Core and execute Greengrass containerized components encapsulating various functions such as camera handling, image pre-processing and model inference for leaf disease detection. The components are logically grouped into *Edge Device Group* for centralized provisioning, versioned deployment and remote updates from the cloud. Communication with the cloud occurs via MQTT over AWS IoT Core.

Both types of edge nodes are equipped with local storage, enabling temporary buffering of sensor data or inference results during connectivity issues.

The sensing layer includes environmental and soil sensors, typically connected via serial ports, analog inputs, or LoRaWAN. Multispectral cameras interface with AI-Capable edge devices through Camera Serial Interface (CSI) (Camera Serial Interface) for high-resolution image acquisition.

This setup represents a reference deployment model that could be adapted to other cloud providers or on-premise environments depending on infrastructure constraints. This architecture establishes the operational backbone of the use case, enabling real-time monitoring and secure traceability workflows, detailed in the following subsections.

4.2 Edge-Assisted Image Analysis for Crop Monitoring

Early detection of crop stress and plant diseases is essential for promoting sustainable and efficient PA, enabling timely interventions that improve yield, quality, and resource optimization. Building on the architecture outlined in Sect. 4.1, the proposed framework integrates AI-based image analysis into routine field operations, particularly through vision-equipped agricultural tractors. These vehicles are outfitted with multispectral cameras connected to AI-capable edge nodes, enabling high-frequency image acquisition during standard activities without introducing additional operational burdens.

On these edge nodes, precompiled models—optimized and distributed by the *AI Model Management* microservice—are deployed as containerized components managed by AWS Greengrass. Each component is responsible for tasks such as image preprocessing (contrast adjustment, noise reduction, spatial normalization) and real-time inference. This setup enables immediate classification of visual plant symptoms (e.g., leaf discoloration, lesions), generating alerts locally and reducing the reliance on continuous cloud connectivity. The proposed approach aligns with the well-evaluated edge-based implementation adopted in [7], where YOLOX-Tiny was deployed on a Jetson Nano B01 for peanut leaf disease detection, achieving 13–28 FPS with low power consumption ($\sim$2.8 W peak) and around 50% latency reduction using TensorRT.

---

[1] (https://developer.nvidia.com/embedded/jetson-nano-developer-kit).

[2] (https://coral.ai/products/accelerator/).

Detected results are published via MQTT and routed through IoT Core to cloud-based services. The Internet of Things (IoT) Rule Engine handles message routing, ensuring that detection outcomes are stored, visualized, or forwarded to relevant business microservices such as `Cultivation` and `Transformation`, or passed to the `Traceability and Audit` layer for certification.

This configuration ensures seamless coordination between local intelligence and centralized analytics while supporting scalability across distributed edge fleets. By embedding inference into regular farming workflows and maintaining architectural alignment with the broader system, this module provides a practical and extensible approach to in-situ crop monitoring.

4.3   Digital Traceability of Field Operations via Blockchain

The traceability layer ensures secure, verifiable, and auditable documentation of agronomic events by integrating blockchain technologies into the PTM process. Building upon the architecture described in Sect. 3.1, it extends the Trust and Integration Layers to support automated data notarization and compliance across the supply chain.

Unlike traditional systems that rely on manual input and centralized storage, the proposed solution automates the acquisition and certification of data from heterogeneous sources, including IoT sensors, image-based disease detection (see Sect. 4.2) and user-generated field reports. Events are normalized, hashed, and logged as immutable records in a permissioned consortium blockchain, ensuring data integrity and tamper resistance. The traceability module leverages Polygon [3], a Layer 2 blockchain built on Ethereum, and offers a cost-effective and energy-efficient solution by supporting up to 7,000 transactions per second and reducing transaction fees to a fraction of a cent, thanks to its Proof of Stake consensus and sidechain architecture, while maintaining full compatibility with Ethereum's smart contract environment. Events are hashed with Keccak-256 and aggregated into Merkle trees, allowing only the root to be notarized on-chain, reducing overhead while ensuring scalable and verifiable traceability. The system adopts a gateway pattern to enable interoperability with both private and public chains, facilitating external certification and visibility when required.

Traceability is maintained across edge and cloud modules. At the edge, classified events (e.g., stress detection, soil anomalies) are validated and forwarded via secure messaging. In the cloud, these are correlated with production events (e.g., batch processing, container operations) managed by the *Transformation* service, producing complete digital records from field to final product. These records are then notarized and versioned by the traceability microservice, which also interfaces with external systems through dedicated connectors.

A key feature is the ability to interface with national institutional platforms such as the *Sistema Informativo Agricolo Nazionale (SIAN)* (https://www.sian.it/). Structured interfaces map validated agronomic activities—such as land use declarations, treatment logs, and quality controls—into formats accepted

---

[3] (https://docs.polygon.technology/).

by SIAN's APIs, simplifying compliance procedures and supporting automated reporting workflows.

By embedding blockchain-based mechanisms into the operational lifecycle and connecting them with national registries, the system enhances transparency, streamlines audits and increases trust among stakeholders. It also facilitates anomaly detection to flag inconsistencies or tampering attempts across the chain.

5   Conclusion and Future Work

This paper has presented a unified cloud-edge architecture for Smart Farming and digital traceability, addressing the operational, scalability and compliance challenges of traditional agrifood systems. Compared to state-of-the-art frameworks that typically address specific segments of the value chain, the proposed infrastructure enables a holistic integration, both vertically, by encompassing the entire process from Cultivation, through Transformation, to Administration and Sales, and horizontally, by incorporating a coherent technological stack that combines edge-based artificial intelligence, sensor networks, blockchain and cloud computing within a unified digital ecosystem. Integration with institutional platforms such as SIAN enhances regulatory alignment and reinforces trust and interoperability among all stakeholders involved.

The Apulian deployment use case confirms the framework's applicability to real-world scenarios, particularly within regional supply chains involving small-holders and cooperative networks. Compared to existing platforms, which are often proprietary or tailored to specific domains, this framework offers an open and adaptable solution that promotes interoperability and scalability across diverse agricultural contexts.

As part of future work, broader validation will be pursued across heterogeneous agricultural contexts to assess scalability and adaptability. Additionally, we plan to enhance the long-term accuracy and responsiveness of the AI components by evaluating two learning strategies. Incremental learning will support periodic retraining of cloud models using updated field data, while federated learning will allow edge devices to train local models and transmit only updates, improving privacy and reducing communication overhead. These enhancements aim to ensure that the system remains adaptive, privacy-preserving, and efficient across diverse operational conditions.

Acknowledgments. The research was supported by *xTech NextHub: Competence Center for Innovative Solutions Development* grant (grant number VTOIFW0), co-funded by Deloitte NextHub S.r.l. S.B. and the European Regional Development Fund for Apulia Region 2014/2020 Operating Program.

Disclosure of Interests. The authors have no competing interests to declare that are relevant to the content of this article.

References

1. Getahun, S., Kefale, H., Gelaye, Y.: Application of precision agriculture technologies for sustainable crop production and environmental sustainability: A systematic review. Sci. World J. **2024**(1), 2126734 (2024)
2. John, S., Arul Leena Rose, P.: Smart farming and precision agriculture and its need in today's world. In: Intelligent Robots and Drones for Precision Agriculture, pp. 19–44. Springer (2024)
3. Karunathilake, E., Le, A.T., Heo, S., Chung, Y.S., Mansoor, S.: The path to smart farming: Innovations and opportunities in precision agriculture. Agriculture **13**(8), 1593 (2023)
4. Kum, S., Oh, S., Moon, J.: Edge ai framework for large scale smart agriculture. In: 2024 27th Conference on Innovation in Clouds, Internet and Networks (ICIN), pp. 143–147. IEEE (2024)
5. Loconte, D., et al.: Serverless microservice architecture for cloud-edge intelligence in sensor networks. IEEE Sens. J. **25**(5), 7875–7885 (2024)
6. Loseto, G., et al.: Osmotic cloud-edge intelligence for IoT-based cyber-physical systems. Sensors **22**(6) (2022)
7. Lv, Z., et al.: Efficient deployment of peanut leaf disease detection models on edge ai devices. Agriculture **15**(3), 332 (2025)
8. Marković, D., Stamenković, Z., Đorđević, B., Randić, S.: Image processing for smart agriculture applications using cloud-fog computing. Sensors **24**(18), 5965 (2024)
9. Nawaz, M., Babar, M.I.K.: IoT and AI for smart agriculture in resource-constrained environments: challenges, opportunities and solutions. Discover Internet Things **5**(1), 24 (2025)
10. Neuhaus, H., Compton, M.: The semantic sensor network ontology. In: AGILE workshop on challenges in geospatial data harmonisation, Hannover, Germany, pp. 1–33 (2009)
11. Ruta, M., Scioscia, F., Ieva, S., Capurso, G., Di Sciascio, E.: Supply chain object discovery with semantic-enhanced blockchain. In: Proceedings of the 15th ACM Conference on Embedded Network Sensor Systems. Association for Computing Machinery, New York (2017)
12. Ruta, M., Scioscia, F., Ieva, S., Loseto, G., Gramegna, F., Pinto, A.: Knowledge discovery and sharing in the IoT: the physical semantic web vision. In: Proceedings of the Symposium on Applied Computing, pp. 492–498 (2017)
13. Sakthi, U., DafniRose, J.: Blockchain-enabled smart agricultural knowledge discovery system using edge computing. Procedia Comput. Sci. **202**, 73–82 (2022)
14. Sarantakos, T., Gutierrez, D.M.J., Amaxilatis, D.: Olive leaf infection detection using the cloud-edge continuum. In: International Symposium on Algorithmic Aspects of Cloud Computing, pp. 25–37. Springer (2023)
15. Soussi, A., Zero, E., Sacile, R., Trinchero, D., Fossa, M.: Smart sensors and smart data for precision agriculture: a review. Sensors **24**(8), 2647 (2024)
16. Ting, L., Khan, M., Sharma, A., Ansari, M.D.: A secure framework for iot-based smart climate agriculture system: toward blockchain and edge computing. J. Intell. Syst. **31**(1), 221–236 (2022)

A Simulation-as-a-Service Engine
for Urban Mobility Digital Twins

Umberto Francesco Carolini[1], Davide Loconte[1], Giuseppe Loseto[2,3], and Floriano Scioscia[1,3]($\boxtimes$)

[1] Polytechnic University of Bari, via E. Orabona 4, 70125 Bari, Italy
`{umbertofrancesco.carolini,davide.loconte,floriano.scioscia}@poliba.it`
[2] LUM "G. Degennaro" University, S.S. 100 km 18, 70010 Casamassima, BA, Italy
`loseto@lum.it`
[3] donkeyPower S.r.l., via E. Orabona 4, 70125 Bari, Italy
`{giuseppe.loseto,floriano.scioscia}@donkeypower.it`

Abstract. The Urban Digital Twin (UDT) paradigm is increasingly adopted to monitor and simulate transport networks for smart city mobility planning and policy-making, as well as for analyzing the integration of innovative transportation technologies and services. Although several mature traffic simulators are available, their integration into broader UDT systems is still limited due to the lack of standardized APIs for scenario definition, management and execution. This paper presents a REST API designed to integrate the SUMO traffic simulator into UDT systems for smart cities, adopting a simulation-as-a-service approach. The proposed framework encapsulates SUMO and exposes its functionalities through an HTTP-based web API, enabling real-time simulation control, scenario modification, and data retrieval. This approach facilitates the development of UDTs which support planning, monitoring, and interactive what-if scenario analysis within microservice architectures. The paper presents integration guidelines of the proposed framework into UDT platforms for smart cities and early experimental evaluations for performance and scalability assessment.

Keywords: Urban Mobility · Smart Cities · Digital Twin · Simulation · SUMO · RESTful API · Microservice Architecture

1 Introduction and Motivation

Urban mobility faces increasing challenges, including congestion, air pollution, and population density growth. At the same time, innovative mobility service paradigms are being introduced, leveraging emerging technologies such as real-time driver assistance [16], vehicular networks [15], autonomous driving, and Unmanned Aerial Systems (UASs) for delivery and passenger transport. To address this growing complexity, simulation tools are commonly used by urban planners and engineers to analyze traffic dynamics and assess the impact of proposed innovations [6]. In this context, the *Urban Digital Twin (UDT)* paradigm is achieving more and more value for researchers and practitioners. A UDT pairs the physical transport infrastructure, equipped with traffic sensors and roadside units, with a digital counterpart that remains synchronized through bidirectional real-time data flows. This digital model makes it possible not only to monitor and analyze the actual infrastructure status, but also to test policies and interventions via simulation without disrupting the actual road network. Although several mature traffic simulators are available, their integration into broader smart city systems remains limited. These tools are typically not designed for real-time interaction or straightforward connectivity with external services. While many smart city applications are based on microservice architectures [11] and web-based communications, traffic simulation is often treated as a standalone component. In particular, there is a lack of frameworks that provide simulation functionalities through REpresentational State Transfer (REST) Application Programming Interfaces (APIs). This paper aims to address this gap by introducing a novel UDT engine prototype, which encapsulates a standard traffic simulator and exposes its functionalities via a REST APIs based on Hyper-Text Transport Protocol (HTTP). The engine supports simulation control, scenario modification, and data retrieval in real time through HTTP requests. This *simulation-as-a-service* design facilitates the integration of traffic modeling into larger systems and supports the development of urban mobility applications, including what-if scenario analysis as well as hardware-in-the-loop simulations and ground tests.

The remainder of this paper is structured as follows. Section 2 reviews related work and provides background on traffic simulation and Digital Twin (DT) technologies. Section 3 describes the architecture and implementation of the proposed REST API framework. Section 4 presents early evaluations in a use case demonstrating the integration and functionality of the system. Finally, Sect. 5 concludes the paper and outlines directions for future work.

2   Digital Twins for Urban Mobility

In recent years, DT technology has gained significant traction as a key enabler for the management and optimization of complex infrastructures, including energy systems and urban environments [7]. A DT is a digital representation of a physical asset, system, or process that enables a wide range of applications, such as what-if simulations, predictive and proactive maintenance, fine-grained control, operator training, and decision support. The development of such systems relies on the integration of several technologies, including Internet of Things (IoT) for real-time data acquisition, cloud, and edge computing for scalable processing, semantic technologies for data integration and interoperability, and Artificial Intelligence (AI) and Machine Learning (ML) for analytics and decision-making [3].

As an application, UDT is essentially a system that models a digital replica of the road network and its users. It mirrors the real environment, which is composed of road infrastructure, vehicles, pedestrians, and their travel behavior, and it is continuously updated based on real-world data. This virtual model enables city planners and decision-makers to simulate a wide range of scenarios and simulate the agents' behavior without disrupting the physical city [12]. By leveraging streams of sensor data and historical information, a UDT models the current physical twin dynamics and predicts future trends. This approach enables more informed urban planning decision making, where understanding the behavior of vehicles, pedestrians and other user agents and how it evolves following infrastructural changes is crucial [5]. Integration with real-time data streams is one of the key features of UDTs systems. In a real world application, the simulation must respond dynamically to incoming data from interconnected vehicles, organized into Vehicular Ad-hoc Networks (VANETs), which enable direct interaction between vehicles and with roadside infrastructure [15], as well as from IoT sensors and traffic management systems [14]. Because of this integration, the UDT takes into consideration the system events like traffic jams, accidents, or road closures. In turn, the simulation can forecast important data, such as expected congestion or average travel times. In the context of urban mobility planning, UDT provides a practical means to evaluate infrastructure changes before implementation. They support the simulation of alternative scenarios, such as the introduction of a tram line or the reconfiguration of an intersection, allowing planners to assess their effects on traffic conditions. This enables the identification of potential issues, such as traffic congestion, and can improve traffic flow [19].

Traffic simulation software plays a central role in these systems. These tools can provide detailed modeling of road networks and its users behavior. *Simulation of Urban MObility (SUMO)* (https://sumo.dlr.de/) is an open-source traffic simulation tool that supports mesoscopic modeling of vehicles, pedestrians, and public transport systems. This tool has been successfully adopted for a wide variety of use cases, such as urban traffic management [8], Intelligent Transportation System (ITS) evaluation [2], and autonomous vehicle testing [18]. By including both microsimulation of individual vehicle behavior and macrosimulation of traffic flow models, it offers high flexibility and accuracy, but its integration into larger software platforms is non-trivial and requires careful handling. SUMO was originally designed for research use and as a standalone application. Real-time interaction is possible via the *Traffic Control Interface (TraCI)* (https://sumo.dlr.de/docs/TraCI.html), a protocol that enables stepwise control and inspection of the running simulation state through a Transport Control Protocol (TCP)-based interface. However, TraCI requires a dedicated client application and low-level command handling, making it difficult to integrate into distributed or service-oriented architectures. These characteristics discourage its adoption in more general-purpose systems [4]. Previous studies have tried to improve simulation integration. For instance, *VSimRTI* [13] and *OMNeT++*-based co-simulation environments [17] offer advanced coordination between SUMO and other simulators. More recently, *SESAM* [10] has proposed a REST-based interface for cloud-hosted SUMO simulations. However, these solutions either focus on restricted domains or require significant effort in terms of configuration and infrastructure management, limiting their applicability in

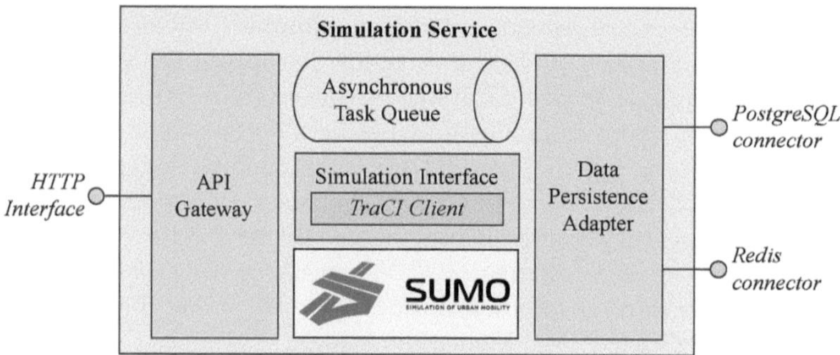

Fig. 1. Simulation service internal architecture

UDT applications for smart mobility. In addition to technical complexity, TraCI is inherently synchronous and tightly coupled to the running simulation, which hinders scalability. The lack of standardized APIs or data exchange formats further limits interoperability with other components. In contrast, this work introduces a REST API engine that abstracts the interaction with SUMO into a stateless, web-accessible service. This enables simulation-as-a-service supporting integration into modular, microservice-based smart city platforms. It reduces the complexity of incorporating real-time traffic simulation into UDT systems and simplifies SUMO usage by abstracting low-level interactions. This also helps lower the learning curve for non-expert users and decision makers.

3   Design and Implementation of a Digital Twin Engine for Urban Mobility

The proposed solution involves the design and implementation of a REST API framework to simplify interaction with SUMO. Web APIs represent the most widely used way to expose application functionalities on Web Clients via Create-Read-Update-Delete (CRUD) operations and are based on a client-server approach that allows one to separate the front and back ends, providing more flexibility in both deployment and implementation. The goal is to provide an accessible and intuitive interface to the simulator for developers and decision-makers, facilitating the entire simulation workflow from network import to scenario execution and data retrieval.

3.1   System Architecture and Integration

The service is designed to be integrated into microservice-based systems. This architectural pattern facilitates the separation of concerns and allows for independent development and deployment of different system components, moreover it allows different components of the system to be replicated to enhance scalability and better utilize distributed computing resources [1]. To match the architectural requirements, the proposed component is stateless, independent and self-contained. As shown in Fig. 1, the component is internally organized in the following layers, each implemented as a separate Python module in the same codebase:

- **API Gateway:** this is the entrypoint of the service. It exposes the HTTP endpoints, performs input validation, and routes the request to the correct internal module to correctly formulate the response.
- **Asynchronous Task Queue:** some requests may involve long running simulations or large I/O operations. Therefore, these are modeled as asynchronous tasks, which are submitted to a task queue and executed as soon as possible. This component ensures service responsiveness by managing the aforementioned tasks without blocking incoming client requests and allowing the main thread to serve different requests.
- **Data Persistence Adapter:** this is an interface layer, configurable at deployment time, that internally manages communication between the service and an external database. By externalizing data persistence, the service remains stateless and can be scaled horizontally, leveraging Database Management System (DBMS) synchronization primitives to prevent data races.
- **Simulator Interface:** this component wraps the logic to communicate with the SUMO executable to launch new simulations and other built-in tools like *netconvert* (https://sumo.dlr.de/docs/netconvert.html) for network processing and TraCI for real-time communication with running simulations.

The service has two main connectors to the external world: the Data Persistence Adapter and the API Gateway. The former connects to a DBMS, while the latter exposes the HTTP interface. Although the current implementation uses *PostgreSQL* (https://www.postgresql.org/) and (*Redis* https://redis.io/) as reference engines for relational and NoSQL databases respectively, other tools can be easily integrated by updating the Adapter component. The Simulator Interface and the integration with SUMO are further detailed in Sect. 3.2. Follows a brief introduction to the primary set of endpoints which expose the key functionalities that allow one to run a complete simulation.

- **Network Management:** this group includes functionalities such as: (i) Importing networks using geographic bounding boxes defined by minimum and maximum latitude and longitude, or by uploading network or *OpenStreetMap (OSM)* (https://wiki.openstreetmap.org/wiki/OSM_file_formats) files. (ii)Retrieving the list of available networks and accessing their details, including *GeoJSON* (https://geojson.org/) representations.
- **Scenario Management:** the main functionality in this group involves the creation of detailed traffic scenarios by specifying the underlying network and a set of common parameters (e.g., vehicle types, car-following models, emission classes) to be included. The scenario creation process involves: (i) generation of custom vehicle distributions; (ii) creation of random trips using a dedicated tool; (iii) route generation through routing algorithms that connect predefined departure and arrival points.

Additional functionalities include listing, downloading, and updating existing scenarios.

- **Simulation Control and Interaction:** this set represents the core of the engine and enables:
  (i) initializing simulations from predefined scenarios; (ii) advancing simulations stepwise; (iii) running simulations to completion with optional vehicle tracking; (iv) dynamically injecting vehicles during runtime; (v) accessing and retrieving simulation results.

Additionally, all SUMO resources, operations, and files are exposed through standard CRUD "low-level" APIs, enabling general-purpose control of the simulator. This design allows interaction with the underlying simulation engine beyond the specific workflows implemented by the aforementioned API set. Additionally, the REST interface is documented using an OpenAPI[1] specification to facilitate system integration.

3.2   SUMO Integration and Scenario Management Services

SUMO, its dependencies, and built-in tools are provided and bundled in the service through the *eclipse-sumo* Python package[2]. This removes the need for any external connection or custom user setup. All operations related to simulation management are handled by the Simulator Interface component, described in Sect. 3.1. When a user starts a simulation, the required SUMO resources and files are generated on demand based on the data stored in the database. The system then launches a separate process that runs the SUMO binary with the correct runtime arguments. Multiple simulations can run and be managed at the same time. Once a simulation is running, the engine communicates with it through a TraCI client. The same approach is used for SUMO's auxiliary tools, which are also executed as separate processes. Their outputs are captured by the Simulator Interface and saved in the database for further use. Real-time control of simulations is made possible through TraCI, which works over a TCP connection using a client-server model. This setup lets external systems monitor and interact with the simulation, stepping through it, pausing or resuming execution, injecting new vehicles, adjusting routes, and retrieving real-time data like vehicle positions, traffic light states, or pollutant emissions. The Simulator Interface wraps TraCI, SUMO, and all related tools as object methods, making it easier to manage the entire simulation lifecycle internally in the system. On top of that, the engine's API Gateway exposes a set of low-level REST endpoints that act as direct bridges to specific SUMO functions. These allow client applications to perform all the previously mentioned actions, such as running a simulation step, getting detailed vehicle data, generating a network from OSM data, or building a traffic demand scenario. These endpoints form the foundation for building custom workflows and integrating with other systems. To support

---

[1] https://openapi.com/.

[2] https://pypi.org/project/eclipse-sumo/.

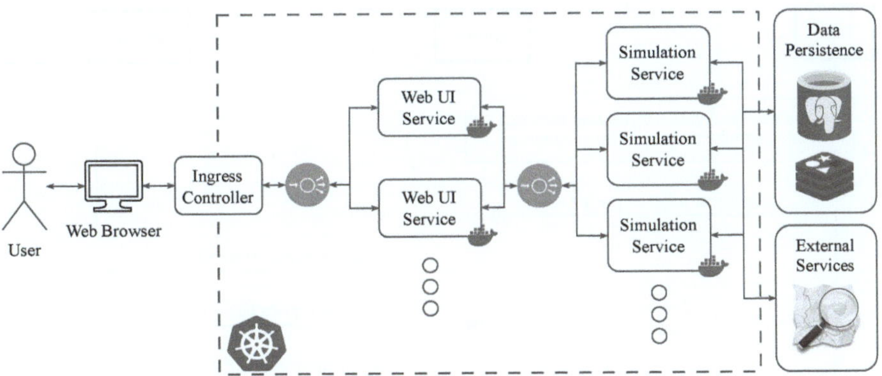

Fig. 2. Deployment diagram for Smart City Scenario

more complex use cases, the framework also provides a set of "high-level" endpoints. These represents actions that would require multiple SUMO actions, such as "close road segment X for Y minutes," or "apply deviation Z." Closing a road dynamically might involve identifying the corresponding edges in the network and issuing commands to reroute traffic or block access. These higher-level features are available through dedicated API Gateway endpoints, making them easy to use from external applications. The API Gateway handles the translation and forwards the necessary instructions to the Simulator Interface.

4 Early Evaluations

This section presents a preliminary experimental evaluation of the proposed engine, focusing on its performance and scalability when executing multiple concurrent simulations. The evaluation aims to demonstrate the feasibility of the approach in real-world smart city planning scenarios.

4.1 Smart City Digital Twin Deployment Scenario

An existing gap identified in Sect. 2 is the lack of a simulation-as-a-service module that can be easily integrated into existing platforms. Figure 2 illustrates a possible deployment of a UDT platform, where the service described in Fig. 1 is encapsulated as the "Simulation Service" microservice. While Docker and Kubernetes are assumed for deployment, the component is technology-agnostic and can be integrated into other platforms. This proposal aligns with software engineering best practices in designing microservice-oriented applications. In particular, the internal services are self-contained, have a single responsibility, and are stateless. This allows each component to scale based on the actual load of the service on the hosting node. Data persistence is offloaded to one or more external managed databases. Some functionalities, such as the network import endpoint, require

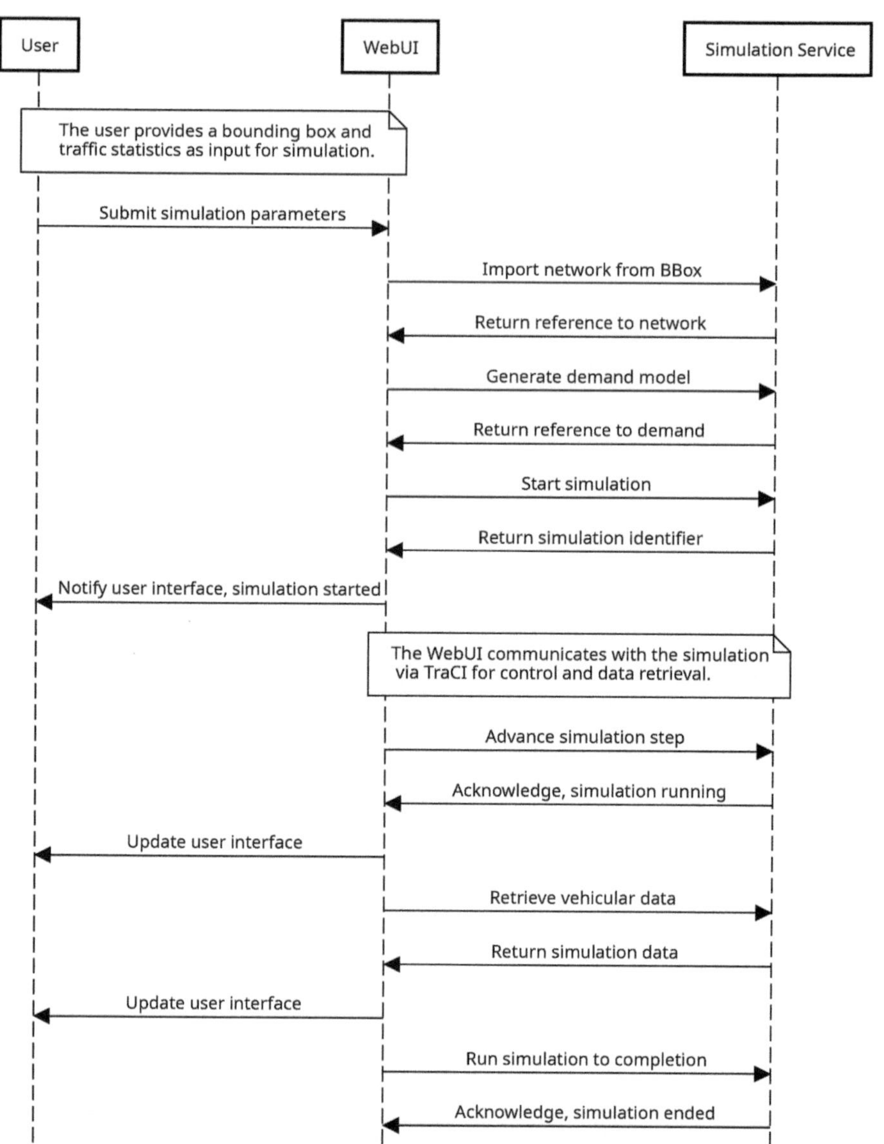

Fig. 3. User interaction for simulation setup, execution, and data retrieval

the simulation service to communicate with external APIs. Those are represented in the architectural diagram as "External Services." To protect sensitive mobility data, the system employs Role-Based Access Control (RBAC), Transport Layer Security (TLS) encryption, OAuth 2.0 authentication, and encrypted storage, with audit logging for traceability and regulatory compliance. The proposed framework is designed to be general-purpose and to support a wide range of use cases. An example of interaction flow between the user and the simulation system is illustrated in Fig. 3. This sequence represents one possible workflow involving network import, demand model generation, simulation execution, and real-time data access. The Web UI acts as human-machine interface, allowing control of the underlying simulation through the TraCI interface.

4.2   Concurrent Simulations and Scalability

Stress tests have been conducted to characterize how the proposed component scales with respect to varying request amount and size. In particular, the tests concerned network generation, scenario creation, and simulation execution endpoints. The testbed device is an Apple MacBook Pro 14[3] equipped with an Apple M1 Pro System-on-Chip featuring 8 CPU cores and 14 GPU cores, 16 GB RAM, 512 GB storage and macOS Ventura 13.6 operating system. Each test has been executed by varying the number of concurrent requests between 1, 3, 5, and 10. The reported results are an average of three measurements. Concerning the request size, a small, a medium, and a large road network have been extracted from a geographic area around the city of Bari, as shown in Fig. 4. In detail, the bounding box for each map extract is reported in Table 1. All simulations have used default parameters, but some runs have included the tracking of vehicle statistics. Collected measurements include CPU and RAM usage measured during each request and latency, that is the total time taken to fulfill each request. Simulation endpoints have been tested with one request per scenario, and mean results are reported. The system generally performs well, showing effectiveness in handling concurrent requests under normal test conditions. As shown in Table 2,

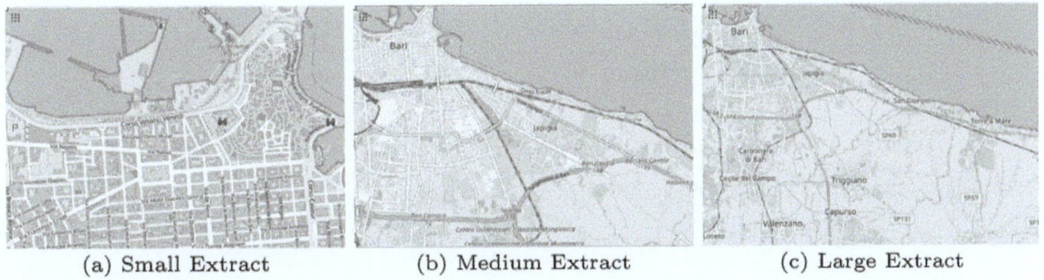

(a) Small Extract   (b) Medium Extract   (c) Large Extract

Fig. 4. Maps extracted from OpenStreetMap for tests

Table 1. Geographical bounds for different area sizes

Size	Min Latitude	Max Latitude	Min Longitude	Max Longitude
Small	41.1179	41.1343	16.8516	16.8883
Medium	41.0839	41.1339	16.8495	16.9771
Large	40.9960	41.1339	16.8417	17.1061

---

[3] https://support.apple.com/en-us/111902.

Table 2. Average results for the `/importByBBOX` endpoint

Requests #	Network	CPU (%)	RAM (%)	Latency (s)
1	Small	15.50	67.70	4.12
3	Small	18.73	67.20	7.82
5	Small	19.62	68.17	7.97
10	Small	21.76	68.44	8.11
1	Medium	26.13	68.80	10.56
3	Medium	30.20	70.57	13.00
5	Medium	31.02	72.62	13.83
10	Medium	33.74	69.53	17.61
1	Large	20.60	68.70	25.91
3	Large	31.40	70.70	25.21
5	Large	44.65	69.60	26.32
10	Large	47.33	71.52	31.22

Table 3. Average results for the `/sumo_scenario/create` endpoint

Requests #	Network	CPU (%)	RAM (%)	Latency (s)
1	Small	12.90	41.20	3.07
3	Small	20.00	43.30	5.57
5	Small	22.40	45.33	8.75
10	Small	43.27	51.78	9.42
1	Medium	16.50	46.13	7.56
3	Medium	22.80	47.24	9.47
5	Medium	24.57	50.98	12.14
10	Medium	46.84	78.88	14.85
1	Large	21.50	56.29	35.56
3	Large	23.55	63.32	38.70
5	Large	29.70	67.30	42.72
10	Large	46.88	75.08	65.99

road network import performance shows some variability, likely influenced by the external OSM *Overpass* API[4] and network connectivity. Using an on-premise API instance may help reduce this effect. However, overall performance trends remain consistent across operations, including scenario generation (Table 3) and simulation execution (Table 4), with similar scaling behavior and resource usage observed throughout.

---

[4] https://wiki.openstreetmap.org/wiki/Overpass_API.

Table 4. Performance Analysis for Simulations

Request #	Network	CPU (%)	RAM (%)	Latency (s)
1	Small	12.4	53.80	2.64
1	Medium	34.83	60.58	63.71
1	Large	59.30	64.10	157.06

5 Conclusion and Future Work

This paper has introduced a modular and extensible framework for managing urban mobility simulations via a REST API interface to the SUMO simulator. The suggested system abstracts low-level simulation functionalities and exposes them through stateless, web-accessible services, allowing for integration of simulation-as-a-service capability into UDT platforms. By virtue of the adherence to microservice architecture principles, every component can scale on its own and communicate asynchronously through common interfaces. Early experiments show that the system is capable of handling concurrent requests and fairly complex simulation scenarios, suggesting that it is scalable and performs well enough to meet the demands of smart city applications. The framework makes it easier to integrate real-time traffic simulation into larger platforms and lowers the entry barrier for developers. Future work will focus on the following points:

- Graphical User Interface: although the simulation-as-a-service component is functional, it lacks a user interface. Future work will include designing and integrating this module to enable user-friendly interaction with the simulation engine and unlock the full potential of the framework.
- Hardware-in-the-loop Integration: hardware-in-the-loop support is needed to allow ground tests of physical vehicles –such as self-driving cars and UASs– in large-scale simulations, so as to assess on-board algorithms in realistic UDT contexts and experiment on vehicle coordination capabilities. Enabling these functionalities requires actuation on road side units, traffic lights and other components of the smart city infrastructure, as well as the extensions of SUMO mobility models to include integrated air-ground mobility. Finally the engine should be optimized for low-latency response in cloud-to-thing deployments [9].
- Validation in Real-World Scenarios: while the current experiments have focused on performance aspects, future research will apply the framework to real use cases of traffic analysis and what-if scenario analysis, in order to prove the benefits of UDT systems in urban planning and the design of innovative mobility services.
- Broader Digital Twin Applications: additional use cases beyond urban traffic simulation, such as energy consumption modeling, environmental impact assessment, and autonomous vehicle coordination with UASs and Roadside

Units (RSUs), will be explored using the extensibility of Eclipse SUMO to demonstrate the framework's applicability across diverse smart city domains.

Acknowledgments. The research was supported by project *SCIAME* (Smart City Integrated Air Mobility Evolution, code F/310305/01-05/X56) funded by the "Partnerships for Innovation" program of the Italian Ministry of Enterprises and Made in Italy, and by the *Digital Enterprise* grant (code NIL6S28), co-funded by Lutech S.p.A. and European Regional Development Fund for Apulia Region 2014/2020 Operating Program.

Disclosure of Interests. The authors have no competing interests to declare that are relevant to the content of this article.

References

1. Bellavista, P., Bicocchi, N., Fogli, M., Giannelli, C., Mamei, M., Picone, M.: Exploiting microservices and serverless for digital twins in the cloud-to-edge continuum. Futur. Gener. Comput. Syst. **157**, 275–287 (2024)
2. Codeca, L., Härri, J.: Towards multimodal mobility simulation of c-its: The monaco sumo traffic scenario. In: 2017 IEEE Vehicular Networking Conference (VNC), pp. 97–100. IEEE (2017)
3. Fuller, A., Fan, Z., Day, C., Barlow, C.: Digital twin: enabling technologies, challenges and open research. IEEE Access **8**, 108952–108971 (2020)
4. Heisig, P., Jeroschewski, S.E., Kristan, J., Höttger, R., Banijamali, A., Sachweh, S.: Bridging the gap between SUMO and Kuksa: using a traffic simulator for testing cloud-based connected vehicle services. In: SUMO User Conference 2019, May 13-15 Berlin, Germany. EasyChair (2019)
5. Herath, M., Alvi, M., Minerva, R., Dutta, H., Crespi, N., Raza, S.M.: Smart city digital twins: A modular and adaptive architecture for real-time data-driven urban management. In: 2024 20th International Conference on Network and Service Management (CNSM), pp. 1–7. IEEE (2024)
6. Ieva, S., et al.: Enhancing last-mile logistics: ai-driven fleet optimization, mixed reality, and large language model assistants for warehouse operations. Sensors **25**(9), 2696 (2025)
7. Ieva, S., Loconte, D., Loseto, G., Ruta, M., Scioscia, F., Marche, D., Notarnicola, M.: A retrieval-augmented generation approach for data-driven energy infrastructure digital twins. Smart Cities **7**(6), 3095–3120 (2024)
8. Kumar, R., Kori, N., Chaurasiya, V.K.: Real-time data sharing, path planning and route optimization in urban traffic management. Multimed. Tools Appl. **82**(23), 36343–36361 (2023)
9. Loconte, D., Ieva, S., Pinto, A., Loseto, G., Scioscia, F., Ruta, M.: Expanding the cloud-to-edge continuum to the iot in serverless federated learning. Futur. Gener. Comput. Syst. **155**, 447–462 (2024)
10. Lopez, P.A., et al.: Microscopic traffic simulation using SUMO. In: 21st International Conference on Intelligent Transportation Systems (ITSC), pp. 2575–2582. Ieee (2018)
11. Loseto, G., Scioscia, F., Ruta, M., Gramegna, F., Ieva, S., Fasciano, C., Bilenchi, I., Loconte, D.: Osmotic cloud-edge intelligence for IoT-based cyber-physical systems. Sensors **22**(6), 2166 (2022)

12. Peldon, D., Banihashemi, S., LeNguyen, K., Derrible, S.: Navigating urban complexity: The transformative role of digital twins in smart city development. Sustain. Cities Soc. **111**, 105583 (2024)
13. Queck, T., Schüenemann, B., Radusch, I.: Runtime Infrastructure for Simulating Vehicle-2-X Communication Scenarios. In: Proceedings of the Fifth ACM International Workshop on VehiculAr Inter-NETworking, pp. 78–78 (2008)
14. Rundel, S., De Amicis, R.: Leveraging digital twin and game-engine for traffic simulations and visualizations. Front. Virtual Reality **4**, 1048753 (2023)
15. Ruta, M., Scioscia, F., Gramegna, F., Ieva, S., Di Sciascio, E., De Vera, R.P.: A knowledge fusion approach for context awareness in vehicular networks. IEEE Internet Things J. **5**(4), 2407–2419 (2018)
16. Ruta, M., Scioscia, F., Loseto, G., Pinto, A., Di Sciascio, E.: Machine learning in the internet of things: a semantic-enhanced approach. Semantic Web J. **10**(1), 183–204 (2019)
17. Varga, A.: OMNeT++. In: Modeling and tools for network simulation, pp. 35–59. Springer (2010)
18. Vrbanić, F., Čakija, D., Kušić, K., Ivanjko, E.: Traffic flow simulators with connected and autonomous vehicles: a short review. Transformation of Transportation, 15–30 (2021)
19. Wu, D., Zheng, A., Yu, W., Cao, H., Ling, Q., Liu, J., Zhou, D.: Digital twin technology in transportation infrastructure: A comprehensive survey of current applications, challenges, and future directions. Appl. Sci. **15**(4), 1911 (2025)